Painting
Landscapes
with Jerry Yarnell

NORTH LIGHT BOOKS
CINCINNATI. OHIO

contents

introduction

If you've ever painted with Bob Ross or Bill Alexander, you're going to love Jerry Yarnell! The adventure begins the moment you pick up a brush. Let Jerry Yarnell show you how to make the most of it! Learn how to create attractive landscapes with skill and confidence, capture the outdoor look and spirit of every season and master composition, design, perspective, value, color and atmosphere. And there are over 30 step-by-step projects for you to

practice on! You'll learn all the tricks and techniques you need to perform magic with paint. Whether you're a beginning artist or a skilled professional, Jerry makes it easy for you to improve, expand your repertoire of skills and build true artistic confidence.

Love to paint? Want to learn? Then grab your paints and brushes and get started!

PAINTING
Magic

**NORTH
LIGHT
BOOKS**

CINCINNATI, OHIO
www.nlbooks.com

Table of Contents

High and Mighty

The Crossing

Tossed by the Waves

Patient Fisherman

Misty Morning Sunrise

Bicycle and the Bluebird

The Stone Wall

No Vacancy

Home from the Market

The Return to Days of Old

The Return to Days of Old
16" X 20" (40.6cm x 50.8cm)

Introduction

When I think about the purpose of this book, I realize that it is all about experience. Once you have reached a point in your art career where you have a good basic understanding of all the technical aspects of painting like composition, design, perspective, negative space, color mixing, values and color coordination in terms of understanding the complementary color system, then it's a practical matter of applying these painting principles by doing numerous studies and practice paintings, until you are comfortable and secure in your understanding of all of them. These paintings are designed to challenge your artistic abilities. Each painting will give you a unique set of artistic challenges to overcome. My goal as an instructor is not only to teach these principles, but to inspire, encourage and help build your confidence. There is a saying by an unknown author: "Success is gained by hard work, discipline, and not a little pain." So, don't be afraid to dive in headfirst and begin to gain experience and confidence.

Terms & Techniques

Before beginning the step-by-step instructions on the following pages, you may want to refresh your memory by reviewing these painting terms, techniques and procedures.

COLOR COMPLEMENTS

Complementary colors are always opposite each other on the color wheel. Complements are used to create color balance in your paintings. It takes practice to understand the use of complements, but a good rule of thumb is to remember that whatever predominant color you have in your painting, use its complement or a form of its complement to highlight, accent or gray that color.

For example, if your painting has a lot of green in it, use its complement, red, or a form of red such as orange, red-orange or yellow-orange. If you have a lot of blue in your painting, use blue's complement, orange, or a form of orange such as yellow-orange or red-orange. The complement to yellow is purple or a form of purple. Keep a color wheel handy until you have memorized the color complements.

DABBING

This technique is used to create leaves, ground cover, flowers, etc. Take a bristle brush and dab it on your table or palette to spread out the ends of the bristles like a fan. Then load the brush with an appropriate color and gently dab on that color to create the desired effect. (See above example.)

DOUBLE LOAD OR TRIPLE LOAD

This is a procedure in which you put two or more colors on different parts of your brush. You mix these colors on the canvas instead of on

To prepare your bristle brush for dabbing, spread out the end of the bristles like a fan.

your palette. This is used for wet-on-wet techniques, such as sky or water.

DRYBRUSH

This technique involves loading your brush with very little paint and lightly skimming the surface of the canvas to add color, blend colors or soften a color. Use a very light touch for this technique.

EYE FLOW

This is the movement of the viewer's eye through the arrangement of objects on your canvas or the use of negative space around or within an object. Your eye must move or flow smoothly throughout your painting or around an object. You do not want your eyes to bounce or jump

from place to place. When you have a good understanding of the basic components of composition (design, negative space, "eye stoppers", overlap, etc.), your paintings will naturally have good eye flow.

FEATHERING

Feathering is a technique for blending to create very soft edges. You achieve this effect by using a very light touch and barely skimming the surface of the canvas with your brush. This is the technique to use for highlighting and glazing.

GESSO

Gesso is a white paint used for sealing the canvas before painting on it. However, because of its creamy con-

Here is an example of poor use of negative space. Notice the limbs do not overlap but are evenly spaced instead. There are few pockets of interesting space.

Here is an example of good use of negative space. Notice the overlap of the limbs and the interesting pockets of space around each limb.

sistency, I often use it instead of white paint; it blends so easily. I often refer to using gesso when mixing colors. Keep in mind that when I use the word gesso, I am referring to the color white. If you don't use gesso for white, use Titanium White paint, which is the standard white that is on the supply list. Please feel free to use it if you prefer.

GLAZE (WASH)

A glaze or a wash is a very thin layer of paint applied on top of a dry area of the painting to create mist, fog, haze, sun rays or to soften an area that is too bright. This mixture is made up of a small amount of color diluted with water. It may be applied in layers to achieve the desired effect.

Each layer must be dry before applying the next.

HIGHLIGHTING OR ACCENTING

Highlighting is one of the final stages of your painting. Use pure color or brighter values of colors to give your painting its final glow. Highlights are carefully applied on the sunlit edges of the most prominent objects in paintings.

MIXING

While this is fairly self-explanatory, there are a couple of ways to mix. First, if there is a color that will be used often, it is a good idea to pre-mix a quantity of that color to have it handy. I usually mix colors of paint with my brush, but sometimes

a palette knife works better. You can be your own judge.

I also mix colors on the canvas. For instance, when I am underpainting grass, I may put two or three colors on the canvas and scumble them together to create a mottled background of different colors. Mixing color on the canvas also works well when painting skies. (Note: When working with acrylics, always try to mix your paint to a creamy consistency that can be blended easily.)

NEGATIVE SPACE

This is the area of space surrounding an object that defines its form. (See example above.)

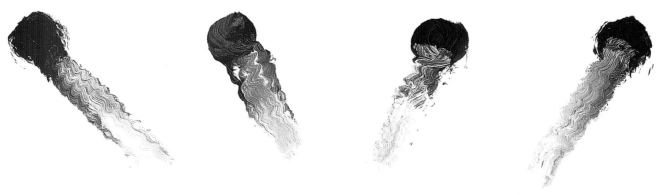

You can change the value of a color by adding white.

SCRUBBING

Scrubbing is similar to scumbling, except the strokes are more uniform in horizontal or vertical patterns. You can use dry-brush or wet-on-wet techniques with this procedure. I use it mostly for underpainting or blocking in an area.

SCUMBLING

For this technique, use a series of unorganized, overlapping strokes in different directions to create effects such as clumps of foliage, clouds, hair, grasses, etc. The direction of the stroke is not important.

UNDERPAINTING OR BLOCKING IN

These two terms mean the same thing. The first step in all paintings is to block in or underpaint the darker values of the entire painting. Then you begin applying the next values of color to create the form of each object.

VALUE

Value is the relative lightness or darkness of a color. To achieve depth or distance, use lighter values in the background and darker values as you come closer to the foreground. Raise the value of a color by adding white. To lower the value of a color, add black, brown or the color's complement.

WET-ON-DRY

This is the technique I use most often in acrylic painting. After the background color is dry, apply the topcoat over it by using one of the blending techniques: drybrushing, scumbling or glazing.

WET-ON-WET

In this painting technique, the colors are blended together while the first application of paint is still wet. I use the large hake (pronounced ha KAY) brush to blend large areas of wet-on-wet color, such as skies and water.

Getting Started

Acrylic Paint

The most common criticism about acrylics is that they dry too fast. Acrylics do dry very quickly through evaporation. To solve this problem I use a wet palette system, which is explained later in this chapter. I also use very specific dry-brush blending techniques to make blending very easy. If you follow the techniques I use in this book, with a little practice you can overcome any of the drying problems acrylics seem to pose.

Speaking as a professional artist, acrylics are ideally suited for exhibiting and shipping. An acrylic painting can actually be framed and ready to ship thirty minutes after it is finished. You can apply varnish over acrylic paint or leave it unvarnished because the paint is self-sealing. Acrylics are also very versatile because the paint can be applied thick or creamy to resemble oil paint, or thinned with water for watercolor techniques. The best news of all is that acrylics are non-toxic, have very little odor and few people have allergic reactions to them.

USING A LIMITED PALETTE

As you will discover in this book, I work from a limited palette. Whether it is for my professional pieces or for instructional purposes, I have learned that a limited palette of the proper colors can be the most effective tool for painting. This palette works well for two main reasons: First, it teaches you to mix a wide range of shades and values of color, which every artist must be able to do; second, a limited palette eliminates the need to purchase dozens of different colors. As we know, paint is becoming very expensive.

So, with a few basic colors and a little knowledge of color theory you can paint anything you desire. This particular palette is versatile, so that with a basic understanding of the color wheel, the complementary color system and values, you can mix thousands of colors for every type of painting.

For example, you can mix Thalo Yellow-Green, Alizarin Crimson and a touch of white to create a beautiful basic flesh tone. These same three colors can be used in combination with other colors to create earth tones for landscape paintings. You can make black by mixing Ultramarine Blue with equal amounts of Dioxazine Purple and Burnt Sienna or Burnt Umber. The list goes on and on, and you will see that the sky is truly the limit.

Most paint companies make three grades of paints: economy, student and professional. The professional grades are more expensive but much more effective to work with. The main idea is to buy what you can afford and have fun. (Note: If you can't find a particular item, I carry a complete line of professional–and student-grade paints and brushes.)

MATERIALS LIST

Palette

White Gesso
Grumbacher, Liquitex or Winsor & Newton paints (color names may vary):

  Alizarin Crimson

  Burnt Sienna

  Burnt Umber

  Cadmium Orange

  Cadmium Red Light

  Cadmium Yellow Light

  Dioxazine Purple

  Hooker's Green Hue

  Thalo (Phthalo) Yellow-Green

  Titanium White

  Ultramarine Blue

Brushes

2" (51mm) hake brush

no. 4 flat sable brush

no. 4 round sable brush

no. 4 script liner brush

no. 6 bristle brush

no. 10 bristle brush

Miscellaneous Items

Sta-Wet palette

water can

no. 2 soft vine charcoal

16" × 20" (41cm × 51cm) stretched canvas

paper towels

palette knife

spray bottle

easel

Brushes

My selection of a limited number of specific brushes was chosen for the same reasons as the limited palette: versatility and economics.

2-INCH (51MM) HAKE BRUSH

The hake (pronounced ha KAY) brush is a large brush used for blending. It is primarily used in wet-on-wet techniques for painting skies and large bodies of water. It is often used for glazing as well.

NO. 10 BRISTLE BRUSH

This brush is used for underpainting large areas—mountains, rocks, ground or grass—as well as dabbing on tree leaves and other foliage. This brush also works great for scumbling and scrubbing techniques. The stiff bristles are very durable so you can be fairly rough on them.

NO. 6 BRISTLE BRUSH

A cousin to the no. 10 bristle brush, this brush is used for many of the same techniques and procedures. The no. 6 bristle brush is more versatile because you can use it for smaller areas, intermediate details, highlights and some details on larger objects. The no. 6 and no. 10 bristle brushes are the brushes you will use the most.

NO. 4 FLAT SABLE BRUSH

Sable brushes are used for more refined blending, detailing and highlighting techniques. They work great for final details and are a must for painting people and detailing birds or animals. They are more fragile and more expensive, so treat them with extra care.

NO. 4 ROUND SABLE BRUSH

Like the no. 4 flat sable brush, this brush is used for detailing, highlighting, people, birds, animals, etc. The main difference is that the sharp point allows you to have more control over areas where a flat brush will not work or is too wide. This is a great brush for finishing a painting.

NO. 4 SCRIPT LINER BRUSH

This brush is my favorite. It is used for the very fine details and narrow line work that can't be accomplished with any other brush. For example, use this brush for tree limbs, wire and weeds—and especially for your signature. The main thing to remember is to use it with a much thinner mixture of paint. Roll the brush in an ink-like mixture until it forms a fine point.

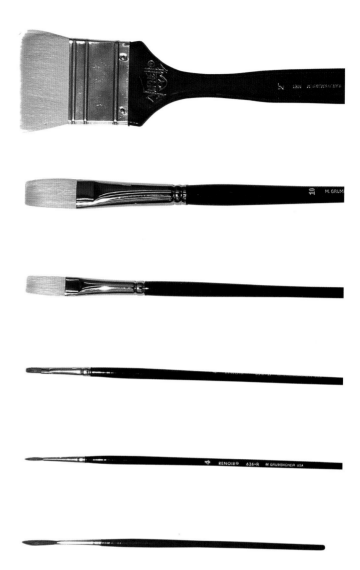

With this basic set of brushes, you can paint any subject.

BRUSH CLEANING TIPS

Remember that acrylics dry through evaporation. As soon as you finish painting, use good brush soap and warm water to thoroughly clean your brushes. Lay your brushes flat to dry. If you allow paint to dry in your brushes or your clothes, it is very difficult to get it out. I use denatured alcohol to soften dried paint. Soaking the brush in the alcohol for about thirty minutes, then washing it with soap and water, usually gets the dried paint out.

The Palette

There are several palettes on the market designed to help keep your paints wet. The two I use extensively are Sta-Wet palettes made by Masterson. Acrylics dry through evaporation, so keeping the paints wet is critical. The first palette is a 12" × 16" (31cm × 41cm) plastic palette-saver box with an airtight lid. This palette comes with a sponge you saturate with water and lay in the bottom of the box. Then you soak the special palette paper and lay it on the sponge. Place your paints out around the edge and you are ready to go. Use your spray bottle occasionally to mist your paints and they will stay wet all day long. When you are finished painting, attach the lid and your paint will stay wet for days.

My favorite palette is the same 12" × 16" (31cm × 41cm) palette box, except I don't use the sponge or palette paper. Instead, I place a piece of double-strength glass in the bottom of the palette. I fold paper towels into long strips (into fourths), saturate them with water and lay them on the outer edge of the glass. I place my paints on the paper towel. They will stay wet for days. I occasionally mist them to keep the towels wet.

If you leave your paints in a sealed palette for several days without opening it, certain colors, such as green and Burnt Umber will mildew. Just replace the color or add a few drops of chlorine bleach to the water in the palette to help prevent mildew.

To clean the glass palette, allow it to sit for about thirty seconds in water or spray the glass with your spray bottle. Scrape off the old paint with a single-edge razor blade. Either palette is great. I prefer the glass palette because I don't have to change the palette paper.

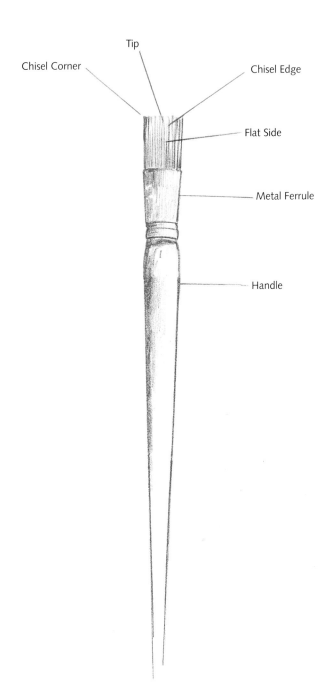

Brush diagram

Setting Up Your Palette

Here are two different ways to set up your palette.

Palette 1

The Sta-Wet 12" × 16" (31cm × 41cm) plastic palette-saver box comes with a large sponge, which is saturated with water.

Lay the sponge inside the palette box. Next, soak the special palette paper and lay it on the sponge. Place your paints around the edge. Don't forget to mist your paints to keep them wet.

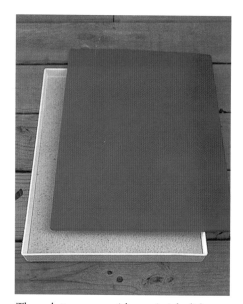

The palette comes with an airtight lid.

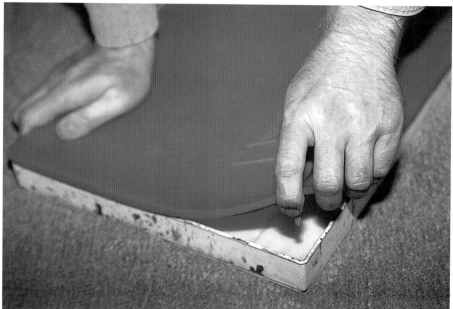

When closing the palette-saver box, make sure the lid is on securely. When the palette is properly sealed, your paints will stay wet for days.

Palette 2

Lay the saturated paper towels on the outer edges of the glass.

Instead of using the sponge or palette paper, another way to set up your palette box is to use a piece of double-strength glass in the bottom of the palette. Fold paper towels in long strips and saturate them with water to hold your paint.

I place my paints on the paper towel in the order shown.

Use the center of the palette for mixing paints. Occasionally mist the paper towels to keep them wet.

To clean the palette, allow it to sit for thirty seconds in water or spray the glass with a spray bottle. Scrape off the old paint with a single-edge razor blade.

Miscellaneous Supplies

CANVAS

There are many types of canvas available. Canvas boards are fine for practicing your strokes, as are canvas paper pads for doing studies or for testing paints and brush techniques. The best surface to work on is a primed, prestretched cotton canvas with a medium texture, which can be found at most art stores. As you become more advanced in your skills, you may want to learn to stretch your own canvas. I do this as often as I can, but for now a 16" × 20" (41cm × 51cm) prestretched cotton canvas is all you need for the paintings in this book.

EASEL

I prefer to work on a sturdy standing easel. There are many easels on the market, but my favorite is the Stanrite ST500 aluminum easel. It is lightweight, sturdy and easy to fold up to take on location or to workshops.

LIGHTING

Of course, the best light is natural north light, but most of us don't have this light available in our work areas. The next best light is 4' or 8' (1.2m or 2.4m) fluorescent lights hung directly over your easel. Place one cool bulb and one warm bulb in the fixture: this best simulates natural light.

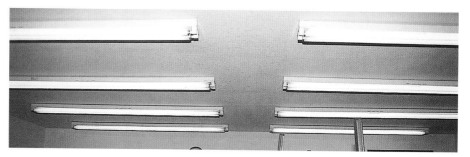

Studio lights

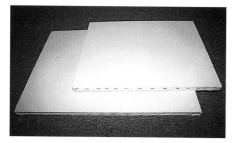

16" × 20" (41cm x 51cm) stretched canvas

Aluminum Stanrite studio easel

SPRAY BOTTLE

I use a spray bottle with a fine mist to lightly mist my paints and brushes throughout the painting process. The best ones are plant misters or spray bottles from a beauty supply store. It is important to keep one handy.

PALETTE KNIFE

I do not do a lot of palette-knife painting. I mostly use a knife for mixing. A trowel-shaped knife is more comfortable and easier to use than a flat knife.

SOFT VINE CHARCOAL

I prefer to use soft vine charcoal for most of my sketching. It is very easy to work with and shows up well. It is easy to remove or change by wiping it off with a damp paper towel.

Spray bottle

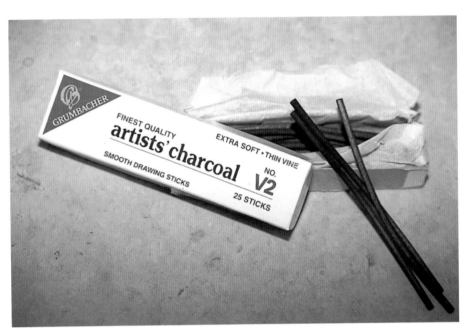

Soft vine charcoal

Palette knives

A Word about Mahlsticks and the Stedi Rest System

All of us at one time or another will have days when we are not as steady as we would like to be. Perhaps you are working on something that requires a lot of close-up detail work, or your painting is still wet and you can't steady your hand on the canvas while painting. The solution to these problems is called a mahlstick. I use it along with a little gadget called a Stedi Rest.

These photos show the use of a mahlstick both with and without the Stedi Rest. Either way, a mahlstick is a "must" for most painters. Really, a mahlstick is nothing more than a dowel rod about 36" (91cm) long that can be purchased from any hardware store. The Stedi Rest must be purchased from an art store. I carry both items at my studio for my students, which can be accessed online at my Web site: www.Yarnellart.com. The mahlsticks I stock are handmade from special woods and finishes.

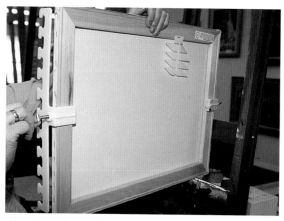

Attaching the Stedi Rest is a simple matter of screwing the bracket on the side of your stretcher strip.

Attaching a Stedi Rest on each side of the painting will give you several different horizontal positions.

Using your mahlstick on only one side of the Stedi Rest will give you several different angles from which to work.

The mahlstick can be used without the Stedi Rest by placing it at the top of the canvas to give you more vertical positions.

Understanding Complements

By the time you begin studying these books, you may have had some experience with the color wheel. However, I have noticed that many students still don't have a clear understanding of complements, the value system and graying colors. I would like to spend a little time discussing these issues as they pertain to landscapes. Note: There is much more in-depth study of the color wheel in my technique book.

Most landscape painters use a color wheel of grayed complements. As you probably know, a standard color wheel is made up of three primary colors—red, yellow, blue—three secondary colors—green, violet, orange—and six tertiary colors (intermediate colors)—red-orange, yellow-orange, yellow-green, blue-green, blue-violet, red-violet. In their pure forms, these colors are too bright to do a traditional landscape. Most artists create their own version of a grayed color wheel. For my color wheel, I use Hooker's Green, Cadmium Red Light and Cadmium Yellow Light as my primary colors, and mix the secondary and intermediate colors from these. Often we need to gray the colors to achieve the desired effect. We gray a color by adding its complement or a form of its complement.

For example, you want to use Hooker's Green, but it looks too intense for a particular area of your painting. Simply add some of its complement, which is found on the opposite side of the color wheel. You could add touches of Cadmium Red Light, Cadmium Orange, red-violet, red-orange, yellow-orange, etc. These are all forms of complements to Hooker's Green. Use this process for all of the colors. To gray purple, add yellows or forms of yellow. To gray orange, add blue or forms of blue, and so on around the wheel.

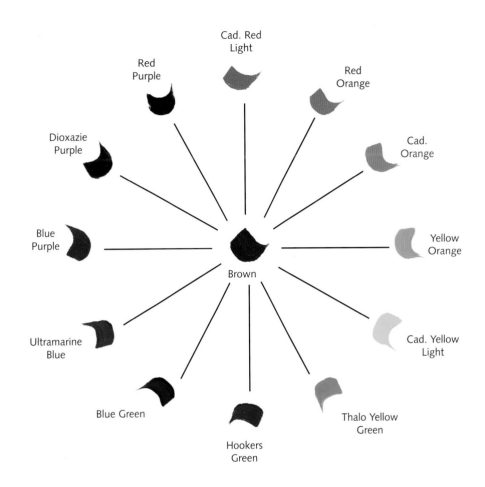

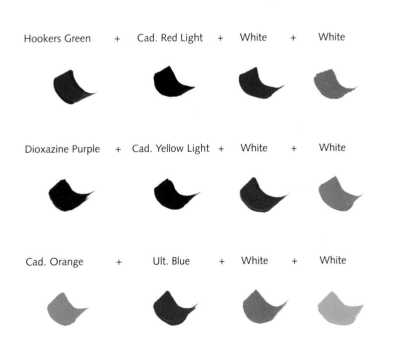

Hookers Green   +   Cad. Red Light   +   White   +   White

Dioxazine Purple   +   Cad. Yellow Light   +   White   +   White

Cad. Orange   +   Ult. Blue   +   White   +   White

The Crossing
16" × 20" (40.6cm × 50.8cm)

The Crossing

My first dream as an artist was to live on a ranch and become a western artist. Well, half of the dream came true. I have had the good fortune of becoming a full-time professional artist; however, the ranch part is still a dream. Nevertheless, I love the West, and find great joy in painting cowboys, horses and cows; and winter is my favorite season. Although I was able to satisfy my personal artistic desires in this painting, its main purpose is to be instructional for you. The main focus is learning to create a cold, snowy atmosphere, along with the clear transparent water. Add subject matter such as the cattle, horse and cowboy, and I think you'll find that this painting will really challenge your artistic abilities. There is much to learn here, so be patient, and you will have great success!

1 Make Charcoal Sketch

Begin with a very basic charcoal sketch using your soft vine charcoal. If you've read my other books, you'll know that I do most of my drawing with a brush, and so all you will need here is just three main contour lines.

2 Underpaint Background Pine Trees

With the high horizon and dense forest, this underpainting is simple. On your palette, using your no.10 hake brush, mix Hooker's Green with a fourth as much purple to make a very dark forest green. Using fairly thick paint, the hake brush and vertical strokes, paint the background solid. Be sure the entire canvas is covered. After it dries you may need to give it a second coat to get complete coverage.

3 Underpaint Water

To the dark green color from the previous step, add a fourth as much Ultramarine Blue. Use your no.10 hake brush to make long horizontal strokes that completely cover the water area. As in the previous step, you may need to give it a second coat after the first coat has dried. Add touches of white for variations in tone and value, and once again, be sure the canvas is completely covered.

4 Underpaint Middle and Foreground Snow

This is also a fairly simple step. First, mix white or gesso, half as much Ultramarine Blue, one-fourth as much Dioxazine Purple, and a small amount of Burnt Sienna. This should create a very clean mauvish gray. Now, take your no. 10 bristle brush and completely block in all of the middle ground and foreground. Make sure the canvas is well covered. Also, notice the irregular strokes along the edge of the forest and the water's edge. Keeping all the edges soft with no hard lines will make a difference later when you highlight the snow.

5 Add Form Shadows on Background Trees

Use the color from the previous step and your no. 10 bristle brush with a straight dabbing stroke to create the form of each pine tree. Notice the different shapes and sizes and interesting pockets of negative space around the trees. Now, add a little more purple and Burnt Sienna to the dark green from step 2. Take your no. 10 flat sable brush and use this color to define each trunk. Be sure these trunks create good negative space, which makes for good composition and eye flow among the trees.

6 Highlight the Snow, Phase 1

I have to admit that the painting looks a little strange at this stage, but never fear, things are going to change quickly. Mix white and just enough orange to slightly tint the white. Using your no. 6 bristle, begin drybrushing in the contour highlights of the snow. This is where your creative juices and artistic license really need to work together. At this point, it is critical that you have excellent eye flow and negative space. Remember, this is only the first phase of highlighting; you will be adding one or two more layers later.

7 Highlight Pine Trees and Add Shadows on Snow

Use the tinted white from the previous step and your no. 6 bristle brush to dab a highlight on the left side of the trees. Now add purple to the snow shadow color, and drybrush in the shadows of the pine trees, being sure to follow the contour of the snow. You will want to keep these shadows very soft. Later on you can refine them and adjust their value and/or color if necessary.

8 Block In Middle Ground Brush

This is a really fun step, but also a very important one. The greatest danger here is making the middle ground too busy. When you add the bushes, be sure you arrange them so that your eye flows gracefully throughout the canvas rather than bouncing from clump to clump. Mix Burnt Sienna with a touch of purple and a bit of white to change the value. Use your no. 6 bristle brush to apply this mixture with a vertical dry-brush stroke, feathering and lightening the pressure as you pull upward. Remember, this is only the underpainting; you will detail the bushes later.

9 Add Rocks and Pebbles to the Shoreline

Here you will begin to get down to the "nuts and bolts" of the painting. I use my no. 4 flat sable brush and a variety of colors to which I've added touches of white to change the values and tones. For example, Burnt Sienna is great by itself, but when you add a touch of white, you get a nice, earthy tan. Add touches of white to all of the colors on your palette—blue, purple, red, green, Burnt Umber, etc.—to make a good variety of colors. Next, simply make small rounded shapes along the water's edge. Notice how the rocks gradually fade out toward the center of the water to create the illusion of transparent water. Now, take Hooker's Green with a touch of purple, and drybrush in a choppy, dark edge to the water.

10 Add Piles of Snow Along the Shoreline

For this step, you will need to remix the snow highlight color: white with just enough orange to slightly tint it. Now, with your no. 4 flat sable brush, place small mounds of snow along the shoreline and on top of some of the rocks. Gradually work the mounds up into the middle ground and out into the water. When you start adding more details, you will add more of these mounds along with more highlights. As always, you need to pay attention to your negative space here. As long as you pay close attention to the rules of good composition, you can add as many of these snow piles as you wish.

11 Highlight Middle Ground Bushes

This is the point where the color really begins to show up in the painting; however, before going any further, take your soft vine charcoal and make a rough sketch of the mountain cabin. This helps establish the proper proportions. Now, take your no. 6 bristle brush and mix Burnt Sienna with touches of red, orange and white. Begin at the top of each bush, and apply this color with a very dry downward stroke. Keep in mind that the sun is coming in from the left side. This will probably be only an intermediate highlight, so don't go overboard here.

12 Block In the Cabin and Add Shadow

First, take some of the original gray that you mixed for underpainting the snow. Use your no. 6 bristle brush or your no. 4 flat sable to block in the roof with a solid coat of gray. Next add a touch of Burnt Sienna to the gray, and block in the right side of the cabin. Add a touch of white to the mixture and block in the left side of the cabin. Don't worry about the details yet, just square it up. Add to the gray a touch of purple, or a little blue if you like, and smudge in the shadow, keeping the edges soft. You will refine this shadow later; for now just be sure the shadow follows the contour of the land.

13 Detail Cabin, Phase 1

The details added to the cabin will differ depending on your own preferences, and you will wait until later to add the final details and highlights. Most of this step will be best accomplished with a no. 4 flat sable brush. Begin by painting on the roof a fairly thick coat of the orange-tinted white color for the snow highlight. Be sure to allow a little bit of the underpainting to show through. Block in the door and windows with a mixture of blue, Burnt Sienna, and purple. Next mix a highlight color of white with touches of orange and Burnt Sienna. Drybrush over the underpainting on the sides of the building to create a weathered wood effect. Add a few fence posts with a mixture of Burnt Sienna, blue, and a touch of white to create the correct value.

14 Sketch Cowboy, Horse, Cows and Tracks

Now you are ready for the exciting challenge of drawing animals and a person. With your soft vine charcoal or a soft charcoal pencil, make a simple but accurate sketch of the horse and rider, the cows, and the location of the tracks. This is an important step because you need to be sure these subjects fit properly into your composition and use of negative space.

15 Underpaint Horse, Cowboy and Cows

The underpainting is the same for the horse and the cows, except that you may choose to make your horse a different color. I used a mixture of Burnt Sienna with a touch of blue and a small touch of white. Because your horse and rider are a little farther back, they should be a slightly lighter value. Your no. 4 flat and round sable work the best here. Simply block in each shape very roughly, using quick, broad strokes. Don't worry about making this perfect; you will make adjustments in the next step. You can use a dark value of whatever color you choose to paint the cowboy's pants and jacket.

16 Add Intermediate Details to Cows, Horse and Cowboy

Here you will need your no. 4 flat and no. 4 round sable. For the cows, mix white, orange and a touch of Burnt Sienna. Apply this color using a quick dry-brush stroke that follows the contours of their bodies. You may have to do this two or three times to get the desired effect. For the heads, mix white with a touch of yellow and use the same dry-brush stroke. The important thing to remember is not to completely cover the underpainting; some of it should show through. The procedure is the same for the cowboy and the horse. Mix the proper highlight color and apply just enough to create the form. Final highlights and details will be added later.

17 Block In Miscellaneous Objects

Here, all you want to do is block in all the remaining objects, such as the fence posts and dead bushes. I used Burnt Sienna mixed with touches of blue and white. The value system of this painting does not create a great deal of depth; however, your fence posts should still be painted a lighter value as they recede into the distance. Next, thin the mixture to an ink-like consistency and use your script liner brush to paint in the small bushes that will add character to the painting.

18 Highlight and "Drift" Snow

Here is where you will really put the light in the painting. Make a creamy mixture of white with a touch of yellow and use your no. 4 flat and your no. 4 round sable brushes to begin "drifting" the snow up around the cabin, clumps of bushes, fence posts and other objects. Don't be afraid to apply the paint thickly so the color stays nice and opaque. You can see that this really adds a lot of sparkle to the painting.

19 Add Miscellaneous Details

Here you will add all of the details that will give the painting its more refined look, such as shadows, weeds, highlights and a glaze on the water. By now, you should be confident that you understand how to finish a painting. For instance, if your water is too dark, apply a white glaze. You can go on to add a wire to the fence posts and individual weeds scattered throughout the painting. Now is the time to add final highlights to the snow and cabin. Remember, the key is to stop before you overwork the painting.

20 Add Final Details to Cows, Horse and Cowboy

What you want to do next is to clean up the forms, add brighter highlights and adjust the shapes of the cows, horse and rider. For instance, if the leg of one of the cows is too fat or crooked, or if the head is a little too large for the body, make those adjustments now. You need to have some underpainting color available for each object. There is a good chance you will need to repaint parts of the cows, horse or cowboy. If so, all you need to do is repaint using the underpaint colors and then add the highlights.

Patient Fisherman
16" × 20" (40.6cm × 50.8cm)

Patient Fisherman

Just outside my studio I have a beautiful small pond surrounded by trees, high weeds and other vegetation. It is a perfect habitat for all kinds of wildlife, especially different types of water birds. Also, the atmosphere created by the pond is wonderful with its many different lighting situations, seasons and other conditions such as fog, mist, haze, ice, etc. This little patch of ground is an artistic paradise. One early misty morning my brother photographed this blue heron that was looking for something to eat. The photo lay on my drawing table for many days until finally it got the best of me, and I had to paint it. This painting has a lot to teach about simplicity, atmosphere and the subtle use of green as the predominant color. These lessons make this painting a true artistic challenge.

1 Make Rough Sketch
First, simply take your soft vine charcoal and make the rough sketch. This is a very simple sketch of a fairly complicated painting.

2 Underpaint Background and Water
When working with this much green and this much water, it is a good idea to completely cover the background with a greenish gray color to get rid of the starkness of the white canvas. First, mix Hooker's Green, and then add one-fourth as much purple, and one-fourth as much white. Now, with your hake brush, have fun covering the background and the water area. Be sure the canvas is completely covered, and don't be afraid to let the brushstrokes show. Also, notice that the area at the shoreline is a little darker.

3 Layering Background Trees, Phase 1
The first thing to do is to gently lay in the first layers of background trees with a color that is slightly darker than the background. This is the first of several layers of trees. When you are happy with your color, take your no. 10 bristle brush and begin dabbing in the first layer using a scumble stroke. Don't worry about creating individual trees just yet. Leave a small opening just to the right of the center because you will be painting some light there later. Just be loose and free and have fun with this step.

4 Layering Background Trees, Phase 2

Next you will repeat the same technique from the previous step with a mixture that is a little darker. You will also begin to establish the basic tree shapes. Take your same mixture and add a little more green and a touch more purple, and add a little touch of Burnt Sienna to warm it up. Now, with your no. 10 or no. 6 bristle brush, begin dabbing in more individual tree and bush shapes. Remember, we are only after basic shapes, so we will not do any highlighting or anything else at this point. Also, remember that this painting will look very rough for these first few steps, so don't panic! Things will begin to change after this step.

5 Underpaint Trees in Water

Now you will move to the water. This step is identical to the two previous steps, except that as you layer the trees, you should use more of a horizontal scumbling stroke; this helps create the suggestion of ripples on the water. Begin with the color that is slightly darker than the background and gently scumble in the reflections of the background trees. Next, slightly darken the mixture and do the same thing again. Remember, keep soft edges and allow some of the background to come through. You will add light and more ripples later on.

6 Block In Tree Limbs

Get ready to switch gears for a little while. Get your no. 4 round sable and your no. 4 liner brush. You may use either or both of these. Take the dark mixture from the previous step and thin it down to an ink-like consistency. Next, carefully block in the background tree limbs and the reflections in the water at the same time. Keep in mind that the reflections in the water have a little bit of a horizontal movement to them. Also, keep an eye on the negative space and variety of shapes. Don't be afraid to darken the mixture a little bit in order for the trees to show up against some of the darker areas of the background.

7 Underpaint Middle Ground Grass

Use the dark inky mixture from the previous step to begin underpainting some of the grasses, mostly in the middle ground. You will want to use your no. 10 or no. 6 bristle brush, and start by scrubbing with a vertical stroke the grass formations on the left side of the painting. If your mixture is too light to show up against the water, simply add a touch more green and/or purple. This is just the underpainting; you will begin highlighting in the next few steps. After you have created the grass formations, reflect that basic shape into the water, keeping the edges soft.

8 Add Light to Background and Water

Finally it's time to liven up the painting. The color you will need is a mixture of Thalo Yellow-Green, white and a touch of the grayish green that you used in the middle ground grass in step 7. Begin in the background by drybrushing in some soft pastel yellow-green then move down to the water and create the same effect. Use horizontal brushstrokes in the water, and a scumbling dry-brush stroke in the tree area. Increase the brightness by simply adding more white and yellow-green; you may need to go over this several times to get the desired effect, but it's worth the effort!

9 Add Ripples to the Water

This is a continuation of the previous step, except now, the strokes will become a bit more controlled. Using a creamy mixture of the same colors as the previous step, take your no. 4 flat sable and your no. 6 flat bristle brushes. Using short, choppy, horizontal strokes, begin applying the ripple effect to the water. I prefer to begin at the base of the painting and work up, lightening the color and pressure as I go, making sure to cover all the water. It's important to make the light much brighter up through the center of the water area. The real danger here is crowdedness, where too many strokes overlap each other. Remember the negative space rule—even in this area of a painting, all of your highlight strokes should have some connection to each other, so your eye will flow instead of bounce across the water.

10 Highlight Background Trees

This is an exciting step. First, mix a creamy mixture of Thalo Yellow-Green, yellow and white. Now, load the very tip of your no. 6 or no. 10 bristle brush with a small amount of color and gently dab on the form highlights of the trees. You may vary the color by adding touches of Thalo Yellow-Green, yellow or white. Also, dab on highlights in the middle ground to create a glow on the grass and bushes. I know you are tired of me mentioning the negative space rule, but it is so important, especially here where you have groupings of trees. Be sure you have good eye flow and that your highlights don't end up being just a bunch of little round clumps.

11 Add Middle Ground Weeds and Darken Shoreline

This is a simple step, but a very important one. Take the dark green mixture that was used for the under-painting in step 7, and thin it to an ink-like consistency. Use your script liner brush to add plenty of tall weeds in the middle ground island that stick out on the left of the painting. Now with your no. 6 bristle brush, scrub in an irregular, darker shoreline, using a mixture of blue, a touch of purple, Burnt Sienna, and a little white to get the correct value.

12 Add Final Highlights on Water

In this step you will be adding very thin slivers of light on top of the water to create a shimmer on the surface. First mix white with a touch of Thalo Yellow-Green and thin it so it is nice and creamy. Then with your no. 4 round sable or your script liner brush, paint thin lines along the surface of the water, using a rocking motion and following the original underpainted ripples. You can see that this really brightens the water and gives it more of a glossy look. You should also put short, choppy highlights along the shoreline.

13 Sketch Large Tree in Foreground

Use your soft vine charcoal to make a simple, accurate sketch of the large tree, keeping in mind good negative space, composition and proportions. This will give you a guide when you paint so there's no guesswork.

14 Block In Large Tree in Foreground

For this step, mix Hooker's Green, purple and a little bit of Burnt Sienna. Use your no. 6 flat bristle brush to block in the tree trunk and larger limbs, then switch to your no. 4 flat sable and block in the intermediate limbs. Lastly, thin the mixture to an ink-like consistency, and use your script liner to finish and taper the limbs. The main thing to remember is that your limbs should have good negative space and plenty of overlap. Also, it's not how many limbs you put in, but rather how you arrange them that can make the tree look too busy or incomplete. While you are doing this, step back occasionally because you can see the negative space problems much better from a distance.

15 Add Foreground Brush and Weeds

Next you will "plant" the tree by scrubbing up some underbrush around its base and smudging in the reflection of the tree into the water. Also add the taller weeds in the foreground and at the base of the tree. I cannot stress the use of good negative space enough at this point! Each clump of grass and all the weeds should be strategically placed to create good eye flow. There is a lot of activity in this painting with all the weeds and tree limbs, so be careful not to make too many; but don't be afraid to add as many as it takes.

16 Final Highlights

This is the tricky area of the painting that I call "accent highlights." Create a mixture of white with touches of orange and yellow. It should be a little on the orange side to complement this color scheme. I usually use my no. 4 round sable for painting these highlights. Because this is a backlit painting, you only want to use short, choppy, broken strokes to add accents just on the edges of the objects. Scatter patches of warm highlights throughout the painting.

17 Sketch In Heron

All you need here is a fairly accurate sketch of the heron, or whatever bird you choose to put here. A sharp piece of soft vine charcoal works best for this step.

18 Underpaint Heron

Mix blue, Burnt Sienna, and touches of white and purple. Then, with your no. 4 flat sable, block in the entire bird. The no. 4 round sable may be the best choice for painting the beak. Now mix black with blue, purple and Burnt Sienna, and use your no. 4 round sable to paint in the stripe on his head, the feather hanging from his head and the little patch on his shoulder.

19 Add Details to the Heron

Brush in just enough highlights and details to give the heron good form. White with a touch of yellow works best for highlighting the outer edge of the bird. Make the mixture creamy, and with your no. 4 round sable, carefully drybrush the highlight on his neck, head and breast area. Use just a touch of orange for his beak. Don't get too carried away with adding details to the bird. I hope you had fun with this painting and can see it has so many possibilities!

High and Mighty
20" × 16" (50.8cm × 40.6cm)

High and Mighty

I am still drawn to the high country. Every chance I get, I go to the mountains to study, research, paint and simply unwind. After living in the mountains and having a studio and gallery in Taos as well as Angel Fire, there is hardly a day that goes by that I don't recall my daily hikes into the wilderness areas of northern New Mexico to photograph and study the deer, elk and other wildlife. Along with the wildlife, there are numerous rock formations and different ground contours that can be a real inspiration as well as a challenge for most artists. As you can see, this painting offers a wide range of rock and ground formations; the different levels of cliffs create the potential to be a compositional nightmare. Be sure that you work out the design aspect of these formations before you get started. Believe me, that little extra effort will really help cut down on frustration later. This is a very satisfying painting because you will walk away feeling as if you have overcome a great challenge when you are finished. Climbing a mountain requires a very slow, careful approach—watching every step and handhold until you reach the top. The same thing applies to painting this landscape. Carefully arrange and rearrange all of the formations using all of the technical tools of composition like negative space, overlap, eyestoppers, etc. until you have completed the task.

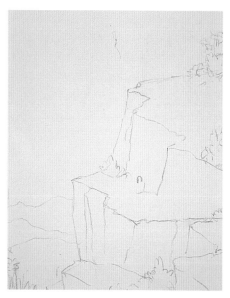

1 Make Charcoal Sketch

Because this is an unusual composition, it's a bit more important here to make an accurate sketch of the basic configuration of the cliff and rock formations.

2 Block In the Sky

You will want a fairly clean sky for this painting, with a few soft clouds; however, since the sky is not the focus, it's best to keep it simple. First, start at the very base of the sky, and with your hake brush and a liberal amount of gesso, paint white about halfway up the sky, adding a touch of yellow and orange as you go up. This will be a very soft pastel horizon color. You don't even have to rinse your brush. Repeat the same process at the top of the sky, starting with gesso, but adding touches of blue, purple and Burnt Sienna as you blend down. When you reach the horizon color, gently blend the two colors together so that there is no hard edge.

3 Add Clouds and Distant Mountains

Use your no. 6 bristle brush with a mixture of white and a touch of orange to scrub in some very soft clouds beginning at the center and working up. This is a dry-brush stroke, so be careful to keep the clouds soft and somewhat scattered. Next, mix three values of a grayish purple mountain color using white, blue, purple and Burnt Sienna. The exact color is up to you—if you like more purple, blue or gray, that's fine; just be sure that you have a light, a middle and a darker value. Begin in the back and make each layer of mountain a bit darker. Like the sky, the mountains are not the feature in this painting, so keep them soft and simple with very little detail.

4 Block In Distant Pine Trees

This is a simple and fairly quick step, but I wanted to single it out so that you can see how important it is. You can use your no. 4 flat sable or the no. 6 bristle brush. The mixture is Hooker's Green, purple and white (your color and value may vary from mine). You'll want to make a couple of different grayish green values; use these colors to dab in some trees of different shapes and sizes. Keep in mind the ever-present challenge of creating good negative space.

5 Underpaint Cliffs, Phase 1

This is where the painting becomes a bit more complicated, and more advanced techniques become necessary. First, use your no. 6 bristle brush for the smaller areas and your no. 10 bristle brush for the more open and larger areas. Mix Burnt Sienna, Ultramarine Blue and a touch of purple. Double- or triple-load your brush, and use short, choppy, vertical strokes to fill in all of the large open areas and small horizontal cracks on the tops of the cliffs. Notice that the canvas is completely covered, but brushstrokes are still visible where the paint varies in thickness.

6 Underpaint Cliffs, Phase 2

This is a practical step of simply defining the edges of the cliffs, adding minor highlights and establishing the basic contour of the cliffs by adding various values of soft highlights. Good use of negative space is absolutely critical here. This is more difficult than it looks! I recommend using a no. 6 bristle and a no. 4 flat sable. Mix a combination of white, orange and a little Burnt Sienna. It's OK for the mixture to be inconsistent in color and value. Beginning on the outer edge of each section, use short, choppy vertical strokes, gradually working back into the crack of the cliff. You should be able to see a contrast between dark and light areas.

7 Underpaint Tops of Cliffs

Our main priority here is to block in the tops of the cliffs, which is important because it helps us to see the entire formation of all of the cliffs as a whole. Underpainting the tops of these cliffs requires loose, free, and somewhat rough brushstrokes. Use your no. 6 bristle and your no. 10 bristle with a mixture of white, Burnt Sienna, purple and orange. Remember, this is only the underpainting, but you still want to be sure that the entire top of the cliff is completely covered. Also notice that this underpainting has a variety of colors.

8 Add Brush and Grass

The goal here is to simply locate the clumps of brush and grasses; this helps to establish the final design of the cliffs, before you add the intermediate details. I generally use my no. 6 bristle brush for this. The mixture is Hooker's Green, Burnt Sienna, purple and white to get the right value. Play with this mixture until you are pleased with the color. Now, use a variety of brush and grass techniques which you have used in previous paintings. Add a good variety of bushes and grasses that complement your existing composition and negative space areas.

9 Finish Background

This really is a fun step; you can truly use your artistic license here, but just be careful not to overdetail or emphasize any of the background subjects. The background cannot overpower the foreground. First, dry-brush a whitish yellow mist on the left side of the painting to soften the edges of the distant mountains. Simply take a touch of white and a little bit of yellow, and with your no. 6 bristle brush, use a dry-brush circular motion and blend out the left side of the mountains into the sky. Then with your no. 4 round sable and a little Burnt Umber with a touch of white, block in the dead pine trees behind the cliffs. Next, you can go ahead and highlight the trees with a touch of orange and white, or even a little Thalo Yellow-Green, using your no. 4 flat sable brush.

10 Highlight Rocks and Pebbles

Now we are getting down to some serious business here. Next you will add a good number of small rocks and pebbles, which is a fairly time-consuming process, so take your "patience pill" and have fun locating the best place for the rocks. Notice that most of them are located at the base of the cliffs. Once again, negative space and good composition are necessary for this to work properly. Use your no. 4 round sable with Burnt Sienna and touches of blue and white for the dark side of the rocks. Use white with a touch of orange for the highlight. Make a good variety of shapes and sizes, and be sure you have plenty of rocks touching and overlapping.

11 Add Miscellaneous Details to Tops of Cliffs

Next you will add the small twigs, branches and individual weeds, but only the most necessary ones at this point. (After you finish detailing the cliffs you will add other branches and weeds in different colors and values.) Mix Burnt Umber with plenty of water to create an ink-like mixture. Now use your script liner brush to add plenty of dead branches, twigs and individual weeds. By now you should have developed good control with your script liner brush. If you like, you can change the color and value for the weeds by simply adding a touch of green, orange, Burnt Sienna, yellow and/or white. Just experiment, have fun, but don't overdo it.

12 Add Cliff Highlights

Putting the final highlights on top of the cliffs will help establish the brightness of the painting. The main color will be a mixture of white and orange with a touch of yellow. The mixture can vary, so don't be afraid to experiment. Now, with your no. 4 flat sable or your no. 6 bristle brush, begin applying the highlights on the more sunlit areas of the cliffs. Don't overhighlight or you will lose the contrast that gives the cliffs their form. Go ahead and highlight some of the rocks as well. How bright you make this is up to you. It may take two or three layers to achieve the desired brightness.

13 Sketch Elk and Dead Tree

Anytime that you add wildlife or any other subject that needs to be anatomically correct, it is important to start with a fairly good sketch. This will go a long way in helping you maintain accuracy of the proportions as you paint. Use your charcoal to sketch in the elk and the large dead tree. Don't be afraid to resketch several times; this is what is so great about using soft vine charcoal: It's so easy to remove.

14 Underpaint Elk and Tree

Your small round and flat sable brushes will really come in handy for this step. For the front part of the elk, use Burnt Umber; for the rest of him, add just a little white to the umber and block in the rest of the body, making sure there is no hard outline around the body. Then use a mixture of blue, Burnt Sienna and purple to block in the dead tree with short choppy, vertical, strokes. On both the elk and the tree, be sure the canvas is well covered with paint.

15 Detail Elk, Phase 1

This is where it will really be necessary to have patience and a good understanding of some of the dry-brush techniques. In this phase, you only want to paint the basic highlights of the elk, establish his form and block in his antlers. First, thin down some Burnt Umber and block in the antlers with your no. 4 round and flat sable. Next, with a fairly creamy mixture of Burnt Umber with touches of white and yellow, drybrush in the intermediate highlights on his back, shoulder and side. Be sure your strokes follow the contours of his body. Smudge a little bit of this color on his forehead and over his eye. That's all for now; you will finish him up a little later.

16 Detail the Tree

Since this tree is in the immediate foreground and serves as the painting's main "eye stopper," it needs to have a good deal of detail work. Notice that it has several colors on it. For the highlight on the left side, use white with a touch of orange, and even a little Burnt Sienna and yellow. I prefer to turn my no. 4 flat sable vertically and use short, choppy, vertical strokes to apply the color. Now add touches of blue, purple, white, red and Burnt Sienna to add color and texture. When you add these colors, don't blend them all together or they will turn to mud, and don't mix them on your palette. Do not completely cover the underpainting; you want some of the dark values to show through and add depth to the bark. For the reflected highlight on the shadowed side of the tree, mix white, purple and blue. Apply just enough to soften the edge of the tree.

17 Final Highlights on Elk

This is a simple but very important step. First, create a creamy mixture of white with a touch of orange for the main highlights. Again, using the smaller brushes, begin adding the very bright accent highlights to the outer edges of the elk. Don't create a solid outline. Use light, feathery strokes, very much like a dry-brush technique, and be sure not to put too much on your brush. You will "plant" the elk later when you pull up the bushes around his legs.

18 Add Final Highlights to Rocks and Pebbles

Now you will create intense light on a good number of rocks and pebbles. The color you will use is a creamy mixture of white with a touch of yellow and maybe a touch of orange. You want to highlight only the rocks that are the most exposed to the light; the others will be in shadowed or subdued light. With either of your small sable brushes, apply the highlights fairly thick so that they will stay opaque. Be careful not to overhighlight.

19 Finish Up

At this point, the painting is almost finished. This final step will be different for each of us. I chose to highlight the bushes, add some leaves to the branches and also a few complementary flowers. I painted a distant eagle to reinforce the theme "high and mighty." Once you have made all of your adjustments and added final highlights, you have one option left that can be used at your discretion: a glaze over the entire painting. This will only be necessary if you want to soften it or add a feeling of haze or mist. I decided not to apply the glaze this time. I hope you had fun with this painting, and that you're looking forward to the next one.

Tossed by the Waves
16" × 20" (40.6cm × 50.8cm)

Tossed by the Waves

I have never lived near the ocean nor have I spent much time there, but like so many artists, the ocean is so exciting to me that I am compelled to paint it. Every so often I have the desire to unleash that excitement onto my canvas. This painting proved to be the perfect challenge because of the focus on action, movement, composition and mood. Believe me, it is more difficult than it looks to take this large body of water and make something very interesting out of it. A good understanding negative space is especially necessary with this painting, so it may be a good idea to review the composition principles before you begin. There is a lot here to challenge you, and I think you'll find the adventure an enjoyable one.

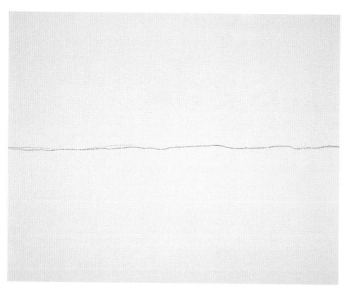

1 Make Charcoal Sketch

How about this for a sketch: a straight line across the center of the canvas! That's all it takes to get this painting started.

2 Underpaint Sky, Phase 1

You will begin with the sky; however, instead of using the hake brush, you'll use your no. 10 bristle brush and a scumbling stroke. First, load your brush with gesso, then add small amounts of blue, purple and Burnt Sienna, and scumble or scrub small sections at a time while working your way across the canvas, making sure to keep the edges soft. Don't be afraid to use plenty of paint. Even though this goes on fairly opaquely, it will require one or two more applications to get full coverage. As you can see, this ends up as a mottled gray sky.

3 Continue Sky, Phase 2

The next step is to build the darker areas in the sky to help create a bit more of a stormy look. Create a mixture of small amounts of blue, Burnt Sienna, purple and a touch of white. This color should be slightly darker than the sky. The technique is pretty much the same as above, except that you should be a little more specific about cloud formations. Again, you will use your no. 10 bristle brush. Have fun creating some exciting, free-flowing clouds.

4 Accent Sky, Phase 3

In this step, the brush technique remains the same as before, you will only change the color and values of the sky area. The best color for this is a soft pinkish highlight of white, red and a touch of blue; this is a nice complement to the gray background. Scumble or scrub soft, light accents of contrasting values against the darker background. Once again, remember to keep soft edges and create good negative space. Don't be afraid to experiment with different combinations of complementary colors to create just the right mood and atmosphere.

5 Underpaint Water, Phase 1

Wow! You can really work out your frustrations in this step! Block in the water with large, loose strokes using your no. 10 bristle brush. In this case it is important to see the brushstrokes, and be sure the canvas is completely covered. The colors you'll need are Hooker's Green, touches of blue, purple, Burnt Sienna and even a touch of yellow now and then. Of course, you will simply add a touch of white when you want to change the value and create a more opaque coverage. Notice that there are several light and dark areas and how the brushstrokes create a dramatic sense of movement.

6 Continue Water, Phase 2

Next you will want to add some intermediate light values to the water and begin to establish a sense of distance in the painting. First, using the no. 6 bristle brush, take a little white and touches of red and blue, then scrub across the horizon, creating a soft, hazy mist. Blend this up into the sky, and then down into the water until the hard edges disappear. As you come forward, switch to the no. 10 bristle brush and add touches of green, blue and purple to the above mixture and begin creating more defined movement in the waves. Bring this color forward a little over halfway, until everything fades together in the foreground.

7 Block In Large Wave
This is a fairly simple but critically important step. The location, size, proportion and color of the large wave are the key factors here. You may want to make a rough sketch with your charcoal to locate it. Then take your no. 10 bristle brush, and use the same combinations of color that you used for the underpainting in step 5 to paint in the wave, carefully blending it into the middle ground water. You will highlight and detail this area later.

8 Highlight Water in Background
With your no. 6 bristle brush, take white with a touch of yellow, and a little blue, and begin creating some turbulence in the water behind the big wave and across the background. Make your strokes choppy and loose. This is a small area, so don't try to create a lot of detail, and keep this choppy water behind the large wave. This will serve to separate the background from the foreground. While you are at it, you may want to use your charcoal to sketch in the small island on the right side.

9 Underpaint Island
For this next step keep in mind that you want to create a sense of distance, so the colors for the island should be the same values as the other colors in that area. I suggest that you use your no. 4 flat sable for this. Mix white, Hooker's Green and a touch of purple and scrub in the suggestion of a rocky shore and distant trees. Next use this color with white and a touch of orange to put a soft highlight on the rocks along the base of the island. There should be only a suggestion of highlights.

10 **Sketch Sailboat**
Next use your charcoal to sketch in the sailboat. It's okay to choose another type of boat as long as it fits the composition. The location of the boat depends on where you put the large wave, so if your main wave is in a slightly different location than mine, be sure to adjust the placement of your boat.

11 **Underpaint the Sailboat**
You will need your no. 4 flat sable brush for this step. First, mix a soft gray of blue, Burnt Sienna, a touch of purple and of course, white. Underpaint the front sails and body of the boat and the lower half of the red sail. Next, mix red with the gray, and underpaint the shadowed side of the large sail. Mix red, orange and a touch of white to paint in the sunlit part of the red sail. Use white with a touch of orange to highlight the white part.

12 **Detail the Boat**
Here, all you need is a good imagination. You can finish the boat just about any way you like; it is important however, to complete the boat before moving on to the next step. Use your no. 4 flat and round sables and your no. 4 script liner for these details using clean and light quick strokes. Don't be afraid to use pure white and pure red to get the clean bright color that you want. Simply brighten the underpainting until you are satisfied with its intensity.

13 Detail Water in Middle and Background

In this step you will add shadows, highlights, mist and motion to the areas around the boat, over to the island, and up to the large wave. Most of this will be done with your no. 4 flat sable and your no. 6 bristle brush. A mixture of white with a touch of yellow works great for the highlight. Your dark mixture will consist of green with touches of blue, purple and white to change the value. Now all you do is intensify the shape and movement of the waves, and place the white caps along the ridges of the waves; this takes a little effort, but it's well worth it.

14 Detail Large Wave, Phase 1

The main thing to accomplish here is to give the wave more of a transparent look along with some minor details. For this you will use your no. 4 flat and round sables. First, take a small amount of Thalo Yellow-Green and a touch of white and carefully drybrush this color at the top of the wave where it begins to break. Next, with white and a touch of orange, dab in the white foam around the outer edge of the wave. Don't outline the wave, just define it. Thin down some white, almost to a wash, and use a toothbrush to spatter some mist around the outer edge of the wave.

15 Detail Large Wave and Foreground

The main goal here is to continue building the wave with dark and light values, and then fade it into the foreground. The base mixture is white, blue and a touch of green; you will change this mixture as needed. Use the underpainting as a guide to darken the darks, lighten the lights and intensify the highlights on the crest of the waves. Then make the large wave look more transparent by adding a touch of Thalo Yellow-Green and a touch of white to the upper part of the wave.

16 Add Mist to Horizon and Highlight Island

This step is an absolute must. You will drybrush in a soft horizon to lighten up the existing one, and create a little more atmosphere and depth. Start by making a wash of water with a touch of white and blue. Use your hake brush or no. 10 bristle brush to paint this wash across the horizon, let it dry and then repeat it if you want your horizon to be more faded out. Then mix a little white with a touch of orange, and use your no. 4 flat sable brush to highlight the rocks on the island.

17 Add Final Highlights to Water

This is probably the most difficult step, not because there are a lot of things to do, but because it is very difficult to know when to stop. The final highlight is a mixture of white and red that's a perfect complement to the bluish gray water. You must carefully decide where to place these highlights, thinking about your composition and creating good negative space. Any of your smaller brushes will work well here, and a creamy mixture will help make the paint flow more easily.

18 Finalize Sailboat Details

This step is really fun because you can just let your own artistic license take over. For me, it is a matter of highlighting and adding minor details. Some things that you might consider are: additional lines to suggest more rigging, brighter highlights, the suggestion of a person or two, additional mist or haze around the boat and maybe even a seagull or two. Just have fun, but don't make the details too crisp. The beauty of this painting is in the suggestion of details.

19 Refine Entire Painting

As is often the case, you may be finished by now; however, adding a few minor things such as a few seagulls, a house on the island or final highlights on the water and boat or even in the sky, may be just the ticket for giving this painting its finished look. So, as I often say, have fun, just don't overdo it. It would be a good idea at this point to stand back and study the foreground water as it moves back toward the large wave. You want to be sure the foreground negative space is not too busy. Your eye should not "get stuck" in the foreground; the composition should lead your eye gracefully and gradually back toward the large wave and the boat. If this isn't the case, you probably have a negative space problem, but don't worry, you can still adjust the values to improve the eye flow.

Misty Morning Sunrise
16" × 20" (40.6cm × 50.8cm)

Misty Morning Sunrise

What a great painting to improve your technique and stimulate your creative juices! The original painting I did of this was a 3' × 4' (91cm × 122cm) museum-type piece that took several days of study, research and painting time. Since this is a much smaller, simpler version, you will be overdoing it if you spend more than a few hours on it. This is a subject that I am very familiar with because I've spent many weekends and summers hiking near and fishing in the many beautiful rivers and streams we are so blessed with in eastern Oklahoma. As a matter of fact, the area has earned the nickname "green country." This painting will challenge even the most seasoned artist. The dense forest, running water, giant rocks and early morning mist will no doubt tickle your creative senses. This is a fairly difficult painting, but it is well worth all the creative energy you can muster up. There are a lot of great learning opportunities in this painting, so catch your breath, settle down and let's get started!

1 Create Charcoal Sketch

As usual, take your soft vine charcoal and make a rough sketch of the main areas of negative space.

2 Underpaint the Background

Here, all you want to create is a very light, grayish white background. There are several layers of values that will go on top of this background. Mix white or gesso, a touch of yellow, purple and blue to create a soft neutral pastel color. Use your large hake brush to paint a very liberal coat of this color on the background. Let this dry completely before going on to the next step.

3 Underpaint Distant Trees, Value 1

You will now begin the layering process for the background trees. First, take your background color from step 2 and slightly darken it with a little more purple and a touch of green. Use your no. 10 or no. 6 bristle brush and scumble in the first layer of distant trees. Start at the bottom and go up, gradually lessening the pressure on your brush until the trees disappear. Keep your edges soft and create good negative space. Don't worry about the trees in the upper left-hand corner.

4 Paint Distant Trees, Value 2

As you probably know by now, the next step is to slightly darken the mixture by adding a little more purple and green, then use your no. 6 bristle brush to scumble in the next layer of distant trees. With each value change, you should become increasingly more aware of the forms of the trees, paying special attention to the negative space. Be careful that the tree area does not become too busy. Also, notice that the leaves go completely off the top of the canvas.

5 Paint Distant Trees, Value 3

As you've anticipated, darken the mixture and scumble in the next layer of distant trees; this is the layer where you will paint the darker foreground trees. Also, you will add the first hint of tree trunks here. Take a small dab of this darker mixture, thin it slightly, then use your no. 4 round sable to carefully paint in the first layer of tree trunks. Next, go back to your no. 6 bristle to scumble in this layer of tree leaves. This time you can be a little more specific about their forms. Notice that you can see all three values; this creates a sense of depth. If you have overpainted too much of the background, you may need to dab in a few areas of value 1 or value 2 to open up some pockets of negative space.

6 Underpaint Water

This is a quick and easy step. Notice that the brushstrokes are mostly horizontal and the canvas is well covered with paint. Do not premix the color on your palette; you want different values and tones. The best way to do this is to put a little of each color on your no. 10 bristle brush and simply blend on the canvas as you go; this will leave a good variety of values and tones. Use blue, purple, green and a little white. Notice how the darker area on the far left gradually fades into a lighter value toward the right side. It's okay for your brushstrokes to show here.

7 Block In Close-up Trees

You will need to mix a large amount of dark green on your palette that will be used for this step and subsequent steps as well. First mix equal amounts of Hooker's Green and purple, making it fairly creamy. If you want your color to be a little warmer, add some Burnt Sienna or Cadmium Red Light. Use your no. 10 bristle brush to paint in the large dark areas. Begin to soften your edges as you get toward the center of the painting; you should create some very irregular rough edges. You will come back later with a smaller brush to add the individual leaves to complete these larger trees. Also notice that I lightened a little bit of the dark color and scrubbed in some underbrush at the base of the background.

8 Underpaint Grasses

All you need here is simply a good but rough grassy effect. Mix a little Hooker's Green, a touch of Burnt Sienna and purple with your no. 10 bristle brush, and with a vertical scrub- like stroke, block in the dark areas of the grass. Then add Thalo Yellow-Green to the mixture and scrub in the lighter areas of the grass. You can add a little white to the mixture for the grass in the background, just be sure that the canvas is completely covered.

9 Add Sunrays, Phase 1

This is the first step in creating the atmosphere of the scene. This is not difficult, but you must have a very light touch and use very little paint. First, mix a creamy mixture of white with a touch of yellow. Then with a very clean and dry no. 10 bristle brush, begin in the upper right corner, apply a small amount of the mixture and begin to drag downward toward the lower left corner until you have created some very strong rays of light. You will touch them up later. You may have to repeat this step several times in order for the rays to show up.

10 **Underpaint the Rocks**
This step is one of my favorites. Use a combination of Burnt Sienna, blue, purple and touches of white to block in all the rock formations with your no. 6 bristle brush. If it helps, sketch in the main or larger rock formations with your charcoal. Keep in mind that these rocks are a major part of the overall composition, so careful placement is critical. You want to create good eye flow with these rocks. Notice how they overlap and touch each other.

11 **Highlight Rocks, Phase 1**
This is a familiar step by now. Mix your highlight color using white with touches of orange and yellow, or you could use a touch of red, just as long as it is a soft, warm highlight. Slightly gray this color by adding a little blue, or even a touch of the color from step 10. Remember, this is only the basic form highlight; the brighter highlights will be added later. Use your no. 4 flat sable for this step and be sure to use quick strokes, being careful not to overwork the rocks.

12 **Add Dark Reflections in the Water**
This is a very quick and simple step. Take the dark green tree mixture from step 7 and add a little more green to it. Use your no. 6 bristle brush to dry-brush in the dark reflections in the water on the left side of the painting. This area will be the "eyestopper" for the left side. Even though this color needs to be very dark, you want to gradually blend it across to the center of the water, making sure there are no hard edges. You can use a variety of dry-brush scumbling strokes to achieve this.

13 Add Ripples on the Water

Now this is where you will start to make some major changes. Mix white with a touch of blue; this should be a very light bluish white color and very creamy. Use your no. 4 flat and round sable brushes to create the ripples; this undoubtedly takes some skill. You want to create movement and at the same time add highlight to the water. The best advice I can give here is not to completely cover up the underpainting. The water is lighter or whiter where it is running and darker where it is calm. Use good judgment, and experiment a little bit. If you overhighlight, just add a few dark areas to open up the negative space again.

14 Block In Fallen Log and Limbs

For this step, mix Burnt Sienna, blue and purple. Sketch the objects in with your charcoal, and then with your no. 4 flat sable brush, block in the fallen log across the water and the large dead limb in front. Once again, use good judgment in regards to composition and negative space. Don't be afraid to add other limbs or logs as you see fit; they can really add interest to the painting. Adding the moss on the foreground limbs adds a wonderful creative touch.

15 Highlight Rocks, Phase 2

Now it's time to begin adding the intense light that gives the painting its name. First, mix white with a touch of orange, then mix white with a touch of yellow. Use both of these mixtures to highlight the rocks. I prefer to use my no. 4 round and flat sable for this. The key here is to only accent the rocks; don't completely paint over the underpainting or the form highlight. You may have to go back to the shadowed side of the rocks and repaint certain parts of them. Since these are river rocks, their edges are slightly more rounded. You will add final details in the final stage of the painting.

16 **Paint Leaves on Large Trees**
This is really not a very difficult step, but it is extremely time-consuming. First take the dark green mixture from step 7 and add just enough white to make it one or two shades lighter than the dark background, and add enough water to make it nice and creamy. You will need only your no. 4 round sable for this step. You will be creating a canopy of leaves over the center of the painting by using a series of overlapping scumbling strokes. Control your brushstrokes carefully to create good negative space. Begin inside the dark area and gradually work your way out. You want to have a good variety of leaves, including clumps, scattered patches and individual leaves. Finally, thin down the same color for use with your script liner brush, and paint the twigs and branches that connect the leaves together. You only want to create the suggestion of individual leaves, so be careful not to overdo the details.

17 **Highlight the Water**
This step takes some courage; in order for this painting to do what it is designed to do, you have to apply this paint very thickly and only accent the areas where the water is in motion. Use your no. 4 round sable brush, and mix a nice, rich creamy mixture of white paint (not gesso) and a very tiny touch of yellow. Apply this mixture around the edges of the rocks where the sunlight falls over the rocks, and highlight the places where the sunlight may fall on the ripples of water. When I say apply the paint thickly, I mean very, very thickly; do not smooth or blend it, simply put it on and leave it. This is the only way it will stay clean and bright.

18 **Drybrush Final Sunrays and Highlights**
Simply repeat step 10; however, this time, be very specific about the location, angle and intensity of the rays. Once the rays are in place, highlight the individual objects where the rays fall, such as the tops of the rocks, pebbles, ripples and grass. Highlight with the appropriate color, white with either yellow or orange; and don't be afraid to make the light extremely bright by applying the paint thickly.

19 Underpaint Deer

First sketch in the deer with your charcoal, then mix a medium gray of white, blue and Burnt Sienna. The value of this color is established by where you place the deer. Use your own judgment; it will be different with each painting. Now simply block him in with your no. 4 flat and round sable brushes, keeping the edges soft. Also, be sure that the size of the deer is appropriate for its location.

20 Detail Deer and Miscellaneous Objects

All you need to do to finish the deer is to give him somewhat of a silver lining and a minor suggestion of detail. Then you will do the same thing with the other objects in the painting, especially the logs, tree trunks and individual weeds. For the deer, you want to add a little bit of color such as Burnt Sienna, then drybrush in some shadows and add some bright accent highlights along his back, legs and antlers. Be sure that the final overall value of the deer fits the location in your painting. Then add reflected light to the rocks, and any other grasses or tree limbs that you feel would complement your painting.

21 Refine the Painting

This is the step where you make all of the necessary changes to fit your particular composition, color scheme and atmosphere; for instance, notice that I rearranged the left immediate foreground. The large limb that was there was too overpowering, so I took it out and replaced it with smaller limbs, added a few more rocks, and then I put a bluish white glaze over the entire painting to help soften it up a bit. If you decide to glaze your painting, be sure to use a very thin wash, and repeat it two or more times if necessary. Good luck; I hope you enjoyed this painting!

The Stone Wall
20" × 16" (50.8cm × 40.6cm)

The Stone Wall

Often our best subjects for paintings can come from vivid and pleasant childhood memories. Not far from my house was a park called Woodward. I recall that it had acres of beautiful trees, walking trails, babbling brooks, ponds and giant rock formations. In the springtime, endless rows of beautifully vivid pink, white and red azaleas would bloom. This was not only a marvelous playground with endless hiding places, but this place continues to influence me and my art career. Several times a year, I go back and study the beautiful surroundings; in fact, if you watch my television show, you will recognize this setting as the subject for some of my paintings. The stone wall was a special place where I used to sit and study and think. The stone stairway, the wall with the dark green foliage and the beautiful pink dogwood is an insatiable challenge for any artist. You may want to take it a step further, and add some wildlife or even some people. No matter how you choose to finish this painting, it is a great study in foliage. I know you will enjoy this one!

1 Make Charcoal Sketch

Make a simple sketch of the basic components of the painting. Once again, a detailed sketch is not necessary; however, a rough idea of the overall composition is very helpful.

2 Underpaint Background

This first step is quite simple, but very necessary. With your hake brush, block in the center area with a soft grayish tone. The best mixture for this is white with touches of yellow, blue and purple. This underpainting needs to be fairly opaque, so be sure that you put the paint on thick and feather the edges into the background.

3 Underpaint First Layer of Background Trees

Now you will begin creating a sense of depth in this painting by scumbling in a very soft layer of trees. The value is slightly darker than the background, and the color is white with touches of purple, green and blue. Make the mixture creamy, then use your no. 10 bristle brush and a haphazard scumbling stroke to block in the first layer of trees. Notice that the edges are very soft and loose.

4 Add Second Layer of Background Trees
This step is identical to step 3, except that the value is darker, and the color is more of a grayish green. Start with the color you used in the previous step and simply darken it with touches of green and purple. Make sure the value fits your painting. Use your no. 10 bristle brush to begin scumbling in a few specific dark tree shapes. Notice the difference in values between the two layers.

5 Add Distant Trunks and Limbs
Take the grayish green you used for the last step and darken it slightly with a little blue and Burnt Sienna. Thin it a bit, and use your script liner brush or your no. 4 round sable to paint in all of the distant limbs and tree trunks. You'll be adding leaves to some of these trees later. Keep in mind that their sizes and forms must be in direct proportion to their locations.

6 Add Underbrush at Base of Trees
Now create a mixture of Hooker's Green with touches of purple and white. Use your no. 6 bristle brush to begin scrubbing underbrush at the base of the trees. As you can see, I have taken this color on up to create more specific trees. As always, create good negative space and keep your edges soft.

7 Underpaint Stone Wall and Steps

All you need to do here is mix a rich brownish gray of white, blue, Burnt Sienna and a touch of purple. Now use your no. 6 bristle brush to underpaint the entire wall and steps. Don't worry about any form shadows or highlights yet. This is a very loose and quick underpainting, so don't worry about exact shapes and forms.

8 Block In Middle Ground Grass

This is a fun step. You're going to create the first sign of good strong light and shadow using your no. 6 or no. 10 bristle brush. Mix Thalo Yellow-Green with a touch of yellow, and beginning at the base of the trees, lay in the sunlit grass with a vertical scrubbing stroke. Next, move down toward the wall and darken the grass with a mixture of Hooker's Green and purple. Gently scrub the two values together, and then stop when you get to the wall where it is darker.

9 Underpaint Foreground

Now, with your no. 6 bristle brush, mix together white, Burnt Sienna and purple; but don't mix the colors completely together. Scrub this color on the foreground making it a little lighter at the base of the wall, and darker as you come forward. Keep your strokes very loose and choppy to suggest dirt. Be sure that the canvas is very well covered. Notice that the purple tone is the predominant color; you want to be sure the purple is very noticeable, but not overwhelming.

10 Add Form Shadow on Wall

All you will do here is create the basic form of the wall and steps; you will work on the stones, highlights and details later. If you haven't mastered good enough brush control to proceed without a sketch, then don't hesitate to get your charcoal and make a rough outline of the steps and wall. Use your no. 6 bristle brush to scrub in the shadowed side of the wall. Now, mix white, purple, Burnt Sienna and a touch of blue. This color should be about two shades darker than the existing wall color. You may want to switch to your no. 4 flat sable brush for the steps. Use quick and loose brushstrokes.

11 Underpaint Foreground Bush

This step is similar to what you did above the wall. Make a mixture of Thalo Yellow-Green and a touch of yellow, and then use your no. 6 bristle brush to begin scumbling the small bush. Darken the mixture as you come forward with more Hooker's Green and purple, and even a touch of Burnt Sienna. This bush is more defined, so give it a fairly good shape; you will refine, detail and highlight it later.

12 Put Stones on Wall

Get ready for a ride on this step because it can be fairly time-consuming and frustrating. To paint the stones in the wall, you will be creating three values of the stone color: a light, a middle and a dark. First mix a basic soft gray tone of white, blue and Burnt Sienna. For the highlight side of the stones, add more white with a touch of yellow or orange. For the shadowed side, add just a little white, plus whatever color you would like to use to darken it, such as red, green, blue or Burnt Sienna. Use your no. 4 flat sable to paint the stones. Once the stones are in place, mix a darker color for the cracks between the rocks. Then go back and make minor adjustments in form, color, shadow or highlight; as usual, you will accent them later. Don't be afraid to experiment, and be careful not to fall into a pattern of making each rock the same and lining them all up in a perfect row.

13 Detail the Foreground

This is a fun step, especially after painting all those stones. In this step you will add highlights, pebbles, rocks and shadows. The main colors for the highlights are white and orange; your no. 4 flat sable brush works best for this. Use very short, choppy, horizontal strokes for the dirt areas, then use small dabs to create a series of overlapping rocks and pebbles. After you have most of the highlights, pebbles and rocks in place, darken the mixture substantially with Burnt Sienna and purple and use your no. 6 bristle brush to drybrush some shadows on the lower left side of the painting. These shadows are being cast by some objects outside the canvas, and their main purpose is to act as "eyestoppers"; keep their edges soft and their shapes irregular.

14 Add Sunlight in Background

This is a very simple but important step. We want to add a soft burst of sunlight coming through the background trees; this will help soften and add a little drama to the background. Simply take some white and a touch of yellow and thin it down some, then with your no. 6 bristle brush, drybrush or scrub in the soft light, gently blending over the edges of the trees. It may not appear that much is happening here; this is an intentional effort to create a subtle light. You may need to repeat this step to achieve the desired effect.

15 Block In Large Tree Trunk

This large tree is the main focus of the painting, so you should first sketch in the main shape of the tree with your charcoal. Mix Burnt Sienna, blue, a touch of purple and maybe a touch of white to change the value. Block in the trunk with your no. 4 flat sable; don't worry about the smaller limbs, you will add them after you leaf the tree. Be sure to double-check the location, proportion and negative space before you continue.

16 Finish the Bushes

This is a practice step of detailing the bushes. Start by mixing two or three values of highlight color. Those colors will vary depending on the effect you want. I mixed Thalo Yellow-Green with yellow and white, Thalo Yellow-Green plus orange, and yellow plus a touch of Thalo Yellow-Green. Keep some of a dark mixture available (Hooker's Green and purple). Now, with your no. 4 round sable brush, begin scumbling in the highlighted leaves on the bushes in the middle and foreground. You may also need to add some darker leaves.

17 Leaf Tree, Phase One

This is where you will create the "heart and soul" of the painting. Mix Alizarine Crimson, a touch of red and a small dab of purple, and use your no. 4 flat sable brush to scumble in the basic shape of the leaf pattern. The most important thing to be mindful of is—you guessed it—negative space, and since this is the underpainting, it's very important to soften the edges of the leaves. This is a good time to stop, stand back and make sure that you are pleased with the composition of each part of the tree.

18 Leaf Tree, Phase Two

There is very little difference between this step and step no. 17. Take the underpainting mixture and add quite a bit of white. Make a second mixture of white with a touch of Alizarine Crimson. You will use these two very light highlight colors for accents. Use your no. 4 round or flat sable brush to begin scumbling in the highlights on the outer edges of each clump of leaves. A few individual comma strokes to suggest individual leaves here and there will add a nice touch. Have fun with this step, but don't overhighlight. Remember, a thicker application of paint will make the highlight brighter.

19 Add Miscellaneous Details

In this step you will add all the miscellaneous details such as small limbs, leaves, flowers, more highlights and grasses. There's quite a bit of room for creativity here; however, I am always ready to stand in favor of simplicity. All you really need to do here is mix a couple of highlight colors such as orange and white, yellow and white, or even Thalo Yellow-Green and white; then use any of your smaller round sable brushes to add the details you feel the best about. Have fun, but don't overdo it. Also, be sure to use a short, choppy, vertical stroke with a mixture of orange and white to suggest bark on the tree.

20 Refine the Painting

Once again, you have reached the point where you need to decide if you're finished with the painting. If you are completely satisfied at this point, you are ready to lay down your brushes; however, I decided to work on two more areas. First, I brightened up the highlights of the leaves on the large tree, and then I roughed up my stones a little more. At that point, I felt the painting was finished. This was a wonderful painting experience for me, and I truly hope that you have learned a lot!

Home from the Market
16" x 20" (40.6cm x 50.8cm)

Home from the Market

Once again, familiar subjects and memories of my days in the Southwest were the main inspiration for this painting. No matter how hard I try, there are just some subjects that I can't get out of my mind until I have put them on canvas; this is one of those subjects. You may have had a similar experience with your favorite subjects. I spent endless hours studying and painting these beautiful old buildings, which are like an oasis in this sometimes harsh environment. The rugged beauty of the soft, earthy tones and textures of the adobe walls with their arched doorways are an inspiration to just about every artist I know. If you haven't had a chance to study these magnificent structures in person, I highly recommend you take a research trip out west, with a camera and sketch pad in hand.

These buildings can be a challenge to paint, especially in this case because of the long stone pathway. This is an ellipse problem that can be a challenging problem even for experienced artists. I will attempt to explain and demonstrate what an ellipse is and how it works before getting started on the painting itself. This is a great painting to experience. Good luck, and, as always, have fun!

Drawing Ellipses

An ellipse is an optical illusion. A round, circular or even a square object that is turned sideways, angled, or is laying down takes on the appearance of an oval or elliptical shape. The best way to clarify this is to show an example. You will need to understand how to draw ellipses for this painting.

Example I
This example shows how a circle becomes an ellipse, and the shape depends on the angle at which it's being viewed by the spectator.

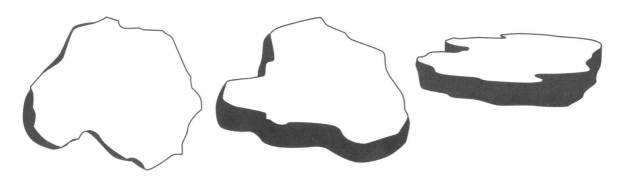

Example II
In the painting *Home from the Market*, the stones on the pathway are all ellipses. The optical illusion here is that when the stone is standing up facing the viewer (far left), it takes on a certain shape; but the same stone lying down looks completely different, more like a true ellipse (far right).

1 Underpaint Sky

For this painting you will need to paint the sky first before making your sketch. This will be a clean, cheerful background color. Load your hake brush with plenty of gesso, start at the horizon and streak it across the base of the sky, using enough water so that it is nice and creamy. Now double-load your brush with yellow and orange and also streak it over the gesso. You don't need to blend this. Now rinse your brush and repeat this step at the top, except after the white gesso, streak on blue, purple and a touch of Burnt Sienna. Quickly blend the base and the top of the sky together so that there is no hard edge.

2 Accent the Sky

Call this whatever you want: clouds, accenting or highlighting. First be sure your underpainted sky is completely dry. Now with your no. 10 or no. 6 bristle brush, scrub in the appropriate highlight for your painting. Most likely the color will be a whitish orange or yellow combination. As you can see, this adds a clean and crisp feel to the sky.

3 Make Charcoal Sketch

Okay, now you can sketch in the main components of the painting, paying special attention to the perspective of the pathway and wall.

4 Underpaint Background Trees
You can create a couple of different trees here. Pine or cedar trees work well for this along with a few bushy trees. For this step, use a no. 6 bristle brush and a mixture of white, purple and green. Of course, this should vary depending on your particular color scheme and value system, so adjust the color accordingly. The main purpose of the trees is to build sort of a framework around the mission.

5 Underpaint Mission and Wall
This is a fairly quick step. Mix a large amount of white, Burnt Sienna and touches of purple and yellow to make a very earthy color. You want to mix plenty of this color because it will be used to underpaint the mission as well as the wall. Use your no. 6 bristle brush with this mixture to scrub in the shape of the mission. For the darker shadowed areas, add a touch of purple to the mixture and switch to your no. 4 flat sable. While you are at it, go ahead and underpaint the wall. Notice that as you come forward, the value gets darker. Also, be sure that the canvas is completely covered in these areas.

6 Underpaint the Pathway
This step is very similar to the previous one, except you will need to gray the mixture by adding a little blue and a touch of purple. Starting back at the mission, use your no. 6 bristle brush to begin blocking in the pathway. Add touches of white at first, and then as you come forward, decrease the amount of white until you are using the mixture in its pure form. As before, be sure the canvas is well covered.

7 Underpaint Wild Flowers

This step is not difficult at all. Just use your no. 10 bristle brush with a mixture of Hooker's Green, purple and Burnt Sienna to block in the entire area, making sure that it is very well covered with paint. Lighten the color a little bit with some Thalo Yellow-Green and a touch of white and do the same thing to the small area of grass on the other side of the wall. Add a little of this lighter green to the edge of the large flower plot to soften and add depth to this area. Now the entire painting is blocked in.

8 Detail the Background Trees

First, with your no. 4 liner brush, mix a medium gray of Hooker's Green, touches of purple and white, and maybe a little Burnt Sienna and paint in a few tree limbs. Experiment with these colors and values to find just the right formula for your particular color scheme. Scumble in a few leaves to give the background a more finished look. After you have placed the large leafy trees, block in a few cedar or pine trees to create some contrast. You will highlight these trees later.

9 Paint In Doors, Windows and Bell

This is another fairly simple step. Just block in the bell with a little Burnt Umber and a touch of white. Either of your small sable brushes will work best here. Then use a medium gray mixture of Burnt Sienna, blue, purple and a little white to block in the doors and windows. Feel free to rearrange the doors and windows to better fit the shape of your building.

10 Highlight Mission, Phase One

I think you'll find this step is a lot of fun. The mission should have the look of hand-finished adobe. First, mix a very light adobe color of white, yellow and just a touch of Burnt Sienna. Load a small amount of paint on the side of your no. 6 bristle brush and use loose dry-brush, scumbling strokes to apply the highlight color to the mission building. It's important to let some of the background show through, so that the surface will look a bit rough. Repeat this step if you need a bit more coverage.

11 Detail the Wall

The wall is in shadow, so it won't be highlighted except on the very top. This is an adobe wall, so our main focus here is to rough it up, to make it look like weathered adobe. The no. 4 flat sable works best for this. Start at the back of the wall and begin drybrushing in various earth tones of Burnt Sienna, yellow, touches of orange and purple and of course a little white. You will do some scrubbing, so if you have an old worn out no. 4 sable, use it; otherwise, you will destroy a new one. Let some of the background show through here as on the mission. Now, with a little of the adobe highlight color, put a cap highlight on the top of the wall, and on the side of the gate.

12 Block In Large Tree Trunk

This is a very quick and fairly easy step. You will be blocking in the large tree, keeping in mind the composition and paying close attention to the arrangement of negative space. If you need to first make a very light sketch with your charcoal, go ahead. You can do most of the painting with your script liner brush, although you may switch to your no. 4 round sable for the main trunk. Make an ink-like mixture of Burnt Umber and water and begin creating the main trunk and then taper out to the smaller branches.

13 Leaf the Large Trees

For this step, start by mixing Hooker's Green, Burnt Sienna and a touch of purple. Add a little white to change the value if needed for your color scheme. Now with your no. 6 bristle brush, begin painting clumps of leaves using a combination of dry-brush, scumbling strokes and some dabbing strokes. The main thing to remember here is to keep the edges of each clump soft and create good negative space. Creating a good underpainting using these basic techniques always makes the following steps easier.

14 Detail Doors, Windows and Miscellaneous Details

Start by making two mixtures: Burnt Sienna with a touch of blue for the dark mixture, and white with a touch of yellow and orange for the light mixture. You may need to add a little white to the dark mixture to soften it. Now take your no. 4 round or flat sable brush and start adding the details you see here, or create some of your own. These details are important to give the mission its character, just don't overdo it.

15 Highlight the Trees

Most of you have done this step many, many times. The highlight mixture will be white, yellow and a touch of Thalo Yellow-Green. I like to use my no. 6 and no. 10 flat bristle brushes for this step. Rough up the tip of your bristles by dabbing them on your table and then put a small amount of the mixture on the tip and begin dabbing the highlights on the sunlit side of each of the clumps. I suggest that you begin the background first and then strengthen the mixture with a little more Thalo Yellow-Green and use it to highlight the larger tree. You may need to repaint the highlight to make the color as bright as you think it needs to be.

16 Paint the Stone Pathway

This is probably the step that will give you the most trouble. It's not the color or the painting technique that will be the problem, but the shape of each rock. These rocks need to appear as if they are lying flat, so you may want to turn back to the demonstration at the beginning of the project to get the ellipses right. Mix white, orange and a touch of yellow for the highlight color. Now beginning at the base of the mission, block in the rocks. The first few rocks are very small, and as you move forward, the rocks get larger and take on more varied shapes. Also, notice the cracks around each rock, and the variation in value of each rock. You can darken the value by thinning the highlight color to almost a wash; it will dry darker than the areas where the mixture is more opaque and thicker. It may take a little practice to get the hang of doing these rocks, but it is well worth the effort.

17 Paint Flowers, Phase One

The first thing to do here is put in the taller weeds with your script brush and an ink-like mixture of Thalo Yellow-Green, orange and a touch of yellow. Then with your no. 4 flat sable brush, dab on spots of white, yellow, pink, purple, orange and red along with any other color you like for different types of flowers. Begin in the background, and come forward until you have covered about half of the flower plot.

18 Highlight Mission, Phase Two

At first glance it may appear that not much has changed; however, if you look closely, you will see exaggerated highlights, more visible brushstrokes and additional highlights that give the mission its glow. Mix white with a touch of yellow and a little orange. Now hunt for the areas where your mission needs a little more highlight and scrub it in with your no. 6 bristle brush; you may even need to work on the wall or even the pathway. Then mix a bluish color, and put a little on the doors to give the mission a little more interest.

19 Sketch in the Woman

All you need to do here is make a simple, accurate sketch of the woman, making sure she has the right proportions and location.

20 Block in the Woman

Next, simply block in the woman's upper outer garment with a deep bluish gray. Block in her dress with a deep maroon, and the bags she is carrying with a dark brown. Use your no. 4 flat sable for this, and don't get carried away with any details. Be sure the canvas is well covered with paint, and keep the edges soft.

21 Highlight Woman

The best advice I can give you here is to use quick, clean strokes of lighter values of the underpainting colors. For example, take the bluish gray color, add lots of white and then with your no. 4 flat sable brush, quickly stroke on highlights to suggest folds, wrinkles and sunlight. Be sure the background color comes through to create the shadows. If you happen to overhighlight, go back and add more shadow color. Repeat this same procedure on the outer areas of the woman. Finally, add touches of a whitish yellow for the accent highlight on the outer edges of her form.

22 Add Flowers, Phase Two

This is really a fun step, and not much different from step 17. Simply mix up your favorite bright color, and use your no. 4 flat and no. 4 round sable to begin painting in the different flowers, making them much larger and more intense in color and detail as you come forward. The very best advice I have for you here, and I know you are tired of hearing this, is to strive for good composition in terms of negative space. Notice most of the flowers are grouped toward the center of the flower plot, so that your eye flows back toward the mission.

23 Finish Up

You may be completely finished here; however, it is a good idea to step back and scan the painting for anything that bothers you. Try to make any of your minor corrections quickly, so that you can get it out of your mind, and move on to the next painting. Try to avoid overworking your painting by remembering the three *P*'s: Don't piddle, play or putter.

The Bicycle and the Bluebird
16" x 20" (40.6cm x 50.8cm)

The Bicycle and the Bluebird

This is a fairly odd, but very interesting painting. I guess it's best described as a composite of several different technical challenges: composition, design, perspective, value, color and atmosphere, combined with a number of different subjects to create a really fun and challenging painting. Having been born and raised in the Midwest, my first idea of interesting subjects to paint were things like old buildings, barns, fences and other nostalgic items found in rural areas. These are all subjects that I never seem to grow out of. I don't paint these things as much as I used to, but every year they manage to appear on a few of my canvases. This is a great study painting; however, there are some hidden dangers, the main one being making the painting too busy. You may want to change some of the subjects or add others; just be careful not to overdo it. Let's get started!

1 Make Charcoal Sketch

Once again, a simple charcoal sketch is all that is necessary to start this painting on its way.

2 Block In Sky

Since this is a gray, overcast day, the sky should be simple and soft. A mixture of white, a touch of blue, Burnt Sienna and orange will give you just the right color to set the mood for this painting. Since there will be no clouds, paint the background solid with your hake brush. Most likely, you will have to give it a second coat after it dries. The exact color of gray that you end up with is up to you.

3 Underpaint the Background Trees, Phase One

Start with the gray sky color and add a touch more blue and orange. Now with you no. 10 bristle brush, scrub in the first layer of background trees. Notice the softness and the variety of shapes. Because this is just the first layer, keep it simple. Softness and good negative space are your main objectives here.

4 Underpaint Background Trees, Phase Two

All you need to do here is repeat the same procedure as in step 3, after you darken the background tree mixture about two shades. Use your no. 10 or no. 6 bristle brush to scrub in some underbrush at the base of the background trees. Once again, negative space is your main concern.

5 Underpaint Cabin

This is a very simple step; however, you need to be fairly accurate with the underpainting, so take all the time you need to get the job done. You will need your no. 6 bristle brush and your no. 4 flat sable and you will mix four basic values for the cabin. I used the background tree mixture we just finished with, and then added touches of Burnt Sienna and purple for the two darker values and touches of white or even a little orange for the two lighter values. There are four basic values: the roof, left side, right side and the chimney and windows. Block in all of these areas, making sure the building is fairly square and is standing up straight. Keep in mind that this is only the underpainting, so it can be a little rough around the edges.

6 Paint Tree Limbs in Background

Now, with your no. 4 script liner brush, create a mixture that is slightly darker than the background trees. Thin it to an ink-like consistency and paint in a few trunks, not too many, and paint in the smaller limbs. These limbs need to be fairly delicate, so be sure to use a very light touch.

7 Underpaint Pathway

For the pathway, just scrub in a middle gray color that's similar to the sky, a mixture of white, blue, Burnt Sienna and orange. Scrub it on fairly thickly using your no. 6 bristle brush. Notice that the edges are rough and irregular. Also, notice that the pathway is much wider at the front, and narrows as it recedes toward the cabin.

8 Underpaint Grass in Middle Ground

You will need your no. 10 bristle brush and two values of paint for this step. Make a large mixture of yellow, orange and a touch of Burnt Sienna and white for the light value. A mix of Burnt Sienna, purple, blue and a touch of white works great for the dark value. Scrub the light mixture on fairly thickly, and while it is still wet, scrub in the dark value beneath it. Now carefully scrub in the two values together while at the same time creating the suggestion of grass, bushes and other brush.

9 Highlight Cabin, Phase One

This is really a detail step; you will use your no. 4 sable brush for most of this. Really, all you do here is create a lighter value of each of the underpainting colors, and then mix it with water until it's creamy. Use gentle vertical strokes to create the suggestion of wood on the front and side of the cabin. For the shingles, use short, choppy strokes, following the angle of the roof. For the chimney, create the suggestion of stones. Now with your no. 4 round sable and a darker mixture, go ahead and add a few accent details to create the suggestion of cracks in the wood, shingles, and between the stones. Don't get carried away with this; you will work on the details later.

10 Underpaint Foreground Bushes and Grass
This step is almost identical to step 8; but for this step you'll need to be more specific about your bush shapes and your value changes. Notice that things become darker as they come forward. I prefer to use my no. 10 bristle brush for this; however, the no. 6 bristle can give you a little more control for the brush that is closer up. Keep an eye on your negative space, your eye flow and where the sunlight falls on the bushes.

11 Detail the Pathway
For the shadow areas, mix Burnt Sienna, blue and a touch of purple. For the highlight, mix white with a touch of orange and maybe a little Burnt Sienna. To create a dirt pathway, use short, choppy horizontal strokes with a no. 6 bristle brush. Sometimes the no. 4 flat sable works better for the smaller details.

12 Highlight Middle Ground Grasses
This step should not be too difficult. A mixture of white, yellow and a touch of orange is a great highlight color for the grass highlights. Use your no. 6 bristle brush to begin dabbing on the highlights of the grass in the middle ground. Put the paint on fairly thickly so that the highlights will remain clean and bright. It's also important to be fairly selective about where you place the highlights. Pick certain bushes and clumps of grass, and dab on the highlights, so that they stand out. This is a small area, so be careful not to overhighlight or you will lose the contrast.

13 Sketch In Fence and Gate

It is important here to be sure that you have a fairly accurate sketch. This is where using the soft vine charcoal comes in handy because you can easily erase it with a damp paper towel. Be sure you are happy with the sketch before proceeding.

14 Block In Fence and Gate

You will need your no. 4 flat sable brush for this step. Block in the fence posts with a mixture of Burnt Sienna and Ultramarine Blue, and add a little white just for painting the more distant posts. As for the gate, use the post mixture and add more blue and quite a bit of white to create a very light gray. Block in the gate pickets, applying the paint fairly thickly.

15 Detail Fence and Gate

Now you will add wire, highlights and minor details to the gate. You will need your script liner brush and your no. 4 round sable for this step. First, make an ink-like mixture of Burnt Sienna and blue. Next, carefully paint in the wire, which is more difficult than it looks and requires a very light touch. Have fun highlighting the fence posts with a mixture of white and orange, and simply add more white to the mixture to highlight the pickets on the gate.

16 Detail Foreground Brush

There is a lot of activity involved in this step, and this is a good place to use your artistic license. You can use a variety of brushes, but mainly your script brush should be used along with your no. 4 round sable and your no. 6 flat bristle. First, block in all the limbs with your script brush, and then with a variety of light or dark values, paint in all of the taller weeds. Remember the contrast rule, light against dark, dark against light. All of the colors in this step are just brighter or darker versions of the colors we have been using. Scrubbing, dabbing and scumbling are the three basic techniques we use to add these details. Don't be afraid to use pure color, like orange or yellow for accenting.

17 Sketch In Miscellaneous Details

Once again, feel free to use your artistic license here. I chose to sketch in a bicycle, cedar trees and an eastern bluebird. Any nostalgic items will be appropriate, as long as they don't interfere with the overall composition. You may want to put a slight point on your charcoal to sketch these items.

18 Paint In Miscellaneous Details

For the cedar trees, mix Burnt Sienna with a touch of blue, maybe a little Hooker's Green and of course, a touch of white to create the right value. Use your no. 6 bristle brush to dab in the trees, which serve to frame the cabin. Use your own judgment for the other objects. Color isn't really an issue here, but the value of the color is; so be sure, wherever you place an object, that the value is correct for its location. By now you should know the value rule for creating depth; however, I will go ahead and give you a brief reminder: As objects recede into the distance they get smaller and less intense in color and value. A grouping of objects will get closer together and, of course, also less intense in color and value.

19 Refine the Painting

As is often the case, you may be done by now. As for my painting, I added smoke from the chimney, a few flowers, additional highlights and distant birds. Have fun, just don't overdo it.

No Vacancy
20" × 16" (50.8cm × 40.6cm)

No Vacancy

Another memory was the inspiration for this painting. A few years ago, we moved to a small farm in eastern Oklahoma. Out by the entrance of our driveway was a huge oversized mailbox attached to an old weathered post, stuck in a cream can, and sitting on some concrete blocks. The mailbox was overgrown with weeds and wild flowers. All of these things combined make for a wonderful subject; however, what really made it interesting for me was that the mailbox was no longer in use, and the lid was wired shut. One day as I was working in the yard, I noticed a male and female cardinal land on top of the box and tug on the wire. This went on for several days, and I finally figured out that they might be wanting to build a nest. So I removed the wire, opened the lid, and before long they began showing up with twigs and pieces of grass. It didn't take me long to get out there with my camera and sketchpad and plan this painting. The original painting is 4' × 5' (122cm × 152cm). Of course, for this lesson I scaled it down to 16" × 20" (41cm × 51cm). This is a great study in painting metal, weathered wood and other textures. I hope you'll have fun with this one!

1 Underpaint Background, Phase One
This may seem like a very unusual way to start a painting; however, what's needed is a loose, free, horizontally mottled background. Also, this painting is unusual because there is no horizon line; it's all background work. All you do here is use your no. 10 bristle brush and pure Hooker's Green and cover the background with long horizontal strokes. Although there are thick and thin spots, be sure the canvas is completely covered with paint.

2 Underpaint Background, Phase Two
The next step is to create a little contour to the ground by adding some subtle contrasting values of color. Start with Hooker's Green and add touches of Burnt Sienna and white, or even a little touch of purple. Now use a variety of horizontal strokes with your no. 10 bristle brush, creating raised places on the ground to give it an interesting contour. Be sure to allow some of the background to show through to create the needed contrast.

3 Add Clumps of Grass
The placement of the clumps of grass is important to the composition of the painting. Begin by mixing Hooker's Green, a touch of Burnt Sienna and a little purple. Now with your no. 10 bristle brush, begin painting in the clumps of grass, using a vertical dry-brush stroke. I can't stress enough the importance of good use of negative space. Keep in mind the location of the mailbox as you place these clumps. As you can see, the larger clumps are closer to the sides to create "eyestoppers."

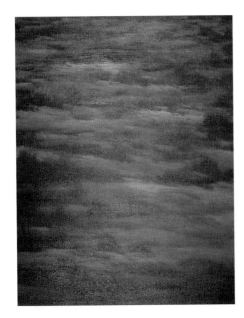

4 Highlight Dirt, Phase One

Now the painting begins to come alive. You will mainly use your no. 6 bristle brush and a variety of earth tones here. Make three mixtures: white with a touch of orange, white with touches of Burnt Sienna and yellow, and white with a touch of yellow. You can also create other light earth tones. Begin highlighting these contours or raised places following the existing contours in and around the clumps of grass, but don't make these highlights too bright yet.

5 Sketch In Mailbox

Because the mailbox is the main subject, it is important to accurately sketch its size, proportions, angle and location. Again, the beauty of working with charcoal is that it is easy to remove if needed. Charcoal may not show up very well against the background, so you may want to substitute a white or light-colored Conte pencil.

6 Block In Rocks and Pebbles

This is really not a difficult step, but it's an exercise in composition to arrange the pebbles and rocks with good negative space. Keep in mind that these pebbles are not the feature, they only accent and complete your background. Block in the rocks with your no. 4 flat sable with a mixture of Burnt Sienna, Ultramarine Blue and a touch of purple. Keep in mind that the sunlight comes in from the right side of the painting, so the shadowed sides of the pebbles are on the left. My advice is that once you have the pebbles blocked in, you should check to see if they interfere with the overall composition. If so, now is the time to make any adjustments.

8 Highlight Grass

For the grass highlights, create mixtures of Thalo Yellow-Green and a touch of orange, Thalo Yellow-Green with a touch of white, and Thalo Yellow-Green with a touch of yellow. Highlighting the grass here requires quick, clean, vertical strokes with your no. 6 or no. 10 bristle brush. Don't be afraid to experiment with different highlight colors. Notice that the highlights are mostly on the tops of the grass clumps.

7 Highlight Rocks and Pebbles

Once your rocks and pebbles are blocked in, add white and a little touch of orange to the color from step 6. Use your no. 4 flat sable brush to quickly highlight the top right side of each rock. If your highlight color is too dull, just add more white and orange, or even a touch of yellow. You may need to go over the highlight two or three times; however, keep in mind that the final highlights are applied in the final step.

9 Add Flowers and Weeds

Next, take the highlight colors from the previous step, thin them down to an ink-like consistency, and use your script liner brush to paint in the taller weeds. Once again, be selective about their placement; they play an important part in the composition. The flowers are simply accents, and you can make them any color you like. With your no. 6 or no. 10 bristle brush, dab in enough flowers to create a good balance of contrast and complements.

10 Block In Mailbox

The next few steps are very quick and easy, so you will be able to fly right on through them. For this step you want to mix Burnt Sienna, Ultramarine Blue and a touch of purple. Use your no. 6 bristle brush to completely cover the outer and inner parts of the mailbox. Be sure you have good coverage, and lighten the outside just a little bit. The mixture should be creamy. Add a little white to change the value for the outside.

11 Block In Post

In this step, use the same basic mixture as in the above step. Add a touch of white to slightly change the value, and block in the light side of the post. Then add a little more blue and Burnt Sienna to darken the mixture for the shadowed side. You should have two distinct values that show a dark and a light side. Now take the dark value, and add a dab in a few dark areas to suggest old weathered wood. Use your no. 4 flat sable or no. 6 bristle for this step.

12 Block In Cream Can

This step will make the cream can appear round. This is nothing more than a basic blending technique. With your no. 4 flat sable, begin at the center of the can with a mixture of Burnt Sienna and touches of blue, purple and white. Use a series of flat scumbling strokes. As you work out toward the edges, add more white directly on the canvas. Since this is an old weathered can, your brushstrokes should be visible to suggest the old, dented, weathered look. Now simply fill in the inside of the can with your dark mixture.

13 Detail Mailbox

Creating the effect of old, weathered metal creates a challenge even for the most seasoned artist. I will explain how I do it, but it is going to take some experimenting on your part. I take my no. 6 bristle brush and mix a base color of white with a touch of yellow. As I start scrubbing in this base color I add very small touches of Burnt Sienna, red, blue and green; look closely and you can see all of these colors in the mailbox. Most likely, you will have to apply two or three layers to get the effect you're after. The final layer is a very bright opaque whitish yellow at the top of the mailbox, just before it curves over to the other side. You can see how the subtle light and dark contrasts create the suggestion of dents or raised areas. Last, with the whitish yellow highlight, accent the rim and outer edges of the mailbox and lid.

14 Detail Post

This is a fun step because I love to paint weathered wood. The best color to use here is white with a touch of orange applied with a dry-brush technique. Load the tip of your no. 4 bristle brush and gently drag the brush downward over the underpainting with a little bit of wiggle, creating the suggestion of woodgrain. Now with your script liner brush and dark mixture of blue and Burnt Sienna, and of course enough water to thin it, add details such as cracks, knots and holes. Finally just have fun adding minor details that you find interesting.

15 Detail Cream Can

In this step you will add minor highlights and the handles to the cream can. I suggest you sketch in the handles with your charcoal, and then use the colors from step 14 to block in the handles, and add highlights with the whitish orange mixture. These details are best accomplished with your sable brushes. Once again, add whatever highlights and details that will best finish out your cream can.

16 Add Foreground Grass

This step should be second nature to you by now. Mix up a variety of light and dark grass colors, and as usual, add water to make the mixture ink-like. Use your script liner brush with long, deliberate strokes to first paint the darker weeds, then add the lighter colored weeds. Notice that there are lots of weeds of differing lengths that overlap each other, which creates a good composition around the base of the cream can.

17 Add Miscellaneous Details

Here you will add the fun details such as the latch, the flag and the reflector. Your sable brushes work best for just about all of your detail work. Underpaint the red objects with a mixture of purple and red, then paint over them with pure red and also perhaps a touch of white to give the color a clean, opaque, intense look. For the other items, use a highlight mixture of white and orange for light details, and blue with Burnt Sienna for darker details. However, do not hesitate to experiment with different values of these two mixtures to finish out the details. Putting some letters inside the box is a nice touch; but if you would rather put a nest in there, be my guest.

18 Underpaint Cardinal

The first thing you need to do here is make an accurate sketch of the cardinal, and then mix red and purple for the underpainting color. Use your no. 4 flat and round sable brushes to completely block in the cardinal. Be sure the outer edges of the body are soft. The soft edges at this stage will make applying the finishing highlight colors much easier, and will keep the bird from looking cut out and pasted on.

19 Detail Cardinal

This step requires a fairly steady hand; in fact, when I paint most of my wildlife, I use a mahlstick and my Stedi Rest (see page 20 for a demonstration of these tools). For the details on the cardinal, mix a creamy mixture of red and a touch of white. Take your no. 4 round sable brush, spread out the bristles a little bit, lightly load the brush and carefully drybrush on the highlights. This takes some practice. Next, add a little more white and a touch of yellow to the red mixture, and put on the final highlights to accent the bird. If you happen to make a mistake, or are not satisfied with your result, just use the dark mixture to paint out that area and start over.

20 **Refine the Painting**
In this final step, I am going to turn you loose with your own "artistic license" to add touches to this painting that will make it your own. Some of the things you might consider adding are flowers, brighter highlights on the mailbox and cardinal, and maybe a few more weeds; but the most important decision you can make is when to quit before you overwork it.

Return to Days of Old
16" × 20" (40.6cm × 50.8cm)

Return to Days of Old

The covered bridge is a wonderful piece of American architecture that still continues to enhance the landscape, especially in the eastern states. I have done a number of covered bridge paintings, each with its own set of challenges, and this one is no different. The main challenge here is perspective. Most covered bridges are long and skinny, and many of them have unique angles and designs that really add to the challenge of creating proper perspective. Although it looks simple, this is a fairly difficult painting. The best advice that I can give you is to work out the perspective of the bridge in relation to the creek and the road. I usually sketch this out full scale on my drawing pad to be absolutely sure that everything is correct. Sketching the bridge requires an understanding of one-point perspective, and it would be well worth your time to do a little review of this technique. You can find good reference material in books in any art supply store.

1 Make Charcoal Sketch

An extremely accurate sketch is not necessary for most landscapes; however in this case, because of the perspective of the bridge and the unique arrangement of the landscape, a fairly accurate sketch is called for.

2 Block In Sky

This is a very simple sky. Simply apply a generous coat of gesso with your hake brush. While the gesso is still wet, add touches of yellow and orange and blend the colors until you have a good, clean, opaque sky. The other option here is to mix this color on your palette and then apply it directly to the sky. I happen to prefer to mix the colors on the canvas, but either way is fine.

3 Block In Distant Hills

Take a little of the sky color and add a touch of purple. Use this color and your no. 6 bristle brush to scrub in the first distant hill. Next, darken the color with a touch of blue, Burnt Sienna and a little more purple. Scrub this next layer in, and notice that I left the top of the hill fairly rough to suggest a tree-covered hill.

4 Block In Middle Ground Trees

Take the hill color you just used and add a little more purple and a touch of Hooker's Green. Be sure the value is two or three shades darker than the hill. Use your no. 10 bristle brush to dab in the trees in the middleground. It's important now to be mindful of the negative space by giving your trees good shapes and forms. Notice that I left a small area blank where the pond will go.

5 Block In Middle Ground

This step is only the underpainting, so you will use your no. 10 and no. 6 bristle brushes to scrub in and scumble in the middle ground area with loose, haphazard strokes just to suggest bushes, brush and grass. The mixture is a combination of yellow, purple, Hooker's Green and Burnt Sienna; notice that the overall color is rather brownish green. Add touches of yellow or white scattered in now and then to create subtle, contrasting light areas.

6 Underpaint Water

For this step, take the underpainting color from step two, and darken with a little more purple and Burnt Sienna. Use your no. 6 bristle brush to scrub a fairly thick line of color along the shoreline, then while it's still wet, begin scrubbing downward into the water. As you move downward into the water, begin adding touches of yellow and white until you have covered the water area. If you don't get good coverage with the first layer, let it dry and repeat this step. Keep all of your edges soft.

7 Block In Bridge

This is where an accurate sketch of the bridge is important. I use my no. 4 flat sable brush for blocking in the bridge. Start with the roof. Mix white with a touch of Burnt Sienna, a little blue and purple. This should be a fairly light value for the sunlit side. Use this color to block in the roof. Next, mix blue, Burnt Sienna and purple and block in all of the very dark areas of the bridge. Now mix Cadmium Red Light and a little purple and/or blue to paint the front of the bridge. Use the same color combination with less purple for the side of the bridge. Use the roof color for the bridge supports. This is a good time to square up the bridge and make sure most of your angles are correct.

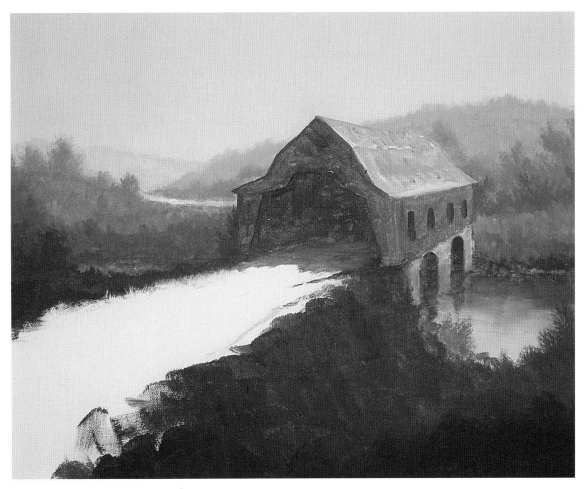

8 Underpaint Foreground

This is a fairly simple step. You will underpaint two different areas: the eroded bank next to the road and the bushes next to the shoreline and in the immediate foreground. The color mixture is Burnt Sienna and touches of blue with a touch of white to slightly lighten it. First, scrub in the bank area. Then darken the mixture with a touch of Hooker's Green and purple, and scrub in the darker bushes in the foreground. This should be a fairly solid coverage, so don't hesitate to give it a second layer if necessary.

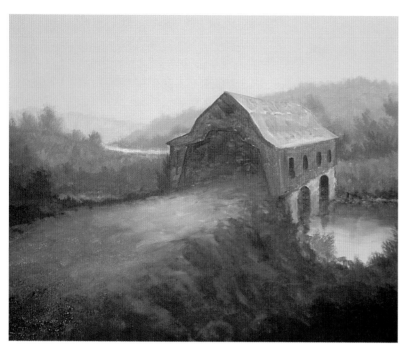

9 Underpaint Road

For this step you will use a mixture of white with touches of Burnt Sienna and purple for the lighter areas of the road. Begin at the back of the road near the bridge and come forward, using short, choppy strokes with your no. 6 bristle brush. As you come forward, begin adding more Burnt Sienna and purple until you reach the foreground. Notice how I put some of the lighter color down the eroded side of the road to suggest rocks and dirt. Everything should be loose and choppy at this stage.

10 Highlight Middle Ground Trees

The painting will really begin to take shape with this step. Use your no. 6 bristle brush and several highlight colors to highlight the trees in the middle ground. I used four different mixtures: Thalo Yellow-Green with a touch of yellow, Thalo Yellow-Green with a touch of orange, Thalo Yellow-Green with a touch of white and Thalo Yellow-Green with a touch of Burnt Sienna. Thalo Yellow-Green alone works well for a highlight if you don't overdo it. Use several different strokes or combinations of strokes (scumbling, dabbing and dry-brushing) to gently highlight the background trees, giving them defined, yet subtle highlights and forms.

11 Highlight Right Side of Bridge

Now you will begin detailing the bridge. Enhance the sunlight on the right side of the bridge with a mixture of Cadmium Red Light and a touch of white. Use your no. 4 flat sable to drybrush vertical strokes to suggest weathered wood and to enhance the red highlight. Now create a shadow color of a little purple and Burnt Sienna to paint in the overhang shadow from the roof. Next, thin this color with water to use with your script liner brush for adding cracks and other details. Use the no. 4 flat sable brush with a mixture of white with touches of yellow and orange to suggest shingles. Add a few cracks and miscellaneous details to the shingles with the script brush and the dark mixture.

12 Detail Front of Bridge

The technique for these details is identical to step 11. The difference is that this is the shadowed side, so all of the details are a subdued color. You will need to use your no. 4 flat and sable brushes and maybe even your script liner brush. First and most important, add the shadow at the overhang of the roof. Detail the door with the trim work, and add a few vertical boards inside the opening. The main objective to keep in mind is to use grayed tones and be very suggestive.

13 Detail Road

This is one of my favorite steps. Begin with a mixture of white and a touch of orange and/or yellow. With your no. 4 flat sable brush, begin at the opening of the bridge and use a series of long horizontal strokes to suggest the wooden floor of the bridge. As you come forward, begin using short, choppy strokes to suggest dirt, pebbles and rocks. Notice that the road gets darker as it comes forward; this is accomplished by allowing more of the background to show through, plus you can darken the mixture with a touch of Burnt Sienna. Next, highlight the eroded side of the road. You have to be creative here to suggest cracks, crevices and rocks embedded in the dirt on the side of the road.

14 Detail Lower Right Foreground

This part of the painting can truly challenge you. You have a variety of objects to deal with (rocks, grass, bushes, highlights, etc.). The best place to begin is with the rocks. Mix white with a touch of orange, and use your no. 4 flat sable brush to define the forms of your rocks with good, clean highlights. Next, add Thalo Yellow-Green to the mixture, and use your no. 6 bristle brush to dab in the highlights of the bushes. Next, adjust the color by adding more yellow, orange or whatever color you feel is appropriate to dry-brush in patches of grass around the rocks to "settle them down." Once again, this is a great place to use your artistic imagination by adding more rocks, bushes and highlights. The main thing is good composition and tonal value as you finish this section.

15 Detail Left Side of Road

This step is similar to the previous one. The first thing we do here is take some of the foliage colors we have been using throughout the painting. I almost always use a bristle brush for most foliage because the bristles can be spread out to create a variety of textures. Use some of the foliage colors you have already been using to add leaves to the tree behind the fence. Then highlight the underbrush. Finally, sketch in the fence with your charcoal, then use a light gray color to block in the fence with your no. 4 round sable brush.

16 Sketch the Remaining Details

No surprise here; use your charcoal to sketch in the horse and buggy, ruts in the road, the fence on the right side of the road and anything else that you want to add. Don't be afraid to add whatever objects you feel will enhance your composition.

17 Block In the Buggy

Once you feel comfortable with your sketch, mix a creamy mixture of Burnt Sienna and Ultramarine Blue and use your no. 4 round sable brush to carefully underpaint the buggy. You might want to use a Stedi Rest and a mahlstick to steady your hand. See page 18 for an example. Finally, slightly lighten the mixture with a little white and block in the fence.

18 Highlight Buggy and Final Details

The main objective here is to highlight the buggy to give it three-dimensional form. Mix white with touches of blue and orange. Now use your no. 4 round sable brush to highlight the buggy. Next, use the same color to highlight the fence. Then mix a little Burnt Sienna with a touch of purple and use your no. 4 flat sable brush to drybrush in the ruts with jerky, broken brushstrokes. Finally, scrub in a shadow under the wagon with this dark mixture.

19 Add Final Details

Now you can hunt and fix, adjust, add or even take away anything that is not technically or artistically correct. Just don't piddle, play or putter. You can see I added flowers and additional highlights to give the painting a little more "snap."

Spring's Song (cropped)
16" x 20" (41cm x 51cm)

PAINT ALONG WITH **JERRY YARNELL**

PAINTING

Techniques

Winter Retreat (cropped)
16" x 20" (41cm x 51cm)

PAINTING

Techniques

NORTH LIGHT BOOKS

CINCINNATI, OHIO

www.artistsnetwork.com

Table of Contents

Winter Retreat

Summer Dreams

Swamp Fisherman

Reminder of the Past

Autumn Fog in the High Country

Spring's Song

You Can See Forever

Texas Bluebonnets
15" × 30" (38cm × 77cm)

Introduction

Like most artists, you begin to expand your horizons as an artist. You begin searching for new ideas, subjects, techniques and ways to make your paintings stand out from the others. In this book my goal is to show you an array of different ideas that you can carry out to make your paintings more interesting and unique to you and your style of painting. I will illustrate to you that adding fog, mist or haze to an otherwise ordinary painting will change it into a painting that has much more eye appeal. You will understand the different applications of reflections in calm water and in moving water and how to create better reflections to help your water look wetter. Even adding simple mud puddles to a dirt road or pathway can dramatically change the atmosphere of your painting. You will also gain an understanding of how to create interesting trees by including dead trees and combining a variety of trees that give your painting good negative space. You will learn how to add final details, such as rocks, pebbles, a variety of grasses, weeds, bushes and other types of foliage that can really bring a landscape painting to life. This will be your opportunity to grab your brushes and create a truly unique work of art. I promise you will have a wonderful experience and a great time.

Terms & Techniques

Before beginning the step-by-step instructions on the following pages, you may want to refresh your memory by reviewing these painting terms, techniques and procedures.

COLOR COMPLEMENTS

Complementary colors are always opposite each other on the color wheel. Complements are used to create color balance in your paintings. It takes practice to understand the use of complements, but a good rule of thumb is to remember that whatever predominant color you have in your painting, use its complement or a form of its complement to highlight, accent or gray that color.

For example, if your painting has a lot of green in it, the complement of green is red or a form of red such as orange, red-orange or yellow-orange. If you have a lot of blue in your painting, the complement to blue is orange or a form of orange such as yellow-orange or red-orange. The complement of yellow is purple or a form of purple. Keep a color wheel handy until you have memorized the color complements.

To prepare your bristle brush for dabbing, spread out the end of the bristles like a fan.

DABBING

This technique is used to create leaves, ground cover, flowers, etc. Take a bristle brush and dab it on your table or palette to spread out the ends of the bristles like a fan. Then load the brush with an appropriate color and gently dab on that color to create the desired effect. (See above example.)

DOUBLE LOAD OR TRIPLE LOAD

This is a procedure in which you put each of two or more colors on different parts of your brush. You mix these colors on the canvas instead of on your palette. This is used for wet-on-wet techniques, such as sky or water.

DRYBRUSH

This technique involves loading your brush with very little paint and lightly skimming the surface of the canvas to add color, blend colors or soften a color. Use a very light touch for this technique.

EYE FLOW

This is the movement of the viewer's eye through the arrangement of objects on your canvas or the use of negative space around or within an object. Your eye must move or flow smoothly throughout your painting or around an object. You do not

want your eyes to bounce or jump from place to place. When you have a good understanding of the basic components of composition (design, negative space, "eye stoppers," overlap, etc.), your paintings will naturally have good eye flow.

FEATHERING

Feathering is a technique for blending to create very soft edges. You achieve this effect by using a very light touch and barely skimming the surface of the canvas with your brush. This is the technique to use for highlighting and glazing.

GESSO

Gesso is a white paint used for sealing the canvas before painting on it.

This is an example of good use of negative space. Notice the overlap of the limbs and the interesting pockets of space around each limb.

This is an example of poor use of negative space. Notice the limbs do not overlap but are evenly spaced instead. There are few pockets of interesting space.

However, because of its creamy consistency, I often use it instead of white paint; it blends so easily. I often refer to using gesso when mixing colors. Keep in mind that when I use the word *gesso* I am referring to the color white. If you don't use gesso for white, use Titanium White paint. Titanium White is the standard white that is on the supply list. Please feel free to use it if you prefer.

GLAZE (WASH)

A glaze or a wash is a very thin layer of paint applied on top of a dry area of the painting to create mist, fog, haze, sun rays or to soften an area that is too bright. This mixture is made up of a small amount of color diluted with water. It may be applied in layers to achieve the desired effect. Each layer must be dry before applying the next.

HIGHLIGHTING OR ACCENTING

Highlighting is one of the final stages of your painting. Use pure color or brighter values of colors to give your painting its final glow. Highlights are carefully applied on the sunlit edges of the most prominent objects in the painting.

MIXING

While this is fairly self-explanatory, there are a couple of ways to mix. First, if there is a color that will be used often, it is a good idea to pre-mix a quantity of that color to have it handy. I usually mix colors of paint with my brush, but sometimes a palette knife works better. You can be your own judge.

I also mix colors on the canvas. For instance, when I am underpainting grass, I may put two or three colors on the canvas and scumble them together to create a mottled background of different colors. Mixing color on the canvas also works well when painting skies. (Note: When working with acrylics, always try to mix your paint to a creamy consistency that can be blended easily.)

NEGATIVE SPACE

This is the area of space surrounding an object that defines its form. (See examples on page 137.)

SCRUBBING

Scrubbing is similar to scumbling, except the strokes are more uniform in horizontal or vertical patterns. You can use drybrush or wet-on-wet techniques with this procedure. I use it mostly for underpainting or blocking in an area.

SCUMBLING

For this technique, use a series of unorganized, overlapping strokes in different directions to create effects such as clumps of foliage, clouds, hair, grasses, etc. The direction of the stroke is not important.

UNDERPAINTING OR BLOCKING IN

These two terms mean the same thing. The first step in all paintings is to block in or underpaint the darker values of the entire painting. Then you begin applying the next values of color to create the form of each object.

VALUE

Value is the relative lightness or darkness of a color. To achieve depth or distance, use lighter values in the background and darker values as you come closer to the foreground. Raise the value of a color by adding white. (See example at right.) To lower the value of a color, add black, brown or the color's complement.

WET-ON-DRY

This is the technique I use most often in acrylic painting. After the background color is dry, apply the topcoat over it by using one of the blending techniques: drybrushing, scumbling or glazing.

WET-ON-WET

In this painting technique the colors are blended together while the first application of paint is still wet. I use the large hake (pronounced ha KAY) brush to blend large areas of wet-on-wet color, such as skies and water.

You can lighten the value of a color by adding white.

Getting Started

Acrylic Paint

The most common criticism about acrylics is that they dry too fast. Acrylics do dry very quickly through evaporation. To solve this problem I use a wet palette system, which is explained later in this chapter. I also use very specific drybrush blending techniques to make blending very easy. If you follow the techniques I use in this book, with a little practice you can overcome any of the drying problems acrylics seem to pose.

Speaking as a professional artist, I think acrylics are ideally suited for exhibiting and shipping. An acrylic painting can actually be framed and ready to ship thirty minutes after it is finished. You can apply varnish over acrylic paint or leave it un-varnished because the paint is self-sealing. Acrylics are also very versa-tile because the paint can be applied thick or creamy to resemble oil paint, or thinned with water for watercolor techniques. The best news of all is that acrylics are non-toxic, have very little odor and few people have allergic reactions to them.

USING A LIMITED PALETTE

As you will discover in this book, I work from a limited palette. Whether it is for my professional pieces or for instructional purposes, I have learned that a limited palette of the proper colors can be the most effective tool for painting. This palette works well for two main reasons: First, it teaches you to mix a wide range of shades and values of color, which every artist must be able to do; second, a limited palette eliminates the need to purchase dozens of different colors. As we know, paint is becoming very expensive.

So, with a few basic colors and a little knowledge of color theory, you can paint anything you desire. This particular palette is very versatile, and with a basic understanding of the color wheel, the complementary color system and values, you can mix thousands of colors for every type of painting.

For example, you can mix Thalo Yellow-Green, Alizarin Crimson and a touch of white to create a beautiful basic flesh tone. These same three colors can be used in combination with other colors to create earth tones for landscape paintings. You can make black by mixing Ultra-marine Blue with equal amounts of Dioxazine Purple and Burnt Sienna or Burnt Umber. The list goes on and on, and you will see that the sky is truly the limit.

Most paint companies make three grades of paints: economy, student and professional. The professional grades are more expensive but much more effective to work with. The main idea is to buy what you can afford and have fun. (Note: If you can't find a particular item, I carry a complete line of professional- and student-grade paints and brushes.)

MATERIALS LIST

Palette

White Gesso
Paints (Grumbacher, Liquitex or Winsor & Newton: color names may vary.)

- Alizarin Crimson
- Burnt Sienna
- Burnt Umber
- Cadmium Orange
- Cadmium Red Light
- Cadmium Yellow Light
- Dioxazine Purple
- Hooker's Green Hue
- Thalo (Phthalo) Yellow-Green
- Titanium White
- Ultramarine Blue

Brushes

2-inch (51mm) hake brush
no. 10 bristle brush
no. 6 bristle brush
no. 4 flat sable brush
no. 4 round sable brush
no. 4 script liner brush

Miscellaneous Items

Sta-Wet palette
water can
soft vine charcoal
16" x 20" (41cm x 51cm) stretched canvas
paper towel
palette knife
spray bottle
easel

Brushes

My selection of a limited number of specific brushes was chosen for the same reasons as the limited palette: versatility and economics.

2-INCH (51MM) HAKE BRUSH

The hake (pronounced ha KAY) brush is a large brush used for blending. It is primarily used in wet-on-wet techniques for painting skies and large bodies of water. It is often used for glazing, as well.

NO. 10 BRISTLE BRUSH

This brush is used for underpainting large areas—mountains, rocks, ground or grass—as well as for dabbing on tree leaves and other foliage. This brush also works great for scumbling and scrubbing techniques. The stiff bristles are very durable, so you can be fairly rough on them.

NO. 6 BRISTLE BRUSH

A cousin to the no. 10 bristle brush, this brush is used for many of the same techniques and procedures. The no. 6 bristle brush is more versatile because you can use it for smaller areas, intermediate details, highlights and some details on larger objects. The no. 6 and no. 10 bristle brushes are the brushes you will use most often.

NO. 4 FLAT SABLE BRUSH

Sable brushes are used for more refined blending, detailing and highlighting techniques. They work great for final details and are a must for painting people and detailing birds or animals. They are more fragile and more expensive, so treat them with extra care.

NO. 4 ROUND SABLE BRUSH

Like the no. 4 flat sable brush, this brush is used for detailing and highlighting people, birds, animals, etc. The main difference is that the sharp point allows you to have more control over areas where a flat brush will not work or is too wide. This is a great brush for finishing a painting.

NO. 4 SCRIPT LINER BRUSH

This brush is my favorite. It is used for the very fine details and narrow line work that can't be accomplished with any other brush. For example, use this brush for tree limbs, wire and weeds—and especially for your signature. The main thing to remember is to use it with a much thinner mixture of paint. Roll the brush in an inklike mixture until it forms a fine point.

With this basic set of brushes, you can paint any subject.

BRUSH CLEANING TIPS

Remember that acrylics dry through evaporation. As soon as you finish painting, use a good brush soap and warm water to thoroughly clean your brushes. Lay your brushes flat to dry. If you allow paint to dry in your brushes or your clothes, it is very difficult to get it out. I use denatured alcohol to soften dried paint. Soaking the brush in the alcohol for about thirty minutes, then washing it with soap and water, usually gets the dried paint out.

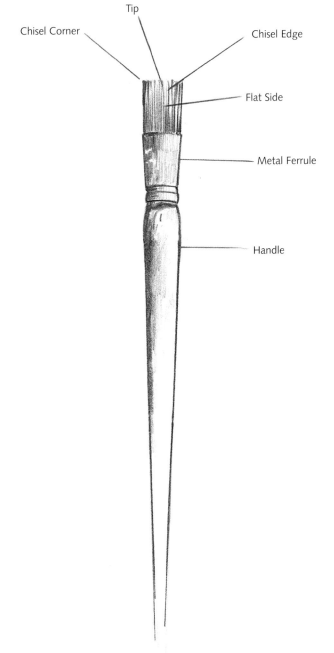

Brush diagram

The Palette

There are several palettes on the market designed to help keep your paints wet. The two I use extensively are Sta-Wet palettes made by Masterson. Acrylics dry through evaporation, so keeping the paints wet is critical. The first palette is a 12" × 16" (31cm × 41cm) plastic palette-saver box with an airtight lid. It seals like Tupperware. This palette comes with a sponge you saturate with water and lay in the bottom of the box. Then you soak the special palette paper and lay it on the sponge. Place your paints out around the edge and you are ready to go. Use your spray bottle occasionally to mist your paints and they will stay wet all day long. When you are finished painting, attach the lid and your paint will stay wet for days.

My favorite palette is the same 12" × 16" (31cm × 41cm) palette box, except I don't use the sponge or palette paper. Instead, I place a piece of double-strength glass in the bottom of the palette. I fold paper towels into long strips (into fourths), saturate them with water and lay them on the outer edge of the glass. I place my paints on the paper towel. They will stay wet for days. I occasionally mist them to keep the towels wet.

If you leave your paints in a sealed palette for several days without opening it, certain colors, such as green and Burnt Umber, will mildew. Just replace the color or add a few drops of chlorine bleach to the water in the palette to help prevent mildew.

To clean the glass palette, allow it to sit for about thirty seconds in water or spray the glass with your spray bottle. Scrape off the old paint with a single-edge razor blade. Either palette is great. I prefer the glass palette because I don't have to change the palette paper.

Setting Up Your Palette

Here are two different ways to set up your palette.

PALETTE 1

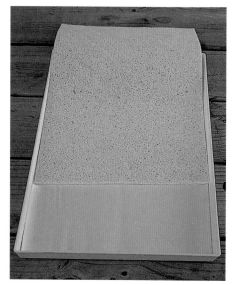

The Sta-Wet 12" × 16" (31cm × 41cm) plastic palette-saver box comes with a large sponge, which is saturated with water.

Lay the sponge inside the palette box. Next, soak the special palette paper and lay it on the sponge. Place your paints around the edge. Don't forget to mist your paints to keep them wet.

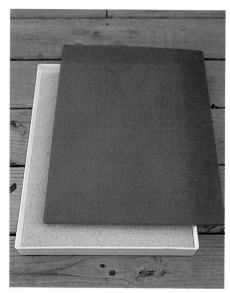

The palette comes with an airtight lid that seals like Tupperware.

When closing the palette-saver box, make sure the lid is on securely. When the palette is properly sealed, your paints will stay wet for days.

Lay the saturated paper towels on the outer edges of the glass.

Instead of using the sponge or palette paper, another way to set up your palette box is to use a piece of double-strength glass in the bottom of the palette. Fold paper towels in long strips and saturate them with water to hold your paint.

I place my paints on the paper towel in the order shown.

Use the center of the palette for mixing paints. Occasionally mist the paper towels to keep them wet.

To clean the palette, allow it to sit for thirty seconds in water or spray the glass with a spray bottle. Scrape off the old paint with a single-edge razor blade.

Miscellaneous Supplies

CANVAS

There are many types of canvas available. Canvas boards are fine for practicing your strokes, as are canvas paper pads for doing studies or for testing paints and brush techniques. The best surface to work on is a primed, prestretched cotton canvas with a medium texture, which can be found at most art stores. As you become more advanced in your skills, you may want to learn to stretch your own canvas. I do this as often as I can, but for now a 16" × 20" (41cm × 51cm) prestretched cotton canvas is all you need for the paintings in this book.

EASEL

I prefer to work on a sturdy standing easel. There are many easels on the market, but my favorite is the Stanrite ST500 aluminum easel. It is lightweight, sturdy and easy to fold up to take on location or to workshops.

LIGHTING

Of course, the best light is natural north light, but most of us don't have this light available in our work areas. The next best light is 4' or 8' (1.2m or 2.4m) fluorescent lights hung directly over your easel. Place one cool bulb and one warm bulb in the fixture; this best simulates natural light.

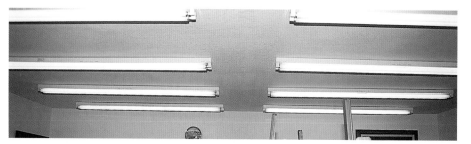

Studio lights

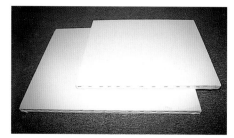

16" × 20" (41cm × 51cm) prestretched canvas

Aluminum Stanrite studio easel

SPRAY BOTTLE

I use a spray bottle with a fine mist to lightly mist my paints and brushes throughout the painting process. The best ones are plant misters or spray bottles from a beauty supply store. It is important to keep one handy.

PALETTE KNIFE

I do not do a lot of palette-knife painting. I mostly use a knife for mixing. A trowel-shaped knife is more comfortable and easier to use than a flat knife.

SOFT VINE CHARCOAL

I prefer to use soft vine charcoal for most of my sketching. It is very easy to work with and shows up well. You can remove or change it by wiping it off with a damp paper towel.

Spray bottle

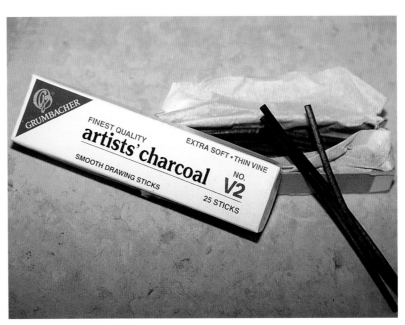

Soft vine charcoal

Palette knives

Glazing

You may have seen me demonstrate washing techniques on my TV show or instructional videos. Most of the time, I am referring to a thin wash of water and a particular color that is applied over a certain area of the painting to create special effects, such as mist, fog, haze or smoke. However, the examples here show how to use glazing to create an intense highlight by applying one glaze on top of another. Glazing is truly an old master's technique, and the results can be phenomenal.

Glazing is an important technique to acrylic artists because the paint dries darker than when first applied. By layering one glaze on top of another, an acrylic artist can control the degree of brightness.

This rock is a good subject to study for practicing glazing techniques. Glazing works on any subject that needs to have a brighter highlight and good three-dimensional form.

1 Underpaint the Rock
First, underpaint the object with its appropriate underpainting color. Be sure the canvas is completely covered (opaque). For this example, use a combination of Ultramarine Blue, Burnt Sienna, Dioxazine Purple, and a little white. Do not premix them all together on the palette to create one color. Instead, mix the colors on the canvas and mottle them so each individual color will show through the glaze. Use a no. 6 bristle brush for this step.

2 Mix Glaze and Apply
Now mix the first layer of highlight color, which I call the "sunshine color." Mix white with a touch of orange and yellow, and thin it slightly with water. The consistency should be like soft, whipped butter. Load a no. 4 flat sable brush with a small amount of paint on the end of the bristles. Gently drybrush the first layer of highlight on the top right side of the rock, carefully blending the highlight color into the underpainting. Be sure the edges are soft, not harsh. Also, some of the background color must show through in order for this process to work.

3 Apply Another Layer

This step and the next step are identical to step 2. Use the same brush and the same highlight color. You will drybrush other layers on top of the first. Be sure each layer is dry before applying the next. Remember, this is a glaze and each layer is a thin layer of paint. Notice that these steps make the rock appear brighter.

4 Add Final Layer

In this final glaze, you may want to be more selective as to where you place the paint. You do not have to cover the entire highlighted area, but notice that the rock is brighter now than the step before. You can add as many layers of glaze as you wish to create the desired effect.

5 Add Details

This is a final detail step and has very little to do with glazing. Seeing the finished product helps you understand the importance of glazing. In this step, you add cracks and crevices, adjust the dark areas in the rock, or make other final touches. My best advice is never to finish an object all in one step. It is best to do things in stages. You will have greater success and have more control over your painting.

A Word About My Mixing Technique

The phrases "a touch of this and a dab of that" can make my instructions sound like a cooking show, but I have adopted this style of mixing because it is well suited for my style of painting. There are two main reasons why this style of mixing works so well. First, I am not a formula painter. Many artists have formulas that they use to premix numerous colors and values before they begin a painting. While this technique is widely used, it is very time-consuming and sometimes frustrating. After all that work, the colors and values may not fit into your color scheme. You may end up remixing or adjusting the color.

Using my technique, for example, gray is a base mixture of white, blue and Burnt Sienna. If I want it to be on the bluish side, I will mix white with blue and a touch of Burnt Sienna, but increase the blue. This makes the blue predominant and creates a bluish gray color. If I want a brownish gray, I mix white with extra Burnt Sienna and just a touch of blue. If I want a purple tint, I add a touch of purple. There are literally hundreds of gray combinations based on the colors that are most prominent. This same technique applies for all color schemes. Experiment with this mixing technique, and you will find it very exciting and helpful to your painting experience.

Another reason I prefer my mixing technique is that as a professional instructor who works with people from all over the world, I've learned there are many different brands of paint. Some brands do not match others, and some paints are weaker in pigment than others. There are three different grades of paint: economy, student and professional grade. A formula mixing technique can't work with all of these different paints. With my technique, adding a touch of this or a larger dab of that is a very quick and easy way to adjust a value or color. With a touch of this and a dab of that, I am not trying to create a tasty dish, but rather trying to simplify your mixing problems.

My mixing technique doesn't require you to measure out your paint.

Painting Fog, Mist and Haze

To the average person, fog, mist and haze may seem relatively dreary; however, to an artist, these atmospheric conditions can create excitement and an opportunity to transform an ordinary painting into an extraordinary work of art. The main focus in these studies is to learn when, where and how to use fog, mist or haze to create the most appropriate effect to your painting.

Imagine an early morning fog rising up from a rolling river or a placid lake. This type of atmosphere can add tremendous interest to an otherwise simple landscape painting. Adding a light mist over an entire painting can create the effect of a damp day or light rain. Learning how to create haze will give you the opportunity to add conditions like dust, smoke or sun rays. These things will add great eye appeal to your artwork and add a professional quality. There are many applications for these conditions and we will discuss only a few of them, but keep in mind the sky is the limit.

Fog

We will begin by learning the proper use, application and technique for creating fog. Painting fog is very much like painting a low-hanging cloud. Acrylic artists easily achieve this effect by using a dry-brush technique, which is the most effective way to create fog. This technique can also be used by oil painters so long as the underpainting is dry.

The most crucial thing to remember about fog is that it is usually located at the base of mountains, in low or depressed areas of a landscape or in valleys between hills or a mountain range.

Fog Studies
Notice in these two examples that the fog at the base of the mountain adds much more interest.

Making Fog

First of all, you want to make sure that you are completely finished with the underpainting or background subjects and that your painting is thoroughly dry. Now, choose the appropriate size and type of brush. Generally you use one of the flat bristle brushes, and only you can decide what size, which depends on the amount of area you need to cover and the location of the fog. A no. 4, no. 6 or no. 10 flat bristle brush will give you a good variety of choices. In this example I will use a no. 6 flat bristle brush.

You must choose the proper color and density of the fog. Let us look at these color swatches to help with this decision. (Note: The key here is to check the color of the subject where the fog will be applied and use a form of its complement.)

When I make fog, I like to use my brush to mix colors, but a palette knife may be your preference. Take a small amount of gesso or white paint and add a very small touch of the appropriate complement. Apply a small amount to the brush and begin at the base of the object you intend to fog. Use a series of overlapping scumbling strokes with a dry-brush technique until you have completely softened all of the edges of the fogged area. Once you have completed this process and it has thoroughly dried, you may repeat the process until you reach the degree of opaqueness that you desire.

Fog Example 1
A blue-gray background would need a slight hint of orange in the fog. This swatch shows you the background color without fog. With the fog added, notice how much softer the background becomes.

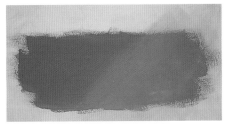

Fog Example 2
If you have a purplish tone in your background, you would want a slight yellow tint in the fog. Please remember you can use many different combinations. If you stick to the basics and use the complements properly, your painting will be pleasing.

Fog Adds Atmosphere
Let us take a look at a finished painting and see how the fog really changes the atmosphere of the painting. Especially notice the soft blended edges.

Three Fog Studies

Take a look at the three versions of this painting and notice the different degrees of opaqueness. In the top example, I've used no fog. In the middle painting, I applied a light fog. In the bottom painting, I used a medium to heavy fog. Remember that the key to good fog is to use a dry-brush scumbling stroke, blending out the edges of the fog so they are very soft. Make sure each layer of fog is thoroughly dry before adding additional layers.

Mist

Mist is another atmospheric condition that really adds great eye appeal and interest to certain paintings. Unlike fog or haze, mist is generally limited to a damp, rainy or snowy atmosphere.

Painting mist is generally a transparent process, and it is applied by using a series of glazes or washes with your large hake brush. Since mist is almost always associated with wet conditions, you will use tones of gray to paint your background. This is really a big help because gray tones make applying the mist easier.

Making Mist

To mix a mist, first take a small dab of gesso or white paint and add enough water until you create a fairly thin transparent wash. This could have a slight tint of red, orange, yellow or even a combination of these colors. Wet the hake brush and squeeze out the excess water with your fingers and form a chiseled edge. Evenly load the brush across the chiseled edge until it is completely saturated with the mist color.

Carefully drag your brush across the surface of the canvas, beginning at the top. Use even pressure and go all the way from the top to the bottom. Gradually move across the canvas, slightly overlapping the previous strokes, until the entire surface is covered. The angle of the stroke is up to you. The more angled the stroke, the windier the weather will appear. Straight or more vertical strokes appear calm.

Once you complete the mist, you can add other atmospheric conditions, such as raindrops or snow. Have fun experimenting. There are many options.

Applying Mist With a Hake Brush

Mist Examples
In these two studies, the example on top has a soft blue-gray background without mist. The study on the bottom has the same background, but I've applied mist.

Haze

Haze is a wonderful complement to any painting. In fact, haze is used in one form or another in most paintings. Let me give you examples of when the technique of creating haze is used: dust kicked up by a passing wind; a pickup truck rumbling on a dirt road; a hazy smoke from a distant forest fire; sun rays breaking through the clouds after a storm; dust kicked up from a thundering herd of horses or animals on a dry African plain. Haze is also used to soften or tone down an entire painting that is too intense or to soften an edge on certain objects, to blur a background or to create depth of field.

Haze Example 1

Notice in this painting the overall softness. The mist not only softens the painting, but it pushes some of the tree limbs and a few of the cardinals farther into the background. The feature cardinal can then be added on top of the haze so that it stands out.

Haze Example 2

Notice how the haze in this detail of a larger painting not only softens the painting, but in this case creates the suggestion of dust kicked up by the horses. This is another wonderful use for haze.

Haze Example 3

In this painting the haze helps to diffuse the glow from the lights, thus giving the painting an almost eerie effect that works well in a night scene.

Making Haze

When you create haze, remember that you can apply as many layers as you desire to create the effect you're after. But each layer must be dry before adding the next layer of haze. Follow along with these steps to see how it's done.

1 Select the Proper Brush
Make sure your painting is completely dry. Select the proper brush. I normally prefer to use my hake brush because a haze usually covers a large area. If you are hazing a smaller area, your no. 10 bristle brush works well.

2 Mix the Haze Color
Mixing the proper haze color is important. It is best to choose a color that blends well with your color scheme and that complements the underpainting. Hopefully by now you know your complementary colors. Mix the haze color with white and plenty of water to create a wash, then add a small amount of the appropriate complement. Wet the area in which you are going to apply the haze. Take your mixture and use crisscross strokes to cover the entire area. Note: It will appear to be slightly milky. This is normal. As it dries, it will turn into a nice soft haze.

3 Make Minor Corrections
Now I'll show you one of the tricks of the trade. There is a good chance that you will haze over an object that you do not intend. To correct this, you immediately take a slightly damp paper towel and blot the area carefully to remove any unwanted haze. You will probably do this more often than not.

Painting Reflections

Painting reflections is one of the most exciting adventures in landscape painting. I would like to take a more in-depth look at painting reflections in calm water, moving water and simple things such as mud puddles. Look at the three studies to the right to see examples from my own artwork.

Painting Calm Water

It is important that you understand that the colors reflected are always those directly above the water area. For example, if you have a gray sky, the underpainting for your water will be a similar sky color. Then objects that are close enough to the water will be reflected, such as mountaintops, trees, grass, rocks and weeds. These objects will be reflected with their original color.

Once the issue of color is settled, the next question that always comes up is, how do I know how long the reflection should be? I can give you a basic rule that will solve most reflection-length problems, and good composition skills should take care of the rest of the problems. Study the simple illustration on the next page to determine the length of your reflection. Then follow along with the steps to see how easy it is to create calm water reflections.

Reflection Study A: Calm Water
The calm water here helps to create a peaceful and tranquil atmosphere, which is the main use for calm water.

Reflection Study B: Moving Water
In this case the moving water creates excitement and action. Use this most often in paintings where action is the main part of the atmosphere.

Reflection Study C: Mud Puddles
Mud puddles add interest to an otherwise dull landscape, and they are great fun to paint. They also help to create the atmosphere of a rainy day or a time just after a passing storm.

LENGTH OF OBJECT

DEAD SPACE

LENGTH OF REFLECTION

Calm Water Reflection Study

After locating the body of water, paint in your objects. Measure the length of an object—for instance, the fence post. Then, beginning at the bottom of the post, measure down directly below into the water and place a mark there. This will be the length of the object reflected in the water.

Note: Be sure you always measure from the bottom of the object, not the edge of the water. Notice how each fence post recedes into the distance the farther from the water's edge it is. Therefore, you see less of each fence post reflected in the water.

1 Paint Background and Reflective Objects

Paint the background for your water, which is generally the same basic color as your sky. After the background dries, paint in each reflective object. Start with the objects that are farthest away from the water. Then add the next closest objects.

Note: Be sure the color of your reflections is a close but toned-down version of the object being reflected. Use a dry-brush stroke, scrubbing to make sure your edges are soft and slightly blurred.

2 Glaze the Water

Once you have completed the reflections, you need to glaze the water with a mixture of water and a touch of white. Using your hake brush, turn it vertically to the canvas; lightly drag it across the water, creating a much softer reflective quality. You can repeat this step if you feel the need.

3 Add Highlights

At this time you can paint in some final accent highlights to give the water a little sparkle. This step is very simple. Take pure gesso and your no. 4 round sable brush and drybrush in some very thin slivers of bright highlights. These horizontal highlights go mostly along the shoreline or any place where the water may be slightly rippled.

Moving or Rippled Water

The techniques we used in painting calm water apply when painting moving water, as well. The main difference is that when you paint the reflections, you use loose, irregular strokes to create blurred edges. Look at the studies on this page to get a better idea of the effect of moving or rippled water.

Keep in mind that there are many variations of moving water, so there is no magic formula for creating perfect water. My job is to give you good technical advice. Then your job is to be very liberal with your artistic license.

Follow along with the steps on the next page to see how to make it all work. I used a no. 4 flat sable brush, no. 4 round sable brush, no. 4 flat bristle brush and a no. 6 flat bristle brush.

Example A: Moving Water

Notice in this autumn painting how the moving water really adds interest and life to the atmosphere. When you don't really have any major activity going on in your painting (in terms of a major center of interest), a little moving water will go a long way in bringing your painting to life.

Example B: Moving Water

In this particular setting, the moving rippled water is actually a major part of the center of interest. The Indians spearing fish in the stream tie the water right into the main focal point.

1 Underpaint the Water

Again, you will paint the water's underpainting using the same sky color. The same process for adding the reflected objects applies here just as it did in the calm-water studies, except for one main difference: As you add the reflected objects, they should be blurred. This begins the process of making the water look like it is moving. A no. 4 or no. 6 bristle brush works best in this step.

2 Add Ripples

Now, at the front of the water we are going to add ripples. We do this by darkening the original sky color by adding more Burnt Sienna, Ultramarine Blue or Dioxazine Purple. Take your no. 6 bristle brush and start at the front of the water area. Use choppy overlapping strokes to create the suggestion of ripples. These should be fairly horizontal strokes. Gradually work your way up toward the shoreline, using less pressure and more space between strokes.

3 Highlight the Ripples

Now, you will highlight the ripples, which will give the water more movement. When you add your highlights, you will use a no. 4 flat sable brush and a no. 4 round sable brush. Mix a very creamy mixture of gesso and a touch of Cadmium Yellow Light or Cadmium Orange. Highlight the edges of the darker ripples. The paint should go on very opaque so it will stay clean and bright. There will be a heavier concentration of these highlights along the shoreline and around the objects in the water such as rocks and grass.

Mud Puddles

It is amazing what a few puddles of water will do for an otherwise ordinary dirt road, pathway or city street. We will not spend much time here because the process is the same as that for painting moving or calm water. The main difference is that puddles are just on a smaller scale. The only other difference is that your road or pathway needs to be completed first. Then you add your puddles on top.

1 Finish the Background
Finish your road or background area. Allow it to dry completely.

2 Add Puddles
Drybrush the basic shape of the puddles using your sky color and a no. 4 or no. 6 bristle brush. Be sure your brushstrokes are fairly horizontal so the puddles appear flat.

3 Add Reflections
Paint in any reflections of any objects that are directly above the puddles. Some puddles may not have any reflected objects, so just using the sky color and a few highlights will be all that is necessary.

Painting Trees

Trees are a major part of most landscape paintings, with the exception of treeless landscapes, such as ocean, desert or sky scenes. Good technical understanding is very important to the composition of a tree. Learning the proper way to underpaint and detail a tree and how to arrange a collection of trees is absolutely necessary in order for your painting to hold its technical, compositional and artistic integrity.

We will look at how to paint both live trees and dead trees. There are hundreds of different species of trees, therefore I am not going to discuss all of the tree types, but rather show you good painting and design techniques that you can apply to any species you choose to paint.

I want you to look at a very common problem when constructing trees. Uniform shape is one of the biggest issues I face when critiquing students' artwork. We are taught in life to line things up, keep things straight and organized. Unfortunately, sometimes we carry these characteristics into our paintings. The best example of this is when painting pine trees, but it also applies to other trees, as well.

Study these two examples to gain a better understanding of how negative space affects the design and composition of your trees.

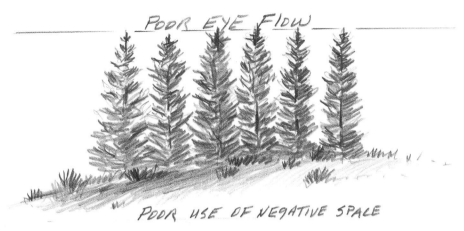

Example A: Poor Composition
In this study, the trees are poorly arranged. Note the negative space is all the same; the trees are all the same height and the same distance apart.

Example B: Good Composition
In this study the trees have the same basic layout as in Example A, but notice the proper use of negative space. This changes the entire look of this collection of trees so that not only are they now compositionally correct, they are also much more appealing to the eye.

Dead Trees

Look at these examples from my own work to better understand working with dead trees. These examples are similar except for the composition and subject matter. The main feature I want you to notice here is the proper use of negative space. This gives each tree good eye flow and interest. Notice the overlapping limbs, which create the negative space. It is how you overlap limbs that makes or breaks your trees. Not only is the individual design of the tree important but also notice the overall view. Observe how each tree works well with the entire composition.

Dead Tree Example A

Notice in this painting how the stump is shifted to the right of the center of interest. It is fairly close to the edge of the canvas, and it leans slightly in toward the center of the painting. This slight shift and leaning creates more interesting negative space around the stump. By adding additional dead limbs, texture and highlights, you create an interesting and unusual object.

Dead Tree Example B

Notice in the painting above how much the dead tree enhances the painting. It acts as an eye stopper on the left side of the painting. It is a major part of the composition. And it adds tremendous interest to the entire setting. Notice how the limbs that overlap the center of the painting help draw your eye into the main focal point or center of interest (the buildings).

Painting Stumps

A dead tree stump can add tremendous character to your painting. However, tree stumps do have their own design problems that we must overcome. Because of its straight cylinder shape, a tree stump is not all that interesting. For this reason we use our artistic license to make a stump really come alive.

Study the sample at right, and then follow along with the steps below. In this painting, the large tree has one main purpose. It is a critical eye stopper that gives the painting its balance. It does have a secondary function of adding interest to the painting, but notice that as large and interesting as the dead tree is, it does not interfere with the main center of interest.

Stump Study

Step 1
First, make a rough sketch.

Step 2
Now, with a no. 6 bristle brush, underpaint the stump, using a mixture of Ultramarine Blue, Burnt Sienna and a touch of purple with a small amount of white. Use short choppy vertical strokes so that it looks rough and textured. Then with a no. 4 round sable brush, add the broken limbs.

Step 3
Highlight the tree using a mixture of white with a touch of orange. Use the no. 4 flat sable brush and once again use short choppy vertical strokes. Be sure you allow some of the background to come through so that you create the effect of rough tree bark.

Step 4
Add the final details: small holes and the reflected highlight. The reflected highlight is a mixture of white, blue and purple. Drybrush this reflected light on the back side of the tree to create soft rounded edges.

Painting Tree Branches

Now we are ready for one of the most exciting aspects of painting leafless trees. For this process you will use a no. 4 script liner brush. We are going to learn how to paint the smaller limbs that finish out a larger tree and also small bushes or saplings. For the sake of practicing, make a mixture of Burnt Sienna, Ultramarine Blue and plenty of water to create an inky mixture.

The way this works is you take your script brush and fully load it by rolling it around in the mixture until the brush comes to a fine point.

Starting at the base of the limb, use heavy pressure and move upward, gradually decreasing the pressure until the limb tapers to a fine point. Use this same process for all smaller limbs, whether they are horizontal, slightly angled or vertical. When you add additional limbs to larger limbs, always start a little farther back on the existing limb and pull the attached limb out or upward.

Never begin painting a limb from the sky area inward, because you will usually leave a blob we call a bird's nest. It takes practice to master this brush, but you will eventually get it. Look at these examples to see how the tree gradually changes.

Tree Limb Study

Painting Live Trees

It is time to learn how to paint live trees. Knowing how to paint a leafed tree can be an asset to your painting, as long as the tree has good three-dimensional form. On the other hand, a tree that has poor form can be a real eyesore.

1 Block in the Trunk
Block in a rough tree trunk with no details, highlights or limbs—only the main trunk and main limbs. You will add the smaller limbs later. Block in the trunk with a no. 4 flat bristle brush with a mixture of Burnt Sienna and blue.

2 Form the Tree
Next, take your no. 10 bristle brush and mix an underpainting color of Hooker's Green, a touch of Burnt Sienna, purple and a little white to soften it. Load the end of the brush and dab straight on the canvas. As you start forming the tree, the most important thing to remember is to make sure your basic tree form has good negative space.

3 Add Highlights
Use the same mixture as in step 2. Change the value slightly by adding orange, yellow and white. You will use the same technique and dab in this value on the sunlit side of the tree. Begin by forming the clumps of leaves that gives the tree its shape. Be careful here because you do not want to overpaint too much of the background color or you will lose the depth in the leaves.

4 Add More Highlights

This step is almost identical to step 3. You will be adding the third and final value to the leaves. Take the same mixture as step 3 and make it much lighter. You need to add white and any or all of the following: yellow, Thalo Yellow-Green or orange. Dab on the final highlight carefully. Do not block out too much of the underpainting.

5 Add Final Details

Now you add final details and highlights. Use your script liner brush to add the final limbs up through the clumps of leaves. Then highlight the edge of the tree with a mixture of orange and white, using your no. 4 flat sable brush. The best advice I can give you is to paint loose and free. Make sure you leave good negative space in, around and through the tree.

Painting Rocks

Painting rocks is one of the more challenging components of a landscape painting. Rocks are also interesting because of their different shapes, colors, formations and sizes. From tiny pebbles to massive boulders, they all play a major role in the compositional makeup of a landscape painting. Let us look at a couple of examples on the right of my own work where rocks played an important role in the overall composition.

In both of these examples notice how the rock formations create balance in the painting. The rocks have good negative space around them. Observe how they overlap or touch each other to create good eye flow and also serve as eye stoppers. You can see how important rocks can be to your painting.

Creating Rocks Step by Step

How do you create a rock? First, know that this rock-painting technique applies to any type of rock or rock formation, color scheme and value system. So once you learn this technique, you can paint almost any rock project that you wish to tackle.

These are the basic steps for creating a good rock. In fact, I will make a small collection of rocks so you can see how to do a variety of rock sizes.

1 Block in the Basic Shapes

Take your no. 6 bristle brush and block in the basic shape of the rocks. Use a mixture of Burnt Sienna, Ultramarine Blue and purple. Add a touch of white to soften. Notice how rough and unorganized the rocks appear.

2 Refine the Rock Shapes

This step is simply to help you find a more accurate shape. We do this with an intermediate-value color by taking a dab of your rock color and adding white with a touch of orange. This will be a very subtle value change. Use a no. 6 or no. 4 bristle brush. Begin forming the shape of the rocks. Be careful not to paint out your background color. At this point you should have a fairly good three-dimensional form to all of the rocks.

3 Create Highlights

Now, we want to intensify the next value so that it almost looks like a highlight color. We do this by adding white and a touch of orange to the value color in step 2. Use a no. 4 flat sable brush or a no. 4 flat bristle brush and apply brushstrokes to the top and sides of the rocks to create form and unique designs within the rocks. The same rule applies: Do not cover up all of your underpainting color.

4 Add Final Details

Here, we add the final highlights and details such as cracks, holes and chips in the rocks. You can use any brush that you want to for this, but your smaller brushes will probably work best. Take the underpainting color for the cracks and then take the value color we used in step 3 and brighten it by adding white, yellow or orange for additional highlights. Have fun experimenting with the final details.

Painting Grass and Weeds

Even though grass and weeds may seem insignificant in the overall picture of a landscape painting, quite frankly they play one of the most important roles. Grass and weeds are like the icing on the cake. They pull the painting together. They can act as eye stoppers and final details, or they can play a major part of the composition. Look at a couple of examples of my finished work, and then I will take you step by step in creating good grasses and weeds.

Keep in mind that there are many different types of weeds and grasses. My effort here is not to identify types of weeds but rather to show you basic techniques that you can apply to any type of weeds you wish to paint. Also, I am showing you only weeds for finishing and detailing your painting.

Notice in these examples how the weeds literally help pull your eye in toward the center of the painting. They also act as eye stoppers, and the taller weeds are a crucial part of the main composition. You must never be afraid to let the weeds do everything they are designed to do.

Creating Grass Step by Step

Look at a few basic techniques for creating good weeds. First of all, you will need a no. 10 bristle brush and your no. 4 script liner brush.

1 Paint Background Grass

The first step is to have a good background of shorter grass to act as a buffer between your underpainting and the taller weeds. Once your underpainting is dry, mix the appropriate color that works well with your color scheme and make it a value that is slightly darker than the underpainting. Take a no. 10 bristle brush and a drybrush technique using an upward motion to create a soft clump of background grass. Be sure the clump has good negative space and has an interesting shape.

2 Paint in Short and Tall Weeds

Using the same color, thin it down with plenty of water to form an inky mixture. Roll your no. 4 script liner in the mixture until it comes to a fine point and paint in the shorter weeds. Next, gradually add the taller weeds. Here again, negative space is critical, so do not be afraid to add plenty of weeds that bend and overlap each other. Of course, weeds can go in all directions. Only you can determine where you place the weeds and their intended use.

Note: When painting the weeds, always start from the bottom up, never from the top down.

3 Mix in Lighter Weeds

Here, you will take the same color used in step 2, but lighten the value by adding white, a touch of yellow or orange. Add the lighter weeds and mix them in among the darker weeds. You can continue making the mixture lighter if necessary to create more of a sunlit effect.

Winter Retreat
16" x 20" (41cm x 51cm)

Winter Retreat

Wintertime—what a great season, especially when snow is the feature. Even though winter is my favorite season, and snow is one of my favorite things to paint, the key reason for doing this painting is to practice some new techniques. For example, for those of you who are having a difficult time mastering the no. 4 script brush, this painting gives you plenty of opportunity to practice one of the most important components of a winter landscape: you guessed it, trees with no leaves. This is a great place to really work out the kinks in your tree-painting techniques. Here, we really concentrate on negative space, eye flow and overlapping of the limbs. This is a great place to practice brush pressure and getting your tree mixture to be the right consistency. This painting also shows you how to glaze in order to create a nice soft hazy effect. Of course, there are many other learning opportunities, as well. So, grab your brushes and settle in for a great painting experience.

1 Create a Rough Sketch

With your soft vine charcoal, make a very loose and rough sketch of the basic ground formations.

2 Underpaint Sky

For this step you will need your hake brush. The first thing to do here is to lightly wet the entire sky area, then apply a liberal coat of gesso; while the gesso is still wet, begin at the horizon and apply pure Cadmium Red Light. Cover the entire sky area until the whole sky takes on the medium pink tone; while this is still wet, beginning at the top, apply pure Ultramarine Blue and blend with a downward criss-cross stroke until the sky takes on a grayish tone. It will turn slightly purple. Don't blend too smoothly, or you will lose the nice brushstrokes that give the sky a little motion. Be sure to leave a nice pinkish glow at the base.

3 Underpaint Water

No surprise here! We paint the water the exact same way that we painted the sky; the only difference is we reverse the application. The dark area is at the bottom of the painting, and the light area is at the top. Notice how everything merges together at the horizon.

4 Add Soft Background Trees
This step is simple but important. Take your no. 10 bristle brush and mix Ultramarine Blue, a touch of Cadmium Red Light and whatever amount of white you need to create a value that is slightly darker than the sky. Now, with a dry-brush scumbling stroke, scrub in a soft background of distant trees. The key here is making sure that they fade out into the sky area with no hard edges. Be sure to give them interesting shapes.

5 Paint Distant Dead Trees
Now for the step that everyone dreads: painting trees with your script brush! We have been through this drill before, so grab your script brush and mix a color that is slightly darker than the background trees. Be sure the mixture is very thin, very much like ink. Now, paint in these delicate distant trees all across the horizon. Notice, the wide variety of shapes, sizes and heights. If you don't remember how to use the script brush properly, refer to the front of the book for that technique.

6 Add Background Cedars

Cedar trees are generally shorter and fatter and have branches that go more upward; therefore, they aren't as interesting as most pine trees. So, you have to use your artistic license to make them a little more interesting. First, take your no. 6 bristle brush and mix Hooker's Green, half as much purple, a touch of Burnt Sienna and whatever amount of white you need to create a value that is slightly darker than the background trees. Now, with a semi-dry brush stroke, scrub in your cedars so that they have good negative space around them as well as different heights.

7 Underpaint Cabin

You can design your own cabin, house or barn, whatever you choose; but whatever you choose needs to be underpainted in soft gray tones. First, you might want to sketch it in with your charcoal. Now, use your no. 4 flat sable brush and mix Ultramarine Blue, a little Burnt Sienna, a touch of purple and enough white to create a value that fits that area of the painting. Block in the two sides, then add more blue and purple to the mixture and block in the roof. Darken the mixture and block in the doors and window.

8 Underpaint Snow

Here, we need to mix a fairly large amount of color, so use your palette knife. Take gesso, half as much Ultramarine Blue, one-fourth as much Burnt Sienna and a small amount of purple; this should be a grayish purple. Now, all you do here is block in all of the snow area all the way to the water. Notice the irregular shapes along the water's edge; also notice that the edges of the snowdrifts on the water are horizontal, which makes the water look flat. Use your no. 10 bristle brush for this step.

9 Underpaint Middle-Ground Trees

This step is one of the more critical ones. Composition is the real issue here. First, mix Ultramarine Blue and Burnt Sienna, with just enough white to change the value. This should be an intermediate value for the middle ground of this painting. Now, take your no. 4 flat sable and block in the main trunks of these trees; then thin the mixture and use your script brush to finish out the trees. Once again, be aware of the placement of each tree and use good negative space.

10 Darken Shoreline and Add Reflections

For this step, take the same color that you used in step 9 for the trees and lighten it slightly with a little white. Now, with your no. 6 bristle brush, scrub in a darker shoreline, then switch to the no. 4 flat sable and scrub in the reflections from any of the middle-ground trees that are close enough to the water to have a reflection.

11 Highlight Snow, Phase 1

Now, let's premix a highlight color of white or gesso, plus a very small amount of orange to slightly tint the white. Take your no. 6 bristle brush and brush in the highlights on the snow and the snowdrifts on the water. The main purpose of this step is to locate the contour of the snow. Creating good eye flow is essential here. The final highlights will be done later. Be sure when you apply this highlight that you use a soft dry-brush stroke so that the edges are soft.

12 Underpaint Clumps of Grass

Now, mix Burnt Sienna with a very small amount of purple and a touch of Ultramarine Blue. You will need to add a touch of white to slightly soften this color. Then, in selected areas throughout the snow and along the water's edge, drybrush in clumps of grass using a vertical stroke. If you are not careful, you can get this too busy. So watch your negative space and overlap some of the clumps, and you will be OK.

13 Underpaint Foreground Trees

Now that we are in the foreground, your values can be much darker. Let's mix Ultramarine Blue with an equal amount of Burnt Sienna. With your no. 4 flat bristle brush, block in the larger foreground trees and the stump, then thin the mixture down and use your script brush to add all of the smaller limbs.

14 Detail Cabin and Cedar Trees

Because we want these objects to remain soft and distant, we don't want to overhighlight or detail. Take your no. 4 flat sable brush and mix white with a touch of orange to tint it, and block in the snow on the roof. Also, smudge a little snow on the cedar trees. Now, slightly soften the left side of the cabin; then, add the chimney, the shadow from the chimney, the smoke from the chimney and the light in the windows. Remember, no major details.

15 Final Reflections On Water

At this point, we need to add reflections from the foreground trees and clumps of grass and any other objects that are close enough to the water to be reflected. Be sure these reflections have soft blurred edges and are slightly lighter than the objects being reflected. Your no. 6 or no. 4 flat bristle brush would work best for this.

16 Add Miscellaneous Objects

This is a great time to add the objects to your painting that give it more character, such as the fallen logs, dead bushes or even some wildlife or people. For me, adding the woodpile and the chopping stump with the ax adds a hint of life to the painting; these are fairly simple objects to add. The main thing to remember is to keep these objects simple without too much detail.

17 Glaze Water

This is a technique we have used before. Its main intent is to soften the water and give it a little more of a gloss or make it appear a bit wetter. First, lightly wet the water area, then create a glaze of water and gesso. Now, take your hake brush and load it evenly across the end, then lightly drag it across the surface of the water with a slight jiggle, which makes the water look slightly rippled. Repeat this step if you think it is necessary.

18 **Highlight Trees and Grass**
This is the step where we add the clean final highlights that give your painting a crisp refined look. For example, you can add thin white lines along the water's edge, also on the edge of your trees; notice the bright whitish orange sunlight. Also, use this same highlight and drybrush some highlights on the tops of the clumps of grass. Now, search through your painting for areas where more light or minor details would finish out the overall composition and brightness in the painting.

19 **Highlight Snow, Phase 2**
This step really makes your snow come alive. All you need here is your no. 4 flat bristle brush. Mix white or gesso and a little touch of orange to tint it, then simply drybrush in some strong bright light on the raised areas of your snowdrifts. Now, drift the snow up against the clumps of grass and tree trunks, which helps to settle them down in the snow.

20 Add Cast Shadows

Here, we need to add the cast shadows from the trees and other objects. The color we need for this is a mixture of white, with a touch of purple, Ultramarine Blue and a little Burnt Sienna. This shadow should be a purplish gray. Now with your no. 4 flat bristle brush, scrub in the shadows, being sure that they follow the contour of the snowdrifts and that they have soft edges. Another important thing here is to be sure that the value is correct. If the shadows are too dark, they will jump off the canvas and overwhelm your painting.

As an option, if you think your painting needs to be softened, or only parts of it such as the background trees, then just mix a glaze of water and a little white. Now, with your hake brush, glaze the area that you want to soften, then take a paper towel to wipe off any areas that you overglazed.

Summer Dreams
16" x 20" (41cm x 51cm)

Summer Dreams

In this fast-paced push-button world, how would you like to find a place like this, where you can go and leave all of your cares behind you for a while? The great thing about being an artist is that you can pick up a paintbrush and create your favorite place without ever leaving your studio. For me, nothing is more peaceful than a cool mountain setting with a running stream or babbling brook. In fact, the point that I want to get across in this painting is how to create running or rippled water. This painting also offers many other practical learning opportunities; things like rocks, live trees, distant mountains and grass will help you expand your artistic library of techniques and practical applications. Keep in mind that there are many different variations of a painting like this, so don't be afraid to experiment. So let's get started. I know you will enjoy this one.

1 Create Basic Sketch

As is usually the case, take your soft vine charcoal and make a rough sketch of the basic composition.

2 Underpaint Sky

For this painting, we want a clean, clear, bluish gray sky with a soft horizon. We begin by slightly wetting the sky area, and then we apply a liberal coat of gesso; while the gesso is still wet, starting at the horizon, take Alizarin Crimson and go over the entire sky until it becomes a light soft pink tone. While this is still wet, starting at the top of the sky, take Ultramarine Blue and a touch of Burnt Sienna. Blend these colors across the top of the sky and then down, until you create a nice soft bluish gray with a soft pinkish horizon.

3 Underpaint Water

Since this is running water, it doesn't have to be a smooth application of color; in fact, you can have a lot of fun with this underpainting. Take your no. 10 bristle brush and a combination of the following colors: Ultramarine Blue, small amounts of Burnt Sienna, Dioxazine Purple and white. Now, using short choppy horizontal strokes, apply these colors and mix them on the canvas, not on your palette. The important thing here is to be sure that your canvas is well covered; also, you don't want to overblend the colors to a smooth texture. It's important to keep your strokes loose and free to suggest movement.

4 Underpaint Background Mountains

For this step, we need to mix a soft distant gray tone. Start with gesso and a touch of Ultramarine Blue, Burnt Sienna and a touch of purple; this should be a light purplish gray. The value is slightly darker than the sky. Now take your no. 6 bristle brush and block in the most distant mountain first, then slightly darken the mixture and block in the second layer of mountains.

5 Underpaint Tree-Covered Hills

Take the mixture you used in step 4 for the second mountain range and darken it slightly, then add a small amount of Hooker's Green to create a grayish green. Now, take your no. 10 bristle brush and use a vertical dry-brush stroke and cover the entire area. The main thing to remember here is to be sure that the canvas is covered completely. Also, notice the treelike shapes along the top of the mountain.

6 Paint Middle-Ground Trees

This is a short but important step. Take the mixture you used in step 5 and darken it slightly with a little more Hooker's Green and a touch of purple. Now, with your no. 6 bristle brush, paint in the basic shape of the trees; you could have a combination of pine, cedar and regular trees.

7 Mist Base of Mountain

Now, we get to use a specialty technique—mist. Take a little bit of gesso and a touch of Ultramarine Blue and Dioxazine Purple. Add enough water to make it slightly creamy. Now, with your no. 6 or no. 10 bristle brush, using a dry-brush circular motion and starting at the base of the mountains, blend upward until the mist fades away.

Note: Be sure the mountain range is completely dry before you begin.

8 Underpaint Middle-Ground and Foreground Grass

This step is going to require a lot of loose Impressionistic strokes. This will be done with your no. 10 bristle brush. Beginning at the base of the mountains, apply Thalo Yellow-Green, touches of orange and maybe a little yellow. The paint must go on fairly thick, with very loose irregular strokes that are mostly vertical, and as you come forward, add Hooker's Green, Burnt Sienna, purple and maybe a little orange here and there. Notice the values become darker and darker as you come forward. Repeat this on each side of the river.

9 Underpaint Rocks

We need to add rocks along the water's edge. Mix on your palette some Ultramarine Blue, Burnt Sienna and a touch of purple with a little white. Now, take your no. 6 bristle brush and simply block in the main shape and location of the rocks. Be sure that you have good compositional balance and negative space.

10 Highlight Mountains

Now, we will highlight both mountain ranges. You will need your no. 4 flat sable and a mixture of white with a touch of yellow and orange. The sunlight will be coming in from the right side, so drybrush highlights using a choppy broken stroke, creating interesting pockets of negative space. Now, add a little more yellow and orange to the mixture and highlight the second mountain range.

11 Underpaint Large Middle-Ground Trees

The first thing you need to do here is create a good skeleton of the tree. I suggest you use Burnt Sienna and Ultramarine Blue, with a little white to create a middle-tone gray. Now, with your no. 4 flat sable brush, block in the main trunk and intermediate limbs. Thin the mixture with water, and take your script brush and add a few smaller limbs. No need to add any tiny limbs to finish the tree; we add them later after we finish the leaves.

12 Leaf Middle-Ground Trees

Now, let's mix Hooker's Green, about one-fourth as much purple and a little white to create a nice soft greenish gray. Now, take your no. 10 bristle brush and dab in the leaves, gradually forming the main shape. You might add miscellaneous smaller trees or bushes at the base of the tree and on the other side of the river.

13 Detail Water

We want to darken the shoreline. With a mixture of Burnt Sienna and Ultramarine Blue, take your no. 6 bristle brush and smudge in a darker edge. It's important to lighten the value as you recede into the distance. Also, as you add the shoreline, be sure to reflect the darker value into the water, kind of like a reflection. Now, take pure white with your no. 4 flat sable brush, make it creamy, and add ripples and movement to the water; these are horizontal choppy concave strokes. Notice the water is more rippled at the back of the river and it becomes calmer as you move forward.

14 Highlight Rocks

Now, we want to mix white, a touch of orange and a little blue to gray it. With your no. 6 or no. 4 flat bristle brush, apply the highlight to the top right side of each of the rocks. You can also add a few highlights to suggest pebbles along the shoreline. Once you have the basic rocks highlighted, you can brighten the mixture and put an accent on the rocks to make them stand out a little more. Brighten the mixture with a little more white, yellow and orange.

15 Highlight Grass

Now here, you have to be fairly creative. We are going to add miscellaneous highlights, flowers and other colors to give the painting a late summer afternoon glow. You will mainly use your no. 6 and no. 10 bristle brushes. It's really sort of hard to explain what to do here, but I'll do my best. The key is to scatter complementary colors to accent the painting. You can add more light to suggest sunlight and add more miscellaneous flowers, as well. The range of colors can be from yellows, oranges, reds, pinks, purples and even light blues. What I normally do is take one of my brushes and dab in the various colors, highlights and flowers throughout the painting, making sure that it has good color balance. A good habit to get into here is to stand back about 5' or 6' (2m) after every few strokes so you can better check your progress and see how your painting comes together.

16 Highlight Large Tree and Bushes

This step requires careful planning. We will apply two highlights to give the trees their form. You will need your no. 10 bristle brush for the larger tree and the no. 6 bristle for the smaller bushes. The primary color will be a mixture of Thalo Yellow-Green and a little bit of orange; you may add a touch of white and/or yellow if you choose. Now, take your brush and dab the highlights on the large tree, being very careful not to cover up too much of the underpainting color. After applying this first layer of highlight, lighten the mixture with a little more white and yellow, and apply this final highlight to give your trees more of a sunlit effect. Don't hesitate to change the color for some of the bushes.

17 Add Final Details

This is where you will add the final things that will give your painting the personality you would like it to have. For myself, I added some tall weeds, additional flowers, highlights and birds. I even added extra color in the water to help tie it in better to the rest of the painting. Remember, a little distance will help you see the painting from a different perspective, and you can make better decisions about final details. As an option, add more mist. Refer to step 7 to refresh your memory on how to do this.

Swamp Fisherman
16" x 20" (41cm x 51cm)

Swamp Fisherman

I could not resist using this piece as an instructional painting; there's just too much good material in it. In fact, I taught this painting in one of my workshops in Florida and it was a great success, so I thought you would enjoy doing it, as well. What makes this painting so different is its unique color scheme, and even though that was not the main intent of this painting, at least you get to see what an important part a color scheme plays in creating a great atmosphere. The main purpose for this study painting is to practice one of the techniques at the front of the book: calm water. As simple as it may seem, painting calm water can be even more challenging than moving or rippled water. The real problem is getting the reflections to have the proper color, value and softness; in moving water, those things are not such an issue, but in calm water, if the reflections are not done correctly, they will overpower the painting and be in direct competition with the main focal point. Hopefully, this painting will help unravel some of these problems and help build your confidence in painting calm water.

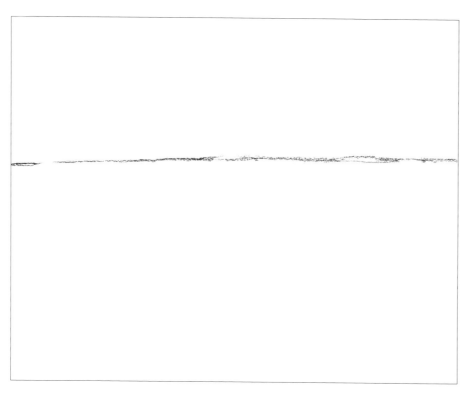

1 Make Basic Sketch
This step is really not that difficult. All you need is a straight line across the canvas, about one-third of the way down from the top of the canvas.

2 Underpaint Sky
This unique color scheme is a lot of fun to work with. The procedure is the same as usual. Lightly wet the sky with water, then add a liberal coat of gesso over the entire sky with your hake brush. While the gesso is still wet, start at the horizon and apply orange with a touch of yellow, blending it all the way to the top. Now, take Ultramarine Blue and a touch of Burnt Sienna; start at the top and blend down until you have faded these colors out near the horizon. You should mix these colors directly on the canvas, not on your palette.

3 Underpaint Water

To paint the water, I am going to ask you to do something a little different here. Turn your painting upside down and repeat the same procedure as in step 2 for the sky. The main thing here is to be sure that the sky and the water are blended at the horizon so that there is no hard edge.

4 Underpaint Background Trees

This first layer of trees is very distant and very soft. Create a mixture of white, Ultramarine Blue, a touch of Burnt Sienna and a touch of purple. Now, with your no. 6 bristle brush, scrub in the first layer of distant trees, keeping them very dry and very soft. Now, thin the mixture with water, and take your script brush and paint in a nice collection of distant dead trees.

5 Sketch in Composition

Now that the background is underpainted, take your charcoal and make a rough sketch of the main components of the composition.

6 Underpaint Shack and Boat Dock

Mix a value of color that is slightly darker than the background trees; this consists of white, with a touch of Ultramarine Blue, Burnt Sienna and purple. Take your no. 4 flat sable brush and block in the shadowed side of the shack; also, block in the shadow under the boat dock and the pier posts. Now, lighten the mixture with a good bit of white and block in the light side of the shack.

7 Detail Shack

Take the dark value that we used for the shadowed side of the shack and add a little purple to it. Now, with your no. 4 round sable brush, paint in the overhang shadows from the roof, the chimney and its shadow, and block in the windows. Take pure yellow and orange, with a little white, and paint in the light in the windows. You can take a little white with your finger and smudge in the smoke from the chimney. If you want to, go ahead and detail the dock, or save it for the final step of miscellaneous details.

8 Add Reflections From Background Trees

This is a short but necessary step. Take the background tree color and add a little white to it. Now, take your no. 6 bristle brush and scrub in the reflections in the water, then take your no. 4 round sable and carefully paint in the dead-tree reflections. Even though most of the shack reflection will be covered later, it's a good idea to paint it in, just in case some of it shows.

9 Underpaint Middle-Ground Bushes and Trees

This step requires a mixture of Burnt Sienna, a touch of purple, white, Ultramarine Blue and a little orange. You should experiment with the mixture until it fits your color scheme. Now, take your no. 10 bristle brush and scrub in the middle-ground bushes, then thin the mixture and take your no. 4 script brush, and paint in the dead trees and smaller dead bushes. This is a good time to take your no. 6 bristle brush and scrub in the reflections from these middle-ground bushes and trees. You should add a little white to the mixture to soften it before adding the reflections.

10 Underpaint Stump and Middle Foreground Bushes

Just darken the mixture used in step 9 by eliminating some of the white, then take your no. 4 bristle brush and block in the stump and the bushes on the left side of the painting. It's important to go ahead and paint in the reflections from the stump and the clumps of grass, so lighten the mixture slightly and scrub in the reflections.

11 Underpaint Foreground Bank and Dirt

For this step, mix Burnt Sienna with a touch of Ultramarine Blue, Dioxazine Purple and a little white to change the value. Now, take your no. 6 bristle brush and, with a comma stroke, block in the bank and gradually fade it into the water. Notice how irregular the edge of the bank is. Now, slightly lighten the mixture with a little white and, using choppy horizontal strokes, block in the top of the bank. You can lighten the mixture with white and a touch of orange and add a few choppy brushstrokes to give the dirt a little more interest.

12 Add Middle-Ground Clumps of Grass

Here, you want to create a mixture of Burnt Sienna, Ultramarine Blue, and a touch of purple and white. This is a fairly dark value, so don't add too much white. Now, with your no. 6 bristle brush, drybrush in the clumps of grass and small bushes along the bank and in the back of the dirt area. Keep in mind that the clumps of grass we put in the water need to be reflected; do this at the same time that you add the clumps. The reflection value is slightly lighter, so add just a touch of white.

13 Add Ripples in Water

What we do here is mix Ultramarine Blue with a little Burnt Sienna and a small amount of white; this should be a deep bluish gray mixture. Add just enough water to make it creamy. Now, take your no. 4 flat bristle brush and, beginning at the bottom of the water, work your way upward, using a series of short choppy horizontal strokes and gradually decreasing your pressure as you go, until this value fades into the lighter value.

14 Add Rocks and Pebbles

For this step, you want to mix white with a touch of orange. If this value is too bright, don't hesitate to add just a touch of blue to slightly tone it down. Now, take your no. 4 flat sable brush and paint small rocks and pebbles along the shoreline and on top of the dirt bank. Be sure you put in enough rocks and pebbles to really tie the shoreline to the water.

15 Block In Large Tree, Add Hanging Moss

Mix Burnt Sienna and Ultramarine Blue and, with your no. 4 flat bristle brush, block in the main structure of the large tree. Now, thin the mixture to an ink-like consistency, take your script brush, and add all the smaller limbs. It is especially important that you have good negative space in, around and through these limbs. This is a good time to add the moss, and it's really quite simple. Take this same mixture without much water, and your no. 6 bristle brush, and drybrush downward from certain limbs and across the top of the canvas. Add moss on the middle-ground trees, but first, lighten the mixture to the proper value.

16 Add Miscellaneous Objects and Details

The main things we are going to put in now are the rowboat in the background, the blue heron standing in the water, and the taller weeds in the foreground. It takes one main mixture to do all of these objects; the only difference is that each of these objects will have a different value. The mixture is Burnt Sienna, Ultramarine Blue and a touch of purple. Now, for the foreground weeds, smudge in a base background, then thin the mixture and, with your no. 4 script brush, paint in the taller weeds. As for the heron and the boat, sketch them first with your charcoal. Now, change the value of the mixture with a little white, and underpaint both objects with your no. 4 flat and/or no. 4 round sable. Using your script brush, add the small dead bushes throughout the painting.

17 Create Final Highlights

This is the step that truly gives the painting its light and life. First, mix white with a touch of yellow and orange. You will probably use two brushes, the no. 4 round and flat sables. Now, it's a matter of applying these highlights in the right areas, such as on the inside edge of your trees and the sunlit ripples on the water. Then, of course, you need to highlight the heron and the rowboat, and gently scrub in their reflections. When you apply these highlights, be sure that they are fairly opaque; this will assure good clean light. However, when you highlight the heron, you will use more of a dry-brush stroke to give a slight impression of feathers.

18 Glaze Painting

This is really an optional step, one we have done before. If you are satisfied with the overall softness of the painting, you can avoid this step; however, if you need to soften your painting, a glaze works great. For this painting, a glaze of water, a little white and a touch of orange works best. Remember, this is a very thin transparent mixture. Now, take your hake brush and apply the glaze to the area you want to soften. Use a damp paper towel to take off any excess or unwanted glaze. Refer to page 146 for a refresher on how to glaze.

Reminder of the Past
16" x 20" (41cm x 51cm)

Reminder of the Past

As you know by now, I love to paint snow. Even though we have already done one snow scene, I thought it would be appropriate to do one in a setting where we could again practice the technique of glazing to suggest a foggy, hazy or misty effect. In a painting like this one, it is absolutely necessary to know how to create a good misty effect so that the snowy atmosphere we want to create will blend in nicely with the rest of the composition and color scheme. Not only does the mist help with the snowy effect, but it also softens the painting and, depending on what color glaze you use, will also help make it a cool or warm atmosphere. This painting also gives you another chance to practice painting tree limbs with your no. 4 script brush. There are also some good value changes in the trees to help create a little depth. So, you will learn a lot in this painting, and not only that, but it is just simply a fun painting to do, especially the old weathered wagon. This could be one of your favorites. Good luck!

1 Underpaint Background

For this step, you need your hake brush. We will block in about the top two-thirds of the canvas; this will be a multicolored background, with a predominately gray overtone. Begin at either side of the painting by applying gesso, with enough water to keep it creamy. As you apply the gesso, add these following colors: Ultramarine Blue, Burnt Sienna, Dioxazine Purple, touches of red and, believe it or not, a little Hooker's Green. Use long vertical strokes that overlap each other, adding the above colors as you go. Do not blend these colors to a solid gray tone. You still want to see hints of each of the colors used, plus you want to see some of the brushstrokes.

2 Underpaint Foreground Snow

What we do here is mix on our palette the underpainting color, which consists of white, half as much Ultramarine Blue, and a touch of Burnt Sienna and Dioxazine Purple. This should be a fairly dark bluish gray; if it leans to the purple side, that's OK. Now, take your no. 10 bristle brush and paint the entire foreground. Be sure the canvas is well covered and that the place where the snow underpainting and background meet has a soft edge.

3 Paint First Layer of Background Trees

To create the layers of depth in this painting, we will need several value changes in the trees. The way we do this is to take the underpainting color for the snow and add enough white to change the value so that it is slightly darker than the background; make it fairly creamy. Now, take your no. 4 round sable and your no. 4 script brush and paint in the first layer of trees. Notice how some of them fade off into the background; this creates the suggestion of mist or haze.

4 Create Second Layer of Background Trees

This step is almost identical to step 3, except the value is a little darker and the trees have a little bit more definite form. You can use your no. 4 round or flat sable and/or your no. 4 script brush. This step will bring you all the way to the large trees on the left. You should have a good variety of values and shapes to your trees at this stage. Notice, however, that there are not many trees on the right side; this step is left out intentionally.

5 Underpaint Large Tree and Stump

You may want to take your charcoal and sketch in the tree and stump on the left. The large tree on the right we will do later. Now, take a mixture of Ultramarine Blue, Burnt Sienna and a touch of purple and, with your no. 6 bristle brush, block in the trees. Finish them out with your no. 4 script brush, thinning the mixture to an ink-like consistency for the script brush work.

6 Highlight Snowdrifts, Phase 1

For this step, you want to create a mixture of white and a touch of yellow and orange; this mixture should be only slightly tinted. Make it fairly creamy, then grab your no. 6 bristle brush and drybrush in the highlights that create the drifts of snow. All you want to do is locate the basic forms of the drifts; we will put the final highlights on later. Keep in mind, as usual, that you have good negative space throughout the drifts so that you have good eye flow; also, notice the soft edges.

7 Sketch In Wagon and Tree

This will be a little test of your drawing skills. Take your charcoal and make a rough but fairly accurate sketch of the wagon and the large tree on the right. Note: Sometimes a soft charcoal pencil is easier to sketch with because you can sharpen it like a pencil and it holds its point better.

8 Underpaint Wagon and Tree

This is not too difficult to do, but you do need to be careful. First, mix a color that has a nice gray tone to it; Ultramarine Blue, Burnt Sienna, and a little white with a touch of purple should do it. Now, with your no. 4 flat bristle brush, block in the body of the wagon and the large dead tree. Don't block in the wheels yet; we actually need to finish the body of the wagon before adding the wheels. See how the top of the tree fades into the background; this helps create the effect of mist.

9 Detail Wagon Body

What you will do here is change the underpainting color to a lighter value by adding a little white. Then, take your no. 4 flat sable brush and drybrush long strokes along the sides of the wagon to suggest weathered wood. You may need to repeat this a couple of times until you are satisfied with the results. Then, take your script brush with a dark mixture of Ultramarine Blue and Burnt Sienna and paint in a few cracks and holes to make the wood appear very old. Now, take the highlighted snow color and paint in some snow on top of the side panels and in the floor of the wagon. Now we are ready for the wheels.

10 **Add Wagon Wheels**
There is no magic formula for painting these wheels. The best thing is to have a fairly accurate sketch, then make a medium-dark mixture of Ultramarine Blue, Burnt Sienna and a touch of white. Make the mixture fairly creamy, then take your no. 4 round sable brush and carefully paint in the wheels. This is a fairly difficult task because of the angle of the wheels, so take your time and be careful! Once the wheel is painted, slightly lighten the mixture and paint the outer rim of the wheel so it looks three-dimensional. You can also paint the snow on top of the wheels, spokes and hubs, as you did on top of the wagon body.

11 **Paint Clumps of Grass**
Now it's time to put in all the clumps of grass. For this, you want to mix Burnt Sienna with a touch of purple and a little bit of blue. Take your no. 6 bristle brush and drybrush in the clumps in the depressed areas of the snow. Keep in mind, this is only the background for the taller weeds to come later. Scatter these clumps so that you have good eye flow throughout the snow.

12 Highlight Snow, Phase 2
This step is fairly similar to step 6, except that we are more specific with the application of the highlights. First, mix the highlight color of white with a touch of yellow. Make it nice and creamy, then take your no. 4 flat sable brush and drift the snow up against the clumps of grass and the tree trunks, along the sides of the trees and against the wagon. Notice how the snowdrifts are on the right side of the trees and clumps of grass; this gives the effect that the wind is blowing from the right to the left.

13 Add Taller Weeds
This is the step that really ties the painting together. Mix a very inky mixture of Burnt Sienna and a touch of purple. Now, take your no. 4 script brush and paint the taller weeds coming out of the clumps of grass we added earlier; then, in selected areas throughout the foreground, add individual weeds. Notice that many of the weeds overlap each other, and some are very stiff and bent over. The idea here is to make the weeds look cold or frozen.

14 Glaze Background

Glazing is something that you should be familiar with by now, but if not, refer to the front of the book for more detailed instruction. Notice here that the glaze has a sharp angle to it, with visible brushstrokes to suggest a slight breeze. Your glaze color here is a mix of white with a slight touch of orange and, of course, plenty of water. Now, evenly load your hake brush and gently skim the surface of the canvas at an angle, until you have created a nice soft directional glaze.

15 Add Snowflakes

This is really a fun step. Simply wet the entire canvas, then with a toothbrush and pure white paint, flick snow onto the wet surface. The individual dots of snow will bleed slightly, creating a variety of sizes of soft snowflakes. You might want to practice this step on a scrap canvas first.

16 Final Snow Highlights

This step is designed to add the final highlights to the snowdrifts and, in fact, add more drifts up against the taller weeds to settle them down. Then, highlight any other area, such as the trees or wagon, to give the painting its final light. For this, use a mixture of white with a slight touch of yellow. Use any brush that fits the area you want to highlight. Generally your sables work best here.

Autumn Fog in the High Country
16" x 20" (41cm x 51cm)

Autumn Fog in the High Country

I can't help but recall my years living in Angel Fire, New Mexico—in my opinion, a true artistic paradise. An early morning fog drifting in and out of the mountain ranges can be enchanting. The great thing about being artists is that we can create this feeling anytime we want to. One of the things that I would really like for you to do is to do this painting without fog, and then do it again with the fog. I think you will be amazed what a difference the fog makes in the atmosphere. Another thing this painting does for you is it gives you another opportunity to practice rocks, mountains and clouds, and it gives you a chance to paint many artists' favorite season, autumn. The aspen trees in this painting also offer you a unique and challenging opportunity. It looks like you might have your work cut out for you, so get ready for another painting experience.

1 Make Rough Charcoal Sketch

We have to begin this painting with a fairly good but rough sketch of the basic layout of the landscape.

2 Paint Sky

Because this painting has a good bit of fog in it, we want the sky to have a soft, warm gray tone to it. So, lightly wet the sky with your hake brush, then apply a fairly liberal coat of gesso. While the gesso is still wet, beginning just above the mountains, use pure orange with a little yellow and blend it all the way up to the top of the canvas. While this is still wet, take Dioxazine Purple and a touch of Ultramarine Blue and, starting across the top, blend downward with large X strokes until you have a very soft blended sky. We will add clouds after we paint the mountains.

3 Underpaint Mountains

Notice the three layers of mountains. We will mix a basic mountain color and change the value for each layer. Mix Ultramarine Blue, a touch of Burnt Sienna, purple and enough white to change the value so that it is slightly darker than the sky. With your no. 6 bristle brush, block in the most distant mountain first. Now, darken the mixture slightly and paint the next layer. And finally, make the mixture a little darker and paint in the final range of mountains. You should have three distinct value changes.

4 Highlight Mountains

Before we can add the clouds and fog, we need to highlight the three layers of mountains. For this, we need to mix white with a touch of yellow and orange; this should be a fairly creamy mixture. Use your no. 4 flat bristle brush and carefully drybrush in the highlights on the first mountain range; keep the highlights fairly soft. Add a little more orange to the mixture and highlight the middle range. The front range doesn't have much highlighting, but it needs enough to define it. Now we are ready for the fog and the clouds.

5 Paint In Distant Pine Trees

These trees are a major part of the fog study. They need to be very soft and muted so that they blend into the fog. First, mix white with a little bit of Hooker's Green and purple; make sure this value is not too dark. Now, take your no. 6 bristle brush and, with a dry-brush vertical stroke, paint in a nice collection of pine trees down toward the center of the painting, ending near the waterfall.

6 Add Fog and Clouds

Mix white with a very small amount of orange, just enough to tint it. Now, take your no. 6 bristle brush and scrub in the clouds; keep the clouds very soft with good negative space. Gradually work the clouds over the first range of mountains, and be sure some of the mountain shows through; now, repeat this in front of the second mountain range. Make sure that there are no hard edges.

7 Paint Waterfall

This is not as difficult as it looks. First, with your no. 6 bristle brush, underpaint the area where the waterfall is with a medium bluish gray mixture of white with Ultramarine Blue and a touch of Burnt Sienna; blend this color into the background so there are no hard edges. Now, with your no. 4 flat sable and pure white, drybrush in the waterfall. Remember, this is a very distant waterfall, so you don't need to add any detail. Keep it simple.

Note: Be sure the bluish gray mixture for the underpainting is completely dry before you add the waterfall.

8 Add Middle-Ground Fog or Mist

The area just below the distant pine trees will be a large patch of fog or mist. We mix this with white and a little bit of Ultramarine Blue. Now, take your no. 10 bristle brush and scrub in the fog, until the entire area is covered.

9 Paint Middle-Ground Pine Trees

For this step, you want to mix Hooker's Green and a touch of purple and white. Adjust the color and the value so that it's not too green or too dark. This is a very important transition step between the background and the foreground, so the value has to be just right. Now, take your no. 4 flat bristle brush and paint in a nice collection of soft middle-ground pine trees. This is a good time to practice your negative space rules; just be sure you have a good variety of shapes and sizes.

10 Underpaint Middle-Ground Meadow

Since this is the autumn of the year, we want to use good clean soft autumn colors, such as yellows, golds, oranges, sienna and soft purples; you will need your no. 10 bristle brush for this. Starting at the top of the hill, apply yellow with touches of Burnt Sienna. Apply the paint very thick across the top of the hill, then, using a vertical stroke, pull upward, creating the suggestion of a grassy mountain meadow. While the paint is still wet, apply successive layers of yellow, orange, Burnt Sienna and purple, pulling each layer up against the other, overlapping each layer slightly to create subtle contrasts. You have to work very fast with this so that each layer blends into the next before it dries. Continue darkening the grass until you reach the foreground. You should have a fairly three-dimensional hill, with three distinct value changes of light, middle and dark.

11 Underpaint Foreground Grass

This step is identical to step 10, except that you will use longer and looser brushstrokes. A slight angle of the grass to the left will give the suggestion of a light breeze. One thing that will be helpful here is to add the shadow from the large aspen trees. Don't be afraid to use loose free Impressionistic strokes. Your no. 10 bristle brush works best here. The best color for the shadow is Burnt Sienna and purple.

12 Underpaint Rocks
Begin with a mixture of Burnt Sienna, Ultramarine Blue, Dioxazine Purple and a little bit of white to soften it. Now, take your no. 6 bristle brush and block in the dark side of the rocks. Once again, create good negative space along with a good variety of shapes, sizes and some overlapping.

13 Highlight Rocks
For this step, mix white with a touch of orange, then add a slight touch of purple to gray the highlight. Remember, all we want to do here is create the basic shape of the rocks. We will add the final highlights later. Use your no. 4 or no. 6 flat bristle brush for this step and quickly apply the highlight to the top right side of each rock. Notice the brushstrokes that show up here; this is what makes rocks look rocky and rough.

14 Block In Aspen Tree Trunks

You may want to sketch in these trunks first with your charcoal. Even though aspen tree trunks are a soft white, we still need to underpaint them with a gray tone. So, mix Ultramarine Blue, a touch of Burnt Sienna and white to create a nice gray. Then, with your no. 6 or no. 4 bristle brush, simply block in the shape of the trunks. Thin the mixture to an ink-like consistency, then take your script brush and add some of the smaller limbs. Add a little white to this mixture to create a lighter value, then go ahead and paint in the aspen trees in the background.

15 Add Foreground Bushes

Notice the bushes on the left of the painting, and around the rocks, and at the base of the aspen trees. You need this darker value to create a contrast against the lighter grass. This mixture is made up of Burnt Sienna and Dioxazine Purple. Make the mixture slightly creamy, then take your no. 10 bristle brush and dab in these bushes.

16 Underpaint Aspen Trees

For this step, we will use Burnt Sienna with a touch of purple. Take your no. 4 flat sable brush and scumble in the larger masses of leaves, keeping the edges of the clumps very soft. Then add occasional individual leaves to help tie the clumps together. Now, you can slightly lighten the mixture with a little white and scumble in the leaves of the aspen trees in the background.

17 Add Small Dead Bushes and Trees

This should be a familiar step by now. So, grab your script brush and create a mixture of Burnt Sienna and Ultramarine Blue, making it very ink-like. Paint in the dead bushes in the foreground, then lighten the mixture slightly and paint in the distant dead pine trees. This would be a good time also to add any additional limbs to your aspen trees.

18 Highlight Aspen Leaves

Here, you want to use a combination of yellow, orange and Burnt Sienna in different combinations and/or as individual colors. Make the mixture creamy, then take your no. 4 flat sable brush and highlight the aspen leaves with a series of overlapping comma strokes. In some places you will want some individual leaves scattered around. Switch to your no. 4 round sable brush to highlight the background aspens.

19 Highlight Tree Trunks

This is a fairly easy step. Mix white with a touch of orange, making it fairly creamy. Then take your no. 4 flat sable brush and, using a series of short choppy strokes, highlight the right side of the trunks. Notice these trunks have little eyes in the bark; leave some of the background showing through to create this effect. Use your script brush to highlight the background aspens.

20 Add Final Details

This is where your artistic license will serve you well. Adding final highlights on the rocks, aspen leaves and pine trees will add the autumn glow that the painting needs. Feel free to leaf some of the dead bushes in the foreground or add a few mountain flowers. And then, of course, the taller weeds in the foreground round out the composition.

Spring's Song
16" x 20" (41cm x 51cm)

Spring's Song

Springtime in Oklahoma, where I am from, means storms and sometimes tornadoes; however, the northeast part of the state where I have my studio is called "green country" and the springtime can be absolutely breathtaking. In this painting, Spring's Song, we are going to practice several techniques. The first thing that you will get to work on is a wide variety of live trees, where you will get to practice some leafing techniques. Another thing you will get to work on is calm water and reflections. One other area that is quite challenging is the use of the color green, one of the more difficult colors to master. In this painting you can see we use a wide range of values and tones of green, which will really help you expand your painting horizons. This is a fairly simple painting in terms of composition, but the trees will challenge you. The key is to keep the trees soft and give them good form, which means, of course, watch your use of negative space. Have fun!

1 Make Rough Sketch

Not much sketching is needed here, just the basic location of the background trees and the lake in the foreground. Your soft vine charcoal works well for this.

2 Paint Sky

We want a clean, crisp and clear sky to help get the early spring look. Begin by lightly wetting the sky with your hake brush, then apply a liberal coat of gesso. While the gesso is still wet, begin at the horizon with pure yellow and blend your way upward until it fades almost to the top. Then, immediately take Ultramarine Blue and a touch of purple and, starting at the top, blend downward until the colors are blended together so that you have a very soft sky. It's OK if the sky turns slightly green toward the center.

3 Paint Water

This step is nearly identical to step 2; the only difference is that you paint upside down. What I like to do here is turn my canvas upside down and paint the water. Simply repeat the process from step 2, and then the water will be ready for reflections.

4 Add Background Trees

Now, this first layer of background trees is very pale to create distance and a bit of a hazy look. For this, mix white with Dioxazine Purple and a touch of Hooker's Green. Now, take your no. 10 bristle brush and dab in a nice formation of distant trees. Notice how pale they are against the yellow horizon.

5 Add Middle-Background Trees

For this step, use the same color we started with in step 4, except you want to darken it a little bit with a little more green and purple. Now, take your no. 10 bristle brush and dab in this collection of trees. Notice the trees in the middle of the painting are much smaller than the trees to the far left. The main thing is to be sure that you have a good variety of shapes and sizes.

6 Paint Cedar Trees

For this step, mix Hooker's Green, a little purple and a little Burnt Sienna. A touch of white may be added to get the correct value. Now, take your no. 6 bristle brush and paint in the cedar trees. These cedar trees are a very important part of the middle-ground composition and overall balance of the painting. It's important that they have soft irregular edges.

7 Paint Middle-Ground Grass

This is a small area and, at the same time, a very big part of the painting. What works best here is a combination of Thalo Yellow-Green and a touch of orange. Now, take your no. 10 bristle brush and apply this paint fairly thick; while it is still wet, put your brush flat against the canvas and push up to create the effect of grass. When you get to the water's edge, add Hooker's Green and a touch of purple and smudge in a darker shoreline.

8 Underpaint Middle-Ground Trees

As you can see, we are getting closer to the front of the painting, so each successive layer of trees gets darker. So, this mixture will made of Hooker's Green, a touch of Burnt Sienna and Dioxazine Purple. Now, take your no. 10 bristle brush and dab in the trees on the left side of the painting. Don't hesitate to make minor value changes within this group of trees by adding more or less of the original colors plus touches of white and Thalo Yellow-Green.

9 Block in Tree Trunks

We need to create a base gray mixture of Ultramarine Blue, Burnt Sienna and a little white. From this base mixture, you can lighten or darken it according to your needs. We are going to paint in all of the tree trunks from the background to the foreground. You may need to use two or three different brushes; probably your no. 4 round and flat sable and your no. 4 script brush will work best. Beginning in the background, start with your lightest value and work your way forward, making each value slightly darker.

10 Underpaint Foreground Grass

Notice the foreground grass on the left of the painting. This area really ties the background to the foreground. We use a combination of colors here to create different shades of green. Begin with Thalo Yellow-Green, touches of yellow and orange, and then add Hooker's Green to help create darker shades. When you get to the water's edge, add a little purple to darken the shade. Use your no. 10 bristle brush and loose vertical strokes to create the suggestion of grass. Be sure as you pull up the grass that you use a soft touch so the grass will have soft edges.

11 Paint Reflections, Phase 1

The reflections in this painting are absolutely the key to its success. The best way for me to explain how to create them is as follows. Look at the objects that are reflected—the background trees, middle-ground trees, cedar trees, tree trunks and grassy areas. Go back to the steps where these objects were created, and in the same order they were created. Take the color and lighten the value by about one degree, then with your no. 4 flat bristle brush, using a horizontal scrubbing stroke, paint in each reflection, making sure the edges are soft and slightly blurred. Once these reflections are finished, we will then finish the rest of the painting and add the final reflections at the end.

12 Add Leaves to Tree Trunks

This step requires careful planning. You can use a variety of greens, but keep in mind this is a spring painting, so you want to keep your greens fairly clean. I suggest a base green of Hooker's Green and a touch of purple. From this base green, you can add touches of Thalo Yellow-Green, yellow and/or white. You can create dozens of spring shades. Then take your no. 10 bristle brush and dab in leaves throughout the painting where the tree trunks are. Remember to change the value of the color to fit the location of the leaves by adding white. You know the rule: lighter in the background, darker as you come forward.

13 Add Final Tree Limbs

Now, with your script brush, take your tree trunk colors and add additional limbs to complete your trees and bushy areas.

14 Add Final Reflections, Phase 2

At this point we need to add any reflections from objects that we have added, such as tree leaves, limbs, grasses, and so on. The technique we use here is the same as in step 11, so you might refer back there for a reminder.

15 Paint Small Rocks Along Shoreline

For this step, take your no. 4 flat sable brush and a mixture of white with a touch of orange; add just a slight touch of blue to gray the mixture. Then, along the shoreline, create the suggestion of small rocks. Just be sure not to line them up in a row with the same shapes and sizes. These rocks are only accents, not features.

16 Highlight Bushes and Trees

This is a good place to have fun with your artistic license. Use a wide variety of highlight colors, such as Thalo Yellow-Green, white, yellow mixed with white, Thalo Yellow-Green mixed with yellow. You can even use some warmer tones by adding a little orange to the above colors. Now, work all through the painting, adding pockets of light to create more complete three-dimensional forms to your underpainted trees and bushes. Also, add highlights to some of the grassy areas. Your no. 6 or no. 10 bristle brush works best for this.

17 Highlight Tree Trunks

For this highlight color, mix white with a touch of yellow and orange. Now, with your no. 4 round and/or no. 4 flat sable, apply a nice clean opaque highlight along the right side of all the tree trunks. On the larger trunks, you may want to create the suggestion of bark by using short choppy vertical strokes.

18 Glaze Water

This is a step most of you have done before; it's really quite simple. Take your hake brush and create a glaze of water and a touch of white. Load your hake brush evenly across the tip. Then, starting from the left to the right, turn your brush vertical to the canvas and gently drag it across the surface of the water with a slight wiggle in the stroke. Now, form a very sharp chisel edge with your brush; take pure white and gently add some thin horizontal highlights along the edge of the shoreline.

19 Add Final Details and Highlights

This is where your own personality takes over. You can add things like complementary flowers, tall weeds or even a small dogwood or redbud tree in the background. The important thing to remember is to use complements of the greens—pinks, reds, oranges and soft purples. Use only accents; it won't take too much to bring your painting to life. You probably will want to use your no. 6 bristle brush to dab in these accents.

You Can See Forever
16" x 20" (41cm x 51cm)

You Can See Forever

This is a very unusual and exciting painting to do. Although we have painted rocks in some of the other paintings, in this painting the rocks are one of the main features. Also notice the tremendous depth in this painting. Many of you struggle with this because you don't understand the proper use of values. In this painting I will teach you how to mix different values to create this kind of depth. We will also practice painting the fog or mist that helps separate the different layers of mountains. And finally, you will learn how to use different shades and values of grays. Gray may seem like a neutral and uninteresting color, but believe it or not, gray is really an artist's best friend. This painting is full of opportunity, so have fun experimenting, and I promise you will be happy with most of your results.

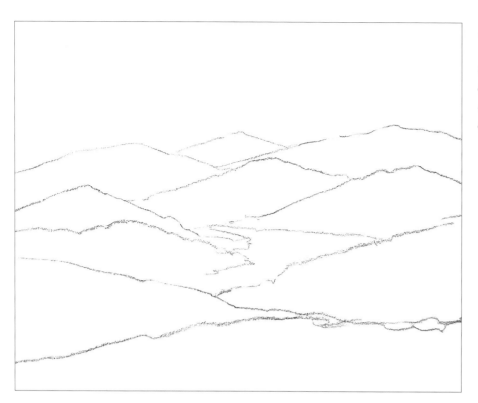

1 Create Basic Sketch
You can see many layers of depth here, so it's important to create a rough sketch showing the different layers. Use your soft vine charcoal for this.

2 Paint Sky
We want a slightly stormy sky here, maybe with a hint of distant rain showers. So, take your hake brush and lightly wet the sky area, then apply a liberal coat of gesso. While the gesso is still wet, take a little orange and paint a soft orange tint over the entire sky. While this is still wet, start on the right side with a mixture of Ultramarine Blue and a little Burnt Sienna. Blend this mixture on the canvas from right to left, gradually fading from dark to light. Once you have blended this, take your brush and use a light angled feather stroke to create the suggestion of distant rain and/or wind.

Note: The next few steps are very similar to each other. As simple as they may seem, each step is critical so that the value is absolutely correct. As we move closer to the foreground, not only do the values get darker, but we begin to add more creative shapes to each hillside.

3 Mix Base Value

All we do in this step is mix our base value color. Take gesso, half as much Ultramarine Blue, a quarter as much Burnt Sienna and a touch of purple. Refer to the color swatch here to check your color and value. Mix a fairly good-sized pile of this, then add just enough water to make it creamy.

4 Scrub in Distant Hill 1

Now, take a little bit of the base value and add just enough white to make it slightly darker than the sky on the left side. Take your no. 6 bristle brush and scrub in the first hill. Be sure it has a nice soft edge; it's OK if part of it blends into the sky.

5 Paint Distant Hill 2

This step is just like step 4, except the shape of the hill is different; also notice that the right side blends into the sky, which helps create the effect of rain or low clouds and fog. Remember to keep edges soft and use your no. 6 bristle brush. The value for this is slightly darker than for hill 1.

6 Scrub in Hill 3

You can see now the process of gradating the values. So, for hill 3, slightly darken the base color and take your no. 6 bristle brush and scrub in a different and unique shape; but notice the top of the hill is beginning to show the suggestion of very faint tree shapes.

7 Add Hill 4

No secret here. Simply darken the value so it is slightly darker than hill 3. Now, you can really begin to see more definite tree shapes. So, after you scrub in the main shape of the hill, take your brush and dab in more recognizable tree shapes.

8 Paint Hill 5

This is the hill just before we reach the lake. Slightly darken your base mixture and scrub in this hill. At this point, you may want to switch to your no. 4 flat sable brush and create even more distinct tree forms. Now, you need to pay close attention to your negative space as you paint in your trees; just keep in mind that soft edges are important with each of these layers.

9 Block in Lake

All we do here is take the sky color that you see above hill 4, which if you remember, is a mixture of white, a touch of orange, blue and Burnt Sienna. With your no. 6 bristle brush, simply block in the water area. Be sure to make the area a little larger than the finished lake will be.

10 Add Hill 6

This hill, as you can see, takes on a much more distinct form, and the trees are taller with more defined shapes. So, as we have been doing, slightly darken the mixture that we used in step 8, then take your no. 6 bristle brush and go to work, being very creative with the shapes and forms.

11 Add Hill 7

This hill is almost identical to hill 6. Of course, the value is slightly darker and the trees have different shapes, but the technique is the same. Notice, though, that these trees are a little more distinct. Continue using the no. 6 bristle brush here, although you may want to switch to your no. 4 flat sable to do the trees.

12 Block in Hill 8

This is the last hill before we get to the foreground. It's a small area, but important nonetheless because it helps to balance the painting. This value is similar to the value used in step 11. Even though it is not much darker, it is enough to make a difference. So, go ahead and block it in with your no. 6 bristle brush, and then we are ready to move into the foreground.

13 Underpaint Foreground Rocks and Bushes

Now that we are in the foreground, we need to change the value and color. So, take the original base color we used for the hills and add Hooker's Green and purple. Be sure this value is very dark. What we want to do here is create a good variety of bushes, clumps of grass and some irregular ground formations. Take your no. 10 bristle brush and dab in these different formations. As you come forward, add touches of white to the mixture to create some soft light areas, then go back to the dark mixture to create some contrasting forms; at the same time, you want to create some basic rock formations. Just darken the mixture we were just using with a little more blue and a little Burnt Sienna. Because this is such a dark foreground, it's important to go ahead and highlight the rocks with a very soft gray to help establish their form; I usually add a little white and orange to the rock color to create this soft gray tone. We will put the brighter highlights on in the next step. This foreground needs a good composition, so keep a careful eye out on your negative space.

14 Highlight Rocks

Highlighting these rocks can be a little tricky. We don't want them to be too bright. So, take the shadow color and add a little bit of white and orange; this will create a nice soft, warm middle-tone gray. Now, with your no. 4 bristle brush, highlight every rock carefully so each has a distinct shape but soft edges. We may add brighter highlights later.

15 Scrub in Mist Between Mountains

For this step, you want to mix a soft mist color. Mix white with a touch of orange and Ultramarine Blue. Now, load your no. 6 bristle brush with a very small amount of this mix and scrub in the mist between the layers of mountains. The key is softness, so be sure you don't leave any hard edges. I discovered that if you thin the mixture down a little bit, it will scrub on easier.

16 Add Final Highlights on Rocks

This is the step that gives the painting a lot of character. For this, mix white with a touch of orange, and a tiny touch of blue to slightly gray it. Then, with your no. 4 flat sable brush, highlight the largest rocks that would be most likely to pick up a little sunlight. Also, add the rocks in the middle ground and along the shoreline. The most important thing to remember here is not to overhighlight; we only want to accent the tops of the rocks.

17 Add Miscellaneous Details

This is a great place to really exercise your artistic license. So, get your script brush and thin the dark mixture down to an ink-like consistency. Now, paint in a good variety of dead bushes, weeds and miscellaneous trees in the background. These bushes have two main purposes: first, to create eye stoppers on each side of the painting, and second, to create good balance within the composition. So, as you probably know by now, keep an eye on your negative space. Also, remember wherever you add a bush, a weed or a tree, you have to change the value for that particular area of the painting.

Covey Raider (cropped)
16" × 20" (41cm × 51cm)

PAINTING

Adventures

NORTH LIGHT BOOKS
CINCINNATI, OHIO
www.artistsnetwork.com

Table of Contents

Giant of the Yellowstone

The Guardian

Evening Prayers

The Silent One

Prairie Giant

Moonlight Canadians

Covey Raider

Moonlight Canadians
16" × 20" (41cm × 51cm)

Introduction

Painting can—and in fact should be—an adventure. But with adventure comes risk, and to grow as an artist you must be willing to take these risks. Work up the courage to add unique subjects to your paintings, such as birds, animals or people. Adding these subjects will create tremendous eye appeal for your paintings. And the adventure doesn't stop there.

I'll show you which brushes to use for realistic fur, feathers and hair, and you'll learn proper brush use and techniques to get the best aesthetic effects.

I'll discuss proper camera use, types of film, ways to combine photos to create a composite and many other photography tips.

And your painting adventure wouldn't be complete without beautiful, rugged mountaintops, unique cloud formations and night scenes. This painting adventure is really going to be exciting!

Terms & Techniques

Before beginning the step-by-step instructions on the following pages, you may want to refresh your memory by reviewing these terms and techniques.

COLOR COMPLEMENTS

Complementary colors always appear opposite each other on the color wheel. Use complements to create color balance in your paintings. It takes practice to understand how to use complements, but a good rule of thumb is to use the complement or form of the complement of the predominant color in your painting to highlight, accent or gray that color.

For example, if your painting has a lot of green, use its complement, red—or a form of red such as orange or red-orange—for highlights. If you have a lot of blue in your painting, use blue's complement, orange—or a form of orange such as yellow-orange or red-orange. The complement of yellow is purple or a form of purple. Keep a color wheel handy until you have memorized the color complements.

DABBING

Use this technique to create leaves, ground cover, flowers, etc. Take a bristle brush and dab it on your table or palette to spread out the ends of the bristles like a fan (see above example). Then load the brush with the appropriate color and gently dab on that color to create the desired effect.

DOUBLE LOAD OR TRIPLE LOAD

To load a brush this way, put two or more colors on different parts of

To prepare your bristle brush for dabbing, spread out the ends of the bristles like a fan.

your brush. Mix these colors on the canvas instead of your palette. Double or triple load your brush for wet-on-wet techniques.

DRYBRUSH

Load your brush with very little paint and lightly skim the surface of the canvas with a very light touch to add, blend or soften a color.

EYE FLOW

Create good eye flow and guide the viewer's eye through the painting with the arrangement of objects on your canvas or the use of negative space around or within an object. The eye must move smoothly, or flow, through your painting and

around objects. The viewer's eyes shouldn't bounce or jump from place to place. Once you understand the basic components of composition—design, negative space, "eye stoppers," overlap, etc.—your paintings will naturally achieve good eye flow.

FEATHERING

Use this technique to blend to create soft edges, to highlight and to glaze. Use a very light touch, barely skimming the surface of the canvas with your brush.

GESSO

Gesso is a white paint used for sealing canvas before painting on it. Because of its creamy consistency

This sketch uses poor negative space. The limbs don't overlap each other, but are evenly spaced so there are few pockets of interesting space.

This sketch uses negative space well. The limbs overlap and include interesting pockets of space.

and because it blends so easily, I often use gesso instead of white paint. When I use the word gesso in my step-by-step instructions, I am referring to the color white. Use gesso or whatever white pigment you prefer.

GLAZE (WASH)

A glaze or a wash is a very thin layer of paint applied over a dry area to create mist, fog, haze or sun rays or to soften an area that is too bright. Dilute a small amount of color with water and apply it to the appropriate area. You can apply the glaze in layers, but each layer must be dry before applying the next.

HIGHLIGHTING OR ACCENTING

Highlighting is one of the final stages of your painting. Use pure color or brighter values to give your painting its final glow. Carefully apply highlights on the sunlit edges of the most prominent objects in your paintings.

MIXING

If you will be using a mixture often, premix a good amount of that color to have handy. I usually mix colors with my brush, but sometimes a palette knife works better. Be your own judge.

I also sometimes mix colors on my canvas. For instance, when I am

underpainting grass, I may put two or three colors on the canvas and scumble them together to create a mottled background of different colors. This method also works well well for skies.

When working with acrylics, always mix your paint to a creamy consistency that will blend easily.

NEGATIVE SPACE

Negative space surrounds an object to define its form and create good eye flow (see above example).

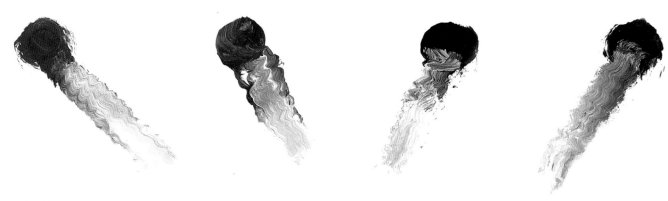

Make the value of a color lighter by adding white.

SCRUBBING

Scrubbing is similar to scumbling (below), but the strokes should be more uniform and in horizontal or vertical patterns. Use a dry-brush or wet-on-wet technique with this procedure. I often use it to underpaint or block in an area.

SCUMBLING

Use a series of unorganized, overlapping strokes in different directions to create effects such as clumps of foliage, clouds, hair, grass, etc. The direction of the stroke is not important for this technique.

UNDERPAINTING AND BLOCKING IN

The first step in all paintings is to block in or underpaint the dark values. You'll apply lighter values of each color to define each object later.

VALUE

Value is the relative lightness or darkness of a color. To achieve depth or distance, use lighter values in the background and darker values closer to the foreground. Lighten a color by adding white. Make a value darker by adding black, brown or the color's complement.

WET-ON-DRY

I use this technique most often in acrylic painting. After the background color is dry, apply the top-coat by drybrushing, scumbling or glazing.

WET-ON-WET

Blend the colors together while the first application of paint is still wet. I use a large hake (pronounced ha KAY) brush to blend large areas, such as skies and water, with the wet-on-wet technique.

Getting Started

Acrylic Paint

The most common criticism of acrylics is that they dry too fast. Acrylics do dry very quickly because of evaporation. To solve this problem I use a wet palette system (see pages 263–265). I also use very specific dry-brush blending techniques to make blending very easy. With a little practice you can overcome any of the drying problems acrylics pose.

Speaking as a professional artist, acrylics are ideally suited for exhibiting and shipping. You actually can frame and ship an acrylic painting thirty minutes after you finish it. You can apply varnish over an acrylic painting, but you don't have to because acrylic painting is self-sealing. Acrylics are also very versatile because you can apply thick or creamy paint to resemble oil paint or paint thinned with water for watercolor techniques. Acrylics are non-toxic with very little odor, and few people have allergic reactions to them.

USING A LIMITED PALETTE

I work from a limited palette. Whether for professional or instructional pieces, a limited palette of the proper colors is the most effective painting tool. It teaches you to mix a wide range of shades and values of color, which every artist must be able to do. Second, a limited palette eliminates the need to purchase dozens of different colors.

With a basic understanding of the color wheel, the complementary color system and values, you can mix thousands of colors for every type of painting from a limited palette.

For example, mix Phthalo Yellow-Green, Alizarin Crimson and a touch of Titanium White (gesso) to create a beautiful basic flesh tone. Add a few other colors to the mix to create earth tones for landscape paintings. Make black by mixing Ultramarine Blue with equal amounts of Dioxazine Purple and Burnt Sienna or Burnt Umber. The list goes on and on, and you'll see that the sky isn't even the limit.

Most paint companies make three grades of paints: economy, student and professional. Professional grades are more expensive but much more effective. Just buy what you can afford and have fun. Check your local art supply store first. If you can't find a particular item, I carry a complete line of professional- and student-grade paints and brushes.

MATERIALS LIST

Palette

white gesso
Grumbacher, Liquitex or Winsor & Newton paints (color names may vary):

- Alizarin Crimson
- Burnt Sienna
- Burnt Umber
- Cadmium Orange
- Cadmium Red Light
- Cadmium Yellow Light
- Dioxazine Purple
- Hooker's Green Hue
- Phthalo (Thalo) Yellow-Green
- Titanium White
- Ultramarine Blue

Brushes

no. 4 flat sable brush
no. 4 round sable brush
no. 4 script liner brush
no. 6 flat bristle brush
no. 10 flat bristle brush
2-inch (51mm) hake brush

Miscellaneous Items

16" × 20" (41cm × 51cm) stretched canvas
charcoal pencil
easel
no. 2 soft vine charcoal
palette knife
paper towels
Sta-Wet palette
spray bottle
water can

Brushes

I use a limited number of brushes for the same reasons as the limited palette—versatility and economics.

2-INCH (51MM) HAKE BRUSH

Use this large brush for blending, glazing and painting large areas, such as skies and bodies of water with a wet-on-wet technique.

NO. 10 FLAT BRISTLE BRUSH

Underpaint large areas—mountains, rocks, ground or grass—and dab on tree leaves and other foliage with this brush. It also works great for scumbling and scrubbing techniques. The stiff bristles are very durable so you can treat them fairly roughly.

NO. 6 FLAT BRISTLE BRUSH

Use this brush, a cousin of the no. 10 flat bristle brush, for many of the same techniques and procedures. The no. 6 flat bristle brush is more versatile than the no. 10 because you can use it for smaller areas, intermediate details and highlights. You'll use the no. 6 and no. 10 flat bristle brushes most often.

NO. 4 FLAT SABLE BRUSH

Use sable brushes for more refined blending, details and highlights, such as final details, painting people and adding details to birds and other animals. Treat these brushes with extra care because they are more fragile and more expensive than bristle brushes.

NO. 4 ROUND SABLE BRUSH

Use this brush, like the no. 4 flat sable, for details and highlights. The sharp point of the round sable, though, allows more control over areas where a flat brush will not work or is too wide. This is a great brush for finishing a painting.

NO. 4 SCRIPT LINER BRUSH

This brush is my favorite. Use it for very fine details and narrow line work, such as tree limbs, wire, weeds and especially your signature, that you can't accomplish with any other brush. Roll the brush in an ink-like mixture of pigment until the bristles form a fine point.

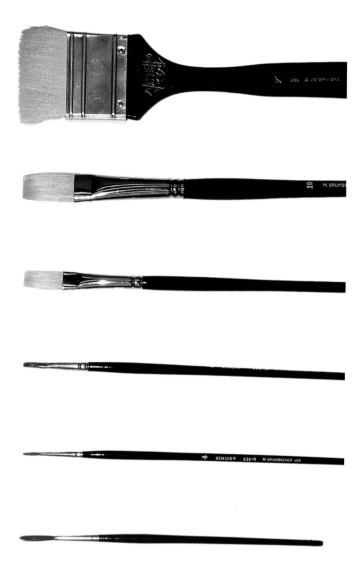

You can paint any subject with this basic set of brushes.

BRUSH-CLEANING TIPS

As soon as you finish your painting, use quality brush soap and warm water to clean your brushes thoroughly before the paint dries. Lay your brushes flat to dry. Paint is very difficult to get out if you allow it to dry on your brushes or clothes. If this does happen, use denatured alcohol to soften the dried paint. Soak the brush in the alcohol for about thirty minutes and then wash it with soap and water.

Palettes

Several palettes on the market are designed to keep paints wet. I use two Sta-Wet palettes made by Masterson. Acrylics dry because of evaporation, so keeping the paints wet is critical. The first palette is a 12" × 16" (31cm × 41cm) plastic palette-saver box with an airtight lid (see page 264). Saturate the sponge that comes with the palette with water and lay it in the bottom of the box. Then soak the special palette paper and lay it over the sponge. Place your paints around the edges and you are ready to go. Use a spray bottle to mist your paints occasionally so they will stay wet all day long. When you are finished painting, attach the lid and your paint will stay wet for days.

My favorite palette is the same palette with a few alterations (see page 265). Instead of the sponge and special paper, I place a piece of double-strength glass in the bottom of the palette. I fold paper towels into quarters to make long strips, saturate them with water and lay them on the outer edges of the glass. I then place my paints on the paper towels. They stay wet for days. I occasionally mist them to keep the towels wet.

If you leave your paints in a sealed palette for several days without opening it, certain colors, such as Hooker's Green Hue and Burnt Umber, will mildew. Just replace the color or add a few drops of chlorine bleach to the water in the palette to help prevent mildew.

To clean the glass palette, allow it to sit in water for about thirty seconds or spray the glass with your spray bottle. Scrape off the old paint with a single-edge razor blade.

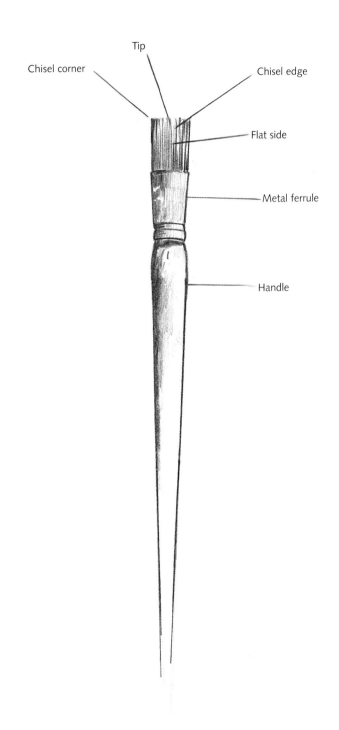

Chisel corner

Tip

Chisel edge

Flat side

Metal ferrule

Handle

Two Ways to Set Up Your Palette

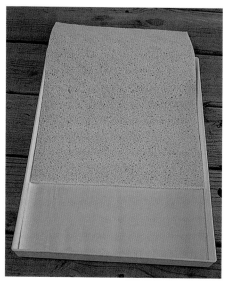

The Sta-Wet 12" × 16" (31cm × 41cm) plastic palette-saver box comes with a large sponge that you saturate with water.

Lay the sponge inside the palette box, soak the special palette paper and lay it over the sponge. Place your paints around the edges. Don't forget to mist them to keep them wet.

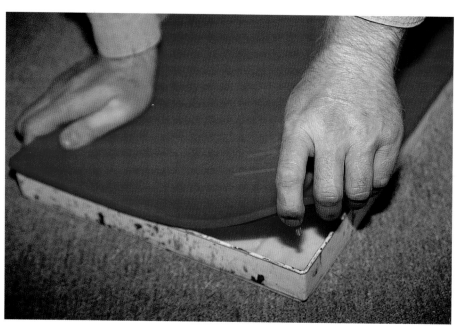

When closing the palette-saver box, make sure the airtight lid is on securely. When the palette is properly sealed, your paints will stay wet for days.

Lay the saturated paper towels around the outer edges of the glass.

Instead of using the sponge and palette paper, you can use a piece of double-strength glass in the bottom of the palette. Fold paper towels in long strips and saturate them with water.

Place your paints on the paper towel strips.

Use the center of the palette for mixing paints. Occasionally spray a mist over the paper towels to keep them wet.

To clean the palette, allow it to sit for thirty seconds in water or spray the glass with a spray bottle. Scrape off the old paint with a single-edge razor blade.

Miscellaneous Supplies

CANVAS

Canvas boards work for practicing strokes, and canvas paper pads work for studies or testing paints and brush techniques. The best surface for painting, though, is a primed, pre-stretched cotton canvas with a medium texture, which you can find at most art stores. As your skills advance, you may want to learn to stretch your own canvas, but 16" × 20" (41cm × 51cm) pre-stretched cotton canvases are all you'll need for the paintings in this book.

EASEL

I prefer a sturdy, standing easel. My favorite is the Stanrite ST500 aluminum easel. It is lightweight, sturdy and easy to fold up to take on location or to workshops.

LIGHTING

Of course, the best light is natural north light, but most of us don't have this light in our work areas. The next best lighting option is to hang 4' (1.2m) or 8' (2.4m) fluorescent lights directly over your easel. Place one cool bulb and one warm bulb in the fixture to best simulate natural light.

Studio lights

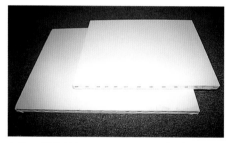

16" × 20" (41cm x 51cm) stretched canvas

Stanrite aluminum studio easel

SPRAY BOTTLE

I use a spray bottle with a fine mist to lightly wet my paints and brushes throughout the painting process. I recommend a spray bottle from a beauty supply store. It's important to keep one handy.

PALETTE KNIFE

I use my palette knife more for mixing than for painting. A trowel-shaped knife is more comfortable and easier to use than a flat knife.

SOFT VINE CHARCOAL

I use no. 2 soft vine charcoal for most of my sketching. It's very easy to work with, shows up well and is easy to remove with a damp paper towel.

Spray bottle

Soft vine charcoal

Palette knives

Adding Wildlife

The most important part of adding wildlife to a painting is to determine if the wildlife will be the focal point of your painting or simply an accent. We'll examine both possibilities.

Wildlife as Accents

First, we'll look at wildlife as an accent or added object within the composition. Landscape artists who want to give their paintings more life and interest can benefit from this use of wildlife.

Paint your landscape without concentrating on the fact that you'll add wildlife later. Once you've finished painting your landscape, refer to your reference material of the wildlife, whether it is a photo or a rough sketch. Decide where you want to place the wildlife within your painting.

Once you've decided on the type of wildlife you're going to use, make a rough sketch over the painting with no. 2 soft vine charcoal. You can wipe soft vine charcoal off dry surfaces with a damp paper towel. If you don't want to wait for the painting to dry, make two or three thumbnail sketches of your basic composition on scrap paper to decide where to place the wildlife. Then paint the wildlife into the painting.

Look at the following examples.

Landscape Without Wildlife
Let's put a deer in this painting. Because the deer is only an accent, don't place it too far forward in the scene or make it too large or too detailed.

Reference Drawing
Use this reference sketch to draw the deer onto the painting. You probably won't find the correct placement the first time, so don't be afraid to sketch it in and wipe off mistakes several times. The following examples are just a few possibilities.

Incorrect Placement
The deer is too close to the side of the painting. It becomes an eye catcher and detracts from the composition.

Incorrect Placement
The deer competes for attention with the focal point, which is the area in front of the waterfall where the logs cross the stream. It overpowers the center of interest and again detracts from the natural eye flow.

Correct Placement
The deer fits nicely into the composition when it is in the background. It does not compete with the center of interest and is not an eyesore.

Final Painting
Once you determine a good location for the deer, paint it in with the correct value and degree of detail. Because this deer is in the background, it should be fairly light and doesn't need too much detail.

Mountain Majesty
18" × 24" (46cm × 61cm)

Follow this simple process when adding wildlife to a painting as an accent:

1. Finish the painting.
2. Choose a wildlife image, a sketch or a photo, from your reference material.
3. Make several rough sketches to determine the placement of the wildlife. Draw over a painting with soft vine charcoal or make several thumbnail sketches.
4. Determine the accurate size of the wildlife in relation to other objects in the same area.
5. Determine the proper value, depending on the placement of the wildlife within the painting.
6. Paint in the wildlife with the right amount of detail.

Wildlife as Centers of Interest

When using wildlife as the center of interest, design the landscape around the wildlife rather than making it fit into the existing landscape.

Wildlife as Accents

Notice how much the swan adds to the painting without competing with the center of interest.

Lonesome Swan
12" × 18" (30cm × 46cm)

Wildlife as Centers of Interest

In this painting, the mother giraffe and her baby form the focal point, and the landscape is secondary.

So That's How It's Done
24" × 30" (61cm × 76cm)

Bad Composition
This composition didn't suit me. Everything lines up too evenly, which creates bad negative space.

Bad Composition
I wasn't happy with this composition either. The fence post and the bird are too centered, which again creates uninteresting negative space. Let's try again.

OK Composition
We're getting closer. I like the two birds and two fence posts, but the composition and negative space still are not quite right. Let's try one more time.

Good Composition
I moved the posts farther apart to create a nice pocket of negative space for the second bird to sit in. I also angled the cross board.

Final Painting
Drawing several thumbnail sketches allows you to study possible compositions and work out any problems in advance of painting.

In this painting, just as in the giraffe painting on page 270, the wildlife is the feature and the landscape is secondary. When wildlife serves as your center of interest, don't neglect good painting habits when it comes to the background. Paint an artistically sound landscape without letting it compete with the wildlife.

Two of a Kind
12" × 16" (30cm × 41cm)

Adding People

The process of adding people to your paintings is identical to our study of wildlife.

Adding people to your landscapes can be very rewarding if done properly. A common concern is the proportion of people or animals in relation to other objects in the painting.

People as Accents

The cowboys and their horses blend well with the center of interest, the church, and they are proportional to other objects on the same plane. Notice that the cowboys and the rest of the landscape do not compete with each other. Compatibility is the key to adding people to your paintings, just as it is when adding wildlife.

Church in the Wildwoods
18" × 24" (46cm × 61cm)

Proportioning With Planes

Once you've completed your landscape and decided where you want to put the people or animals, draw a horizontal line all the way across the canvas with no. 2 soft vine charcoal at the height at which you want to place the figure. Look at every object on the plane formed by this line. Make sure your person or animal is in proportion to the other objects *standing on* that plane. Common sense plays a vital role in this process.

Every object on your canvas stands on a plane, and each object must appear in proportion to every other object standing on the same plane. As an object recedes into the distance, it becomes smaller, and other objects on the same plane also become smaller. With a little practice you'll master your observation skills and begin to relate objects to each other using proportion and planes.

Planes and Proportions

I decided to add a person next to the cabin in this drawing. I drew a line across the canvas with soft vine charcoal. Good judgment tells me that the person cannot be larger than the cabin, and he or she must be small enough to fit through the door. If I wanted to place the person closer to the foreground, I would draw another line and make the person proportional to other objects on the new plane.

Objects should be the same proportion as other objects *standing on* the same plane. For example, the figure closest to the foreground should be the same proportion as the rocks on the same line, not the post closest to the foreground, which sits on another line/plane.

Painting Fur, Feathers and Hair

Bristle Brush

Bristle brushes have very stiff, coarse hairs. This brush works best for blocking in or underpainting an animal's form before adding details. It's very tough, so you can use it to scrub, scumble and smudge. It's too coarse and stiff to create soft fur, feathers or hair. You'll use a bristle brush for underpainting. I use two bristle brushes—a no. 4 and a no. 6. Don't hesitate to experiment with other sizes to see what works best for you. Bristle brushes come in two bristle lengths, long and short. I prefer long bristles because they are more flexible.

Sable Brush

Most artists who paint fur, feathers and hair use a sable brush. The sable brush is flexible, holds its form and has very fine hairs that work well for extreme detail. It's more expensive than other brushes but well worth the investment.

A sable brush is very delicate, so you can't treat it as harshly as you can a bristle brush. It comes in several varieties, such as blended—50 percent sable, 50 percent synthetic—and pure red kolinsky sable. Whatever fits your price range will do.

I use two medium-quality sables that I manufacture—a round and a flat. The no. 4 round and no. 4 flat sable brushes are my favorites, but I also use larger brushes for bigger projects.

Synthetic Brush

A cheaper alternative to the sable brush is the synthetic brush. A synthetic brush has man-made bristles designed to feel like the more expensive red sable. It falls short of a sable brush in flexibility and control and is more useful for painting coarser hair and fur.

Whenever I mention a sable brush in a demonstration, though, feel free to substitute a synthetic brush. You may be quite satisfied.

Brushes
The most commonly used brushes for fur, feathers and hair are shown from left to right: no. 4 flat bristle, no. 6 flat bristle, no. 4 flat sable and no. 4 round sable.

When to Use These Brushes

Contemplation
20" × 16" (51cm × 41cm)

Hair

I underpainted the long, flowing hair on this ballerina with a rich, brown tone using a no. 6 flat bristle brush. Then, I took my no. 6 synthetic brush to add the highlights and form. I switched to a no. 4 round sable brush to paint in the stray hairs. The hair is a bit more impressionistic, so I used loose, feathery strokes with a fairly creamy mixture.

Fur and Feathers

I needed a sable brush for the detail work on these studies because the fur and feathers are much more refined than the ballerina's hair. I underpainted the base body form with a no. 4 flat bristle brush. I mixed the highlight color until it was slightly creamy. Then, I loaded the end of the brush and used light, short, feathery strokes to suggest the hair on the deer and the feathers on the hummingbird.

Painting Mountains

Most artists love to paint mountains. They're intriguing and exciting and definitely adventurous. They can be difficult as well as the most rewarding subjects you could ever learn to paint. Knowing what makes a bad mountain can help you understand what makes a good one.

Start with a good design. The most common mistake when painting mountains is making each mountain or range similar in shape. Repetition of shapes seems to be a part of human nature, but it can be a disaster when composing an interesting mountain range.

Poor Use of Negative Space
Notice how uninteresting this arrangement is. All of the peaks are the same. Repeating the shape of even the most beautiful mountain in the world will ruin a composition.

Proper Use of Negative Space
This arrangement is much more interesting. Unusual pockets of negative space and overlapping peaks create better eye flow and make the scene much more appealing and fun.

1 Draw Basic Sketch

Apply a liberal coat of gesso over the sky. While it is still wet, add touches of Cadmium Yellow Light and Cadmium Orange at the horizon and blend about a quarter of the way to the top of the canvas. Add Ultramarine Blue and touches of Burnt Sienna at the top of the canvas and blend down with large crisscross stokes. Where the colors meet, feather them together with a hake brush.

Getting down to business, create a basic sketch of the mountains over the washes you painted for the sky with no. 2 soft vine charcoal. Work out your mountain design in advance to get the mountain off on the right foot.

2 Mix Base Gray

Mix three values—one for each mountain range in this exercise—to create depth. The mountains will get lighter as they move back in the painting. Mix a base gray color of Titanium White (gesso), some Ultramarine Blue, a touch of Burnt Sienna and just a little Dioxazine Purple. I like a slightly purple gray because it helps create depth. Your base color does not have to match this swatch perfectly.

3 Underpaint Distant Mountain Range

To create the most distant value, add enough Titanium White (gesso) to some of the base gray mixture to make it slightly darker than the sky. Use a no. 6 flat bristle brush to scrub in the basic shape of the first mountain range, keeping the edges fairly soft.

4 Underpaint Middle Mountain Range

Take some more of the base gray mixture and add less Titanium White (gesso) to make this mixture slightly darker than the color you mixed in step 3. Use a no. 6 flat bristle brush to scrub in the second mountain range.

5 Underpaint Closest Mountain Range

Again add a little less Titanium White (gesso) to the base mixture to make it slightly darker than the color you used in step 4. Scrub in the closest mountain range using a no. 6 flat bristle brush.

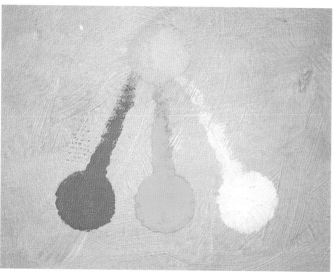

6 Mix Highlight Color

Mountains can be all different colors. This mixture—Titanium White (gesso) and a touch each of Cadmium Yellow Light and Cadmium Orange—is a basic highlight color. Don't be afraid to experiment with other colors.

7 Highlight Distant Mountain Range

Establish the direction of the light source before you add highlights. The light in this demonstration shines from the upper right. Make some of the highlight mixture slightly creamy, and load a small amount on the end of a no. 4 flat sable brush. Start at the top of the first mountain range, and using short, choppy dry-brush strokes add highlights to give the mountain its form. Make sure your strokes have a left-to-right movement to indicate the light source. Keep the edges of the highlights soft so they blend into the base color. Whenever you're highlighting, use negative space well. Don't repeat the same highlight shapes. This is a common mistake and an easy one to fall into. Make subtle changes in the directions of your strokes as you go.)

8 Highlight Middle Mountain Range

The middle mountain range is the largest of the three, so it will have the most details. Brighten the highlight mixture with more Cadmium Yellow Light and Cadmium Orange. Again, paint unique and interesting highlight shapes with a no. 4 flat sable brush.

9 Highlight Closest Mountain Range

Again brighten the value slightly and use a no. 4 flat sable brush to highlight the mountain range closest to the foreground. Be careful not to make it too busy.

10 Add Finishing Touches

To finish the painting, you could add snow, fog, mist or haze to create an interesting mood. You may choose just to brighten the highlights. I chose to add fog between the mountain ranges and brighten the highlights on the middle mountain range. Just experiment and have fun!

Painting Night Scenes

This is an area of painting that has intrigued artists forever. The secret to a good night scene is *contrast*. You just have to know how to make contrast work properly so the painting takes on the characteristics of night and the season.

You can best learn to paint a night scene when it is in a winter setting. Night scenes have rich, dark colors and values; soft, warm, glowing light from stars, the moon, windows, a street lamp or a campfire; silhouettes; well-defined forms in shadows and cast shadows; silver linings or accent highlights on the edges of objects and few or no details.

So how do you put all of these components together to create a night scene? Following is an example of how to do just that. The demonstration for *Evening Prayers* on page 302 will take you through a more in-depth, step-by-step process.

Watercolor Study
I painted this watercolor study to prepare for a larger acrylic painting. Notice the warm glow and the soft haze surrounding the light from the windows and street lamp. This haze really adds to the mood of the scene.

Light Study
To create this glow, paint the actual light with an opaque mixture of Cadmium Yellow Light and Cadmium Orange. Then, add a small amount of Titanium White (gesso) to the mixture and smudge in a little bit of a haze around the light with a very dry brush.

1 Mix Sky Color
The most important component in a night scene is, obviously, the sky. Mix Ultramarine Blue and touches of Dioxazine Purple, Burnt Sienna and Hooker's Green Hue.

2 Underpaint Sky
Paint in the sky with the mixture from step 1 using a hake brush. Add a mixture of Titanium White (gesso) and a touch of Cadmium Orange at the horizon line. Blend the mixture about halfway up the sky, keeping the edges very soft.

3 Underpaint Trees
Using a no. 4 flat bristle brush and the original sky mixture, paint in a small collection of trees. Keep the edges soft so the contrast is not too harsh. Use a no. 4 script liner with an inky version of this mixture to paint the dead trees.

4 Add Moon and Stars

Use a no. 4 flat sable brush and a mixture of Titanium White (gesso), touches of Cadmium Yellow Light and Cadmium Orange and a hint of Ultramarine Blue to slightly gray the mixture to block in the moon's shape. Dab in the stars with a no. 4 round sable brush. Drybrush some very faint light rays, pulling paint from the stars while they are still wet.

5 Underpaint Snow

Block in the snow with a mid-tone gray mixture of the base sky mixture and Titanium White (gesso). After this dries, highlight the snow with a mixture of Titanium White (gesso) and a touch each of Cadmium Yellow Light and Cadmium Orange.

6 Add Trees and Shadows

Add a couple of trees and a few clumps of grass with the base sky mixture. Make this mixture slightly lighter with Titanium White (gesso), and drybrush shadows from all of the trees with a no. 4 flat bristle brush. Make sure you follow the contour of the snow when painting the shadows.

7 Add Highlights

Using a no. 4 round sable brush, highlight the edges of your trees with a thin sliver of a thick, opaque mixture of Titanium White (gesso) and a touch each of Cadmium Yellow Light and Cadmium Orange. Apply highlights with thick paint to make them stand out.

Painting Clouds

Clouds can be one of the most effective components in a landscape painting, but they also can be a compositional nightmare. It would be impossible to discuss all of the different types of cloud formations in these few pages. Instead I will teach you the basic techniques for painting clouds, which you can apply to any cloud formation you choose to paint.

Choose the proper type of cloud formation before you begin painting. Look at your overall composition and determine the focal point. From there, decide what type of cloud formation will work with that focal point. If the landscape is the focal point, keep the sky relatively simple. On the other hand, if you want the sky to be the focal point, keep the landscape simple to prevent competition between the two.

Clouds as Accents

The most common type of clouds are light clouds scattered throughout the sky over a darker blue or blue-gray background. These clouds have simple shapes, good composition and no shadows underneath them. Instead they blend into the background. Use this type of formation when the sky is not the feature and you want movement and interest that don't overpower the painting. It's a versatile type of formation that you probably will use often.

Clouds as Centers of Interest

These clouds form a more significant part—possibly the focal point—of the painting's composition. You can create tremendous effects with this type of cloud formation. There is an extreme contrast between light and dark values. You can apply a wide variety of color schemes to these clouds.

1 Underpaint Sky

Lay down a soft, medium-value background. Use a hake brush to apply a liberal coat of gesso over the entire area. While it is still wet, apply a small amount of Cadmium Orange at the horizon line and blend it up into the sky. Apply a blue-gray mixture of Ultramarine Blue and a touch each of Burnt Sienna and Dioxazine Purple, starting at the top and blending down until you blend the two tones together. The blue-gray mixture will appear dark until blended with the gesso.

2 Underpaint Clouds

Mix Titanium White (gesso) and a touch of Cadmium Orange as a light complement to the gray tone. Load the end of a no. 6 flat bristle brush with a small amount of the mixture and drybrush the cloud formations, carefully blending the bottom of each cloud into the background. Good composition is critical here; make sure you have good negative space. Once the paint has dried, you can repeat the step to brighten the clouds.

3 Add Shadows

Place a deeper, darker shadow under the clouds to give them definition and three-dimensional form and to suggest a stormy atmosphere. Notice the change in the mood. Create a soft gray mixture of Titanium White (gesso), Ultramarine Blue, a touch of Burnt Sienna and a touch of either Cadmium Red Light or Dioxazine Purple. Adjust the value to suit the mood and to fit other values in the painting. Use a no. 6 or no. 10 flat bristle brush to scrub in shadows at the base of each cloud. If necessary, thin the mixture slightly so it will blend more softly.

4 Add Highlights

You can add more highlights or values to create other layers of clouds to suggest depth.

Using Photography for Reference

Photography is a wonderful tool for gathering reference material. Paintings you create from your own photographs are your own, original, unique creations.

Let's take a look at the equipment. I'm not a professional photographer, but I've learned the necessary skills that apply to my work as a professional artist.

Camera and Lens

Most artists prefer a quality 35mm camera. The camera that works best for me is the Pentax P30 T with a Takumar-A Zoom 28mm to 80mm three-in-one lens.

I don't have to carry multiple lenses, and it's easy to operate and reasonably priced. I tend to damage lenses more often than I would like because I often use my camera in extreme conditions. Replacing this lens is easier on the checkbook.

This lens also has a macro, which takes extremely close-up shots, such as a lady bug on a leaf or a dew drop.

Film

Photography is much easier when you understand film speed. I like to paint from prints rather than slides, so I use regular film. I use 200-speed film as an all-purpose film because it works well for both overcast and sunny days. I use 100-speed film in normal sunlight. 400-speed film works for most lighting situations, but it works best for low-light situations, such as late evening. Keep film of all different speeds on hand.

Research

Now let's look at the research process: A painting starts with an idea. Once you've decided on a subject, a color scheme, values, a season and atmosphere, begin gathering reference material for these particular elements. I have a large collection of photographs on file, and I catalog them by subject. If I have exhausted my files and haven't found what I need, I grab my camera and head to the great outdoors to photograph the rest.

Sketch Pad and Reference Materials
Once I have gathered all of my reference materials, I spread them out in front of me with a sketch pad.

When I have gathered my reference materials, I make several thumbnail sketches of different compositions using combinations of several photos. For example, you may use a mountain from one photo, a tree from another, a lake or stream from another and a unique sky formation from another to make a composite sketch of these elements.

A good understanding of basic composition is very important when using reference photos. Artists don't generally copy their photos exactly. They use reference photos to get ideas, and then use artistic license to create your their own works of art.

Look at the following photographs. Each has different subjects I would like to include in my painting. I combined elements from each photo to create a composite sketch with good composition.

Reference photos

Composite Sketch
I combined the cloud formation from photo 1, the barn and wire from photo 2, the dead tree on the left from photo 3, some cows from photo 4, the fence post from photo 5 and miscellaneous landscape items from photo 6 to draw this sketch.

Your imagination plays a vital role in creating a good composite sketch. Even when you have reference photos for most of the objects, you will have to use your imagination for some things, such as rock formations, land contour, shadows and negative space for good eye flow. Color scheme, value and atmospheric conditions determine these factors as you compose the painting. Grab a bunch of photos and have fun composing your next painting!

Thumbnail
I used the reference photos at left and the thumbnail sketch above to paint the final painting on page 289.

Reference photos

High Country Falls
12" × 24" (30cm × 61cm)

Giant of the Yellowstone
16" × 20" (41cm × 51cm)

Giant of the Yellowstone

Every year in early May, the gates of Yellowstone National Park open for spring. I try to plan a workshop or research trip each year to study the wildlife and landscape. During one particular trip, a forest fire had been burning for several days. Smoke had settled in the forest and mixed with the fog, and a light mist was born. As the sun rose above the pine trees and tried to shine through the thickening haze, it created a unique, almost eerie color combination. As I sat on a log watching this phenomenon, a giant moose emerged from the mist and began grazing along the edge of the Madison River. I took several good photos. What a perfect subject and atmosphere for an instructional painting in this book! In this demonstration, you'll study a truly unique animal and have a great opportunity to practice drawing and painting a large animal.

1 Draw Basic Sketch
Make a rough sketch of the basic components of the landscape with no. 2 soft vine charcoal. You don't really need to sketch in the moose yet.

2 Paint Sky
Apply a liberal coat of gesso over the entire sky with a hake brush, making sure the paint is fairly creamy. While it is still wet, use slightly angled, vertical strokes to brush in Cadmium Yellow Light and Cadmium Orange over most of the sky. Apply Ultramarine Blue and touches of Burnt Sienna and Dioxazine Purple with long, vertical strokes, leaving irregular patterns of dark and light values. Notice how soft the blended edges are.

3 Underpaint Water

Follow the same process and use the same colors to underpaint the water. You'll add reflections later. Keep the blended edges soft.

4 Paint Distant Pine Trees

This is the only element of the painting that will provide depth. Mix Titanium White (gesso), a touch of Dioxazine Purple, a touch of Burnt Sienna and a very slight touch of Ultramarine Blue, making the value slightly darker than the sky. Scrub in the basic shapes of the pine trees with this mixture and a no. 4 flat bristle brush. Notice how they almost blend into the background.

5 Paint Middleground Pine Trees

Mix a good-sized batch of Dioxazine Purple; touches of Cadmium Yellow Light, Burnt Sienna and Ultramarine Blue; and just a little Titanium White (gesso). Add just enough water to make the mixture fairly creamy. These trees have very little detail. They're very suggestive and actually impressionistic. Scrub in the pine trees with a no. 6 flat bristle brush. Use a variety of shapes and sizes and plenty of good negative space.

6 Paint Reflections

Even though this body of water is very calm, the reflections still should have a bit of a rippled edge simply to make the water appear wetter. Slightly lighten the mixture from step 5 with a little Titanium White (gesso). Scrub in the reflections with horizontal dry-brush strokes and a no. 6 flat bristle brush. You don't need to duplicate the pine trees exactly. Just make them similar.

7 Add Sun's Glow

Add the strong backlighting behind the trees that really adds atmosphere to the painting. With very dry no. 4 and no. 6 flat bristle brushes, scrub in a mixture of Titanium White (gesso) and a little Cadmium Yellow Light behind the trees, in the sky and in the water. As you brush this color on, be sure to blend the edges into the background so there are no hard edges. You may need to repeat this step two or three times because you are using a dry-brush stroke.

8 Paint Shoreline

Slightly darken the pine tree color. Then paint in some suggestions of irregularly shaped rocks, vegetation and a few fallen logs with a no. 4 or no. 6 flat sable. Don't be afraid to put in quite a bit of scattered debris along the shoreline. It will add authenticity to the painting. Add some subtle highlights to these forms with a mixture of Titanium White (gesso), a touch of Cadmium Orange and a touch of the pine tree color to make them appear a bit more three-dimensional. Just be careful not to overhighlight!

9 Add Dead Trees

Darken the pine tree mixture from step 5 to make two new values—one for the distant tree trunks and a darker value for the dead trees on the bank. Make the mixtures very creamy. Add a nice collection of trees of different shapes and sizes in the background and along the shoreline with a no. 4 round sable or no. 4 script liner.

10 Glaze Water

Load a hake brush evenly across the chisel edge with a thin glaze of water and a bit of gesso. Holding the brush perpendicular to the canvas, drag it across the surface of the water. You can create a ripple effect by wiggling the brush as you drag it.

11 Underpaint Foreground Grass

Darken the pine tree mixture from step 5 with more Ultramarine Blue, Burnt Sienna and a little Dioxazine Purple. You can add a touch of Hooker's Green Hue to this mixture if you wish. Paint in a nice, opaque foreground against the water with a soft, irregular edge using a no. 10 flat bristle brush.

12 Underpaint Dead Tree

Block in the stump with a no. 6 flat bristle brush and a mixture of Burnt Sienna, Ultramarine Blue and a touch of Dioxazine Purple. Be sure to cover the canvas well.

13 Sketch Moose

Sketch in the moose with no. 2 soft vine charcoal. If you need to practice, sketch it on a piece of paper first and then transfer it to the canvas.

14 Underpaint Moose

Block in the entire body of the moose with a no. 4 flat sable brush and a mixture of Ultramarine Blue and Burnt Sienna. Change the value slightly with Titanium White (gesso) when needed. Keep your edges soft here.

15 Highlight Stump

Add Titanium White (gesso) and Cadmium Orange to the original stump mixture to create a nice, soft midtone highlight. Use short, choppy, vertical strokes with a no. 4 flat sable brush to suggest weathered wood or bark. Let the highlight fade into the base color as you move around the tree until the tree looks round. You'll add brighter highlights later.

16 Add Details to Moose

Refer to the tips for painting fur on page 275 before you begin this step. Make a creamy mixture of Titanium White (gesso) and touches of Cadmium Orange, Cadmium Yellow Light, Ultramarine Blue and Burnt Sienna to slightly gray the mixture. Load just a little of the mixture on the end of a no. 4 flat sable brush and, beginning at the top of the moose's body, use short dry-brush, feathery strokes to follow the contour of the body. Allow some of the underpainting to come through so the hair will have a little depth to it. We'll add final highlights later. If you make a mistake, paint over the area with the base color and repeat this step.

17 Add Foreground Grass

Really loosen up on this step. Roll a no. 4 script liner in an inky mixture of Ultramarine Blue, Burnt Sienna, a touch of Dioxazine Purple and, if you wish, a little Hooker's Green Hue until the brush comes to a point. Put in a variety of overlapping weeds. Don't be afraid to put in a lot. It makes the grass look wild and realistic.

18 Highlight Grass

For this step, change the value of the mixture you used in step 17, adding a lot more Titanium White (gesso) and touches of Cadmium Yellow Light and Cadmium Orange. Make sure the mixture is very inky, and, using a no. 4 script liner, cover the underpainting with a variety of shapes, sizes and lengths. Add plenty of overlapping, bent and angled weeds. Don't hesitate to add variety by changing the value or color with a little more Cadmium Yellow Light or Cadmium Orange.

19 Add Final Details

Give the painting a little sparkle. Use one basic highlight color for this step. Using a no. 4 round sable brush, apply a silver lining—a mixture of Titanium White (gesso) and a touch of Cadmium Yellow Light and/or Cadmium Orange—on the edges of the main objects, such as the dead pine trees, the stump, the moose and the moose's antlers. Apply these highlights with opaque layers so they will stay nice and bright.

This painting probably challenged you, but paintings like this can really help build your confidence, so keep up the good work!

Evening Prayers
16" × 20" (41cm × 51cm)

Evening Prayers

By now you know that I love painting winter scenes and especially snow. In this painting, though, I want to teach you how to paint night scenes. Refer to the list of characteristics of night scenes on page 280. This painting provides a great opportunity to work on contrast, the key component of night scenes. It also allows you to work on atmosphere—in this case a cold, crisp night. The warm light from the windows and the cast shadows on the snow add to the interest and the feeling of the snowy night scene. You get a warm feeling when you look at this painting, even though the scene is of a cold night. The smoke from the chimney and the soft glow from the windows make this building an inviting place to spend a long, winter evening. Join me and you will learn a lot from this painting.

1 Draw Basic Sketch

There is not much detail to this sketch. It serves only to help you see where everything should go, so keep it simple.

2 Underpaint Sky

This is a great color scheme. Lightly wet the sky and then apply an even coat of gesso with a hake brush. While it is still wet, apply Ultramarine Blue and Burnt Sienna. Mix these on the canvas instead of your palette. Mix them together all over the sky until you have a nice, rich, dark gray. Then mix in a little Dioxazine Purple to add a snowy atmosphere.

3 Drybrush Clouds

Scrub in some cloud masses with a no. 10 flat bristle brush and a mixture of Ultramarine Blue, Burnt Sienna, a little Titanium White (gesso) and a touch of Alizarin Crimson to create a soft, midtone gray. Scatter the clouds throughout the sky, keeping the edges soft. Don't make the clouds too bright. You just need enough contrast to make the clouds stand out from the background.

4 Paint Background Hill

Add just enough Titanium White (gesso) to a mixture of Ultramarine Blue and touches of Burnt Sienna and Dioxazine Purple to lighten the value so it is just slightly darker than the sky. Scrub in the soft range of hills with a no. 6 flat bristle brush. Notice that they almost fade into the background.

5 Paint Background Pine Trees

These pine trees are slightly darker than the background hills, so add just a little Dioxazine Purple and a touch of Hooker's Green Hue to the mixture from step 4. Paint in these trees with a no. 4 flat bristle brush. You don't need any detail here; just suggest the forms. Also make sure you have good negative space around the trees.

6 Underpaint Snow

Make a mixture of Ultramarine Blue, touches of Burnt Sienna and Dioxazine Purple and just enough Titanium White (gesso) to make a rich, purple gray. Underpaint the entire foreground with a no. 10 flat bristle brush. Make sure you cover the canvas well.

7 Add Snow to Pine Trees

Dab snow on the pine trees to give them form with a no. 4 flat sable brush and a bluish gray mixture of Titanium White (gesso), touches of Ultramarine Blue and Dioxazine Purple and a little Burnt Sienna. Don't overpaint or the trees will lose their forms.

8 Underpaint Church

You'll establish the basic values of the church in this step. Block in the dark side with a no. 4 flat bristle brush and a mixture of Burnt Sienna, touches of Ultramarine Blue and Dioxazine Purple and just enough Titanium White (gesso) to gray the mixture. Add a little more Titanium White (gesso) to the mixture and block in the light side of the building. Add even more Titanium White (gesso) and a little more Dioxazine Purple and block in the roof, door, windows, steeple and soft shadow from the roof's overhang.

9 Highlight Snow

Dry-brush in the highlights to give the snow its contour with a no. 6 flat bristle brush and a mixture of Titanium White (gesso), a touch of Cadmium Orange and just a touch of Ultramarine Blue to gray it. Leave pockets of negative space to create depressions in the snow. You'll add grass and bushes here later. Also paint the rest of the shadows from the roof's overhang.

10 Block In Clumps of Grass

Drybrush in clumps of grass with a no. 10 flat bristle brush and a fairly creamy mixture of Burnt Sienna and a touch of Dioxazine Purple. The clumps should fit nicely into the depressions you created in step 9. Overlap some of the clumps to create good negative space.

11 Add Details to Church

Paint the snow on the roof and the side of the steeple with a no. 4 flat sable brush and a mixture of Titanium White (gesso) and a slight touch of Cadmium Yellow Light. Drybrush a little of this color onto the front of the church to give it a little more light. Dab in the light in the windows with a mixture of Cadmium Yellow Light and a touch of Cadmium Orange. Add any other details you wish, such as a chimney with smoke coming out of it, icicles dripping from the corners of the roof, windowpanes, a cross on the top of the steeple, etc.

12 Add More Snow Highlights

Highlight the tops of the snowdrifts in the middleground and background with a no. 4 flat bristle brush and a mixture of Titanium White (gesso) and a touch of Cadmium Yellow Light. Don't put too many highlights in the foreground, but don't be afraid to add some brighter patches of snow, such as in front of the church. Just make sure your value system stays balanced. Blend carefully, making sure to leave no hard edges.

13 Add Miscellaneous Details

Really have fun with this step. Add the taller weeds throughout the clumps of grass with a no. 4 script liner and an inky mixture of Ultramarine Blue and Burnt Sienna. At the same time, add miscellaneous dead bushes to act as eye stoppers on each side of the scene. Add the fence and the dead pine trees in the background. Add any other details that you'd like to the church as well.

14 Add Final Highlights

Dab in highlights on the pine trees and block in the moon with a no. 4 flat sable brush and a mixture of Titanium White (gesso) and a touch of Cadmium Yellow Light. Drift snow up against the weeds with a no. 4 round sable brush and the same mixture to accent them. Add a few highlights to the top of the roof, the fence and some of the dead pine trees. Keep most of the light in the middle background surrounding the church, though. Dry-brush some of the highlight color around the edge of the moon, carefully blending into the background.

This was an exciting painting and a great learning experience. It also can make a great winter holiday card. Keep up the good work. I look forward to working with you on our next painting adventure.

The Guardian
16" × 20" (41cm × 51cm)

The Guardian

Just the thought of painting a large bird of prey and all the feather details scares most people. But I've simplified the eagle's form and adjusted the details to make it simpler for you. I've been studying birds for many years and have spent endless hours photographing, sketching and illustrating these phenomenal creatures. Just relax and enjoy the learning process. This painting is about not only the eagle, but also the wonderful mountain range, the great cloud formation and the dead pine tree that the eagle is perching on. Practice will help perfect your technique. You may end up painting the eagle over two or three times, but the experience and the result will be worth it. This is a fun painting, and your confidence will be sky-high when you finish it.

1 Draw Basic Sketch

Once again, make a rough sketch of the main composition with no. 2 soft vine charcoal. Even though you'll paint over it, the sketch helps you picture the painting on your canvas.

2 Underpaint Sky

Lightly wet the sky, then apply a liberal coat of gesso with a hake brush. Starting at the horizon, blend Cadmium Yellow Light and Cadmium Red Light halfway up while the gesso is still wet. Add Ultramarine Blue and a little Burnt Sienna at the top of the canvas and blend downward until you meet the horizon color. Carefully blend over the horizon color until you create a fairly dusty color in the middle of the sky. Keep all blended edges soft, and make sure you have a variety of subtle color changes.

3 Underpaint Clouds

Create a soft gray mixture of Titanium White (gesso), Ultramarine Blue, a touch of Burnt Sienna and a touch of Cadmium Red Light. Scrub in the shadowed part of the cloud formations with this mixture and a no. 6 flat bristle brush. You may need to make the mixture slightly creamy, but make absolutely sure all of the cloud edges are soft.

4 Paint Tops of Clouds

Scrub in the tops of the cloud formations with no. 4 and no. 6 flat bristle brushes and a fairly creamy mixture of Titanium White (gesso) and a touch of Cadmium Orange. Notice the good negative space around the clouds and the depth created by overlapping them.

5 Highlight Clouds

Be a little more careful and a bit more precise in this step. Add a little more Titanium White (gesso) and a touch of Cadmium Yellow Light to the mixture you used in step 4. Carefully highlight the very tops of the clouds with this new mixture and a no. 4 flat sable brush. Don't apply too many highlights, but make sure the paint is opaque so it stays nice and bright.

6 Underpaint Background Mountains

Redraw the sketch lines for the large mountain that you painted over in step 2. Make a mixture of Titanium White (gesso), touches of Ultramarine Blue and Burnt Sienna and a little Dioxazine Purple. Make sure the value is slightly darker than the blue part of the sky. Scrub in the first range of distant mountains with this mixture and a no. 6 flat bristle brush, keeping the mountain range simple and soft.

7 Underpaint Large Mountains

The mountain is a major feature in this painting, but it still is in the distance, so you don't want to make it too dark. Make a mixture of Titanium White (gesso), Ultramarine Blue and touches of Burnt Sienna and Dioxazine Purple, adjusting the value so it is slightly darker than the background mountain. Block in the mountain with this mixture and a no. 6 flat bristle brush, making sure you have some unique shapes along the edges. These will come in handy when you add highlights.

8 Highlight Large Mountains

After the paint dries, wipe off any charcoal lines from the top of the large mountain that you did not paint over in the last step. Make a fairly creamy mixture of Titanium White (gesso) and a touch of Cadmium Orange for the highlights. Add highlights to the mountain with a no. 4 flat sable brush, beginning at the top and using short, choppy dry-brush strokes. Don't put too much paint on your brush or the highlights will be too bright. If you need to increase the brightness, just repeat the strokes.

9 Underpaint Middleground Mountains

This step is a bit challenging. Make a grayish green mixture of Titanium White (gesso), Burnt Sienna, Ultramarine Blue and touches of Dioxazine Purple and Hooker's Green Hue. Make the value slightly darker than the value of the large mountain. Dab in suggestive forms of pine trees across the top of the mountain with this mixture and a no. 4 flat bristle brush held perpendicular to the canvas. Change the color and darken the value of the mixture by adding a little more Dioxazine Purple and Titanium White (gesso). Block in the rest of the mountain using short, choppy strokes to suggest rocky ground.

10 Add Details to Middleground Mountains

Add more Titanium White (gesso) and a touch of Cadmium Orange to the first mixture from step 9 to create a soft highlight color. Suggest rugged, rocky ground formations with a no. 4 flat bristle brush. Let some of the background color show through to add three-dimensional form to the rock formations. You'll add final highlights later.

11 Underpaint Foreground Pine Trees

Make sure you use good negative space around the pine trees in this step. Fill in the entire foreground with a nice, rich, greenish gray mixture of Hooker's Green Hue, Burnt Sienna and a touch of Dioxazine Purple. I used a no. 6 flat bristle brush, but you may feel more comfortable with a no. 4 flat bristle. Carefully place the pine trees to create a path for the eye to follow. Notice that the trees are not detailed but just suggested with fairly soft edges.

12 Sketch Tree and Eagle
You don't normally need a very accurate sketch for landscapes, but you do for this eagle. You can use a soft charcoal pencil instead of no. 2 soft vine charcoal if you want a sharper point. When the paint from step 11 is dry, sketch the tree and eagle lightly.

13 Underpaint Dead Pine Tree
With a no. 6 flat bristle brush, blend Ultramarine Blue, Burnt Sienna and a little Dioxazine Purple together on the stump, not on the palette. Use short, choppy, vertical strokes to create texture. Make sure no canvas shows through.

14 Add Details to Dead Tree

Make a fairly creamy mixture of Titanium White (gesso) and touches of Cadmium Orange and Burnt Sienna. Apply this mixture with a no. 4 flat sable and short, choppy, vertical strokes, beginning on the right and gradually working across to the dark side of the tree. Leave some dark areas showing through to create depth in the bark. With a mixture of Titanium White (gesso) and touches of Ultramarine Blue and Dioxazine Purple, drybrush the reflected highlights on the left side of the tree to make it appear rounder. Add some darker areas to suggest cracks and holes in the bark. You'll add final highlights later.

15 Underpaint Eagle

Make a mixture of Burnt Sienna and Ultramarine Blue for the dark body and a gray mixture of Titanium White (gesso), touches of Ultramarine Blue and Dioxazine Purple and a little Burnt Sienna for the head and tail. Block in these areas with a no. 4 flat sable brush. Don't create a hard outline, but make sure you cover the canvas. Add a little Cadmium Orange to the gray mixture and block in the beak and talons.

16 Add Details to Eagle

Practice this step on a scrap canvas before trying it on this painting. Make a creamy, light tan mixture of Titanium White (gesso), Burnt Sienna and a slight touch of Ultramarine Blue. Load just a little of this mixture on the end of a no. 4 flat sable brush and drybrush suggestions of feathers. Start at the bottom and work your way up. Leave some dark spaces between brushstrokes to separate the feathers. Don't block out all of the underpainting or you'll lose depth. Use the same technique and the same brush with pure Titanium White (gesso) for the head and tail. Repeat these strokes two or three times to create brighter highlights if you wish. Highlight the beak, talons and eye with a no. 4 round sable and a mixture of Cadmium Orange, touches of Cadmium Yellow Light and Titanium White (gesso). Add Ultramarine Blue and Burnt Sienna to the mixture for any really dark areas, such as the shadow underneath the beak. With a no. 4 script liner, put a few thin accent highlights on the edges of some of the feathers with a little Titanium White (gesso) and Cadmium Orange.

17 Add Final Details and Highlights

This step differs for each artist. If you're happy with the highlights and details, you don't need to do much now. I used no. 4 flat and round sable brushes for this step. I highlighted the large mountain with a mixture of Cadmium Orange and Titanium White (gesso). I highlighted the middleground pine trees with a mixture of Hooker's Green Hue and Titanium White (gesso). I highlighted the rock formations in the middleground with a mixture of Titanium White (gesso), Cadmium Yellow Light and Cadmium Orange. I added some dark pine trees in the foreground to serve as eye stoppers with a mixture of Hooker's Green Hue and Dioxazine Purple. I added a few light bushes at the base of the dead pine tree and a few brighter highlights on the eagle and dead pine tree.

This painting probably challenged you a bit more than the others, but what a terrific learning experience it was! Don't hesitate to try this one again. The results will improve each time, so keep up the good work!

The Silent One
16" × 20" (41cm × 51cm)

The Silent One

This painting brings back many memories from the beginning of my art career. I did a painting similar to this almost twenty years ago as a study of fur. A rabbit like this is an excellent study because there are not a lot of complicated body parts and angles to take your attention away from the fur. It turned out to be one of my most popular paintings, so I turned it into a limited edition print and it became a bestseller. If you have an interest in wildlife art and want to begin showing and selling it, start with small animals, such as rabbits, squirrels and chipmunks. They are fairly easy to paint and sell very well. This painting will help you get a handle on brush control—pressure, paint thickness, angle of the brush and dry-brush strokes—things that are critical to painting good fur. There are some bonus lessons here as well. Painting weeds, especially close, tall ones like these, is great fun and extremely challenging. Notice what a great addition to the atmosphere they are.

1 Paint Background

Have fun with this step. Lightly wet the background, and then paint on a liberal coat of gesso with a hake brush. While the gesso is still wet, add Ultramarine Blue, Burnt Sienna, Cadmium Yellow Light, Cadmium Orange, Dioxazine Purple, Cadmium Red Light and a little Hooker's Green Hue in long, vertical, slightly overlapping strokes. Don't blend these colors on your palette. Just put them on the canvas in any order and slightly blend the lines together for a gradated look.

2 Underpaint Snow

Underpaint the rest of the canvas with a no. 10 flat bristle brush and a nice, midtone, purplish gray mixture of Titanium White (gesso), Ultramarine Blue and touches of Burnt Sienna and Dioxazine Purple. Make sure you have a fairly soft edge where the underpainting meets the vertical background strokes.

3 Highlight Snow

Give the snow some interesting contour and softness. Don't make this layer too bright because you'll add final highlights later. Drybrush in the basic contour of the snow with a no. 6 flat bristle brush and a creamy mixture of Titanium White (gesso) and a touch of Cadmium Orange. Make the blended edges very soft.

4 Paint Large Background Weeds

The weeds in this painting come in a good variety of sizes, shapes and angles. Make a base color of Burnt Sienna, Titanium White (gesso), Ultramarine Blue, a touch of Dioxazine Purple and a little Hooker's Green Hue. Thin this mixture substantially, and paint in these tall weeds, switching among a no. 4 flat sable, a no. 4 round sable and a no. 4 script liner. Occasionally change the value—by adding a little Titanium White (gesso)—and the color of the mixture.

5 **Highlight Background Weeds**
Using the same techniques and any or all of the brushes you used in step 4, paint in some light-colored weeds with a fairly thin mixture of Titanium White (gesso) and touches of Cadmium Orange and Cadmium Yellow Light. Leave some weeds unhighlighted and paint new weeds with this highlight mixture to add depth and variety.

6 **Sketch Rabbit**
Make an accurate sketch of the basic shape of the rabbit, but don't worry about detail. If you need to work out the shape before drawing over your painting, sketch the rabbit on a sketch pad, and then transfer the drawing onto the canvas with graphite paper and a tracing pencil.

7 Underpaint Rabbit

Underpaint the rabbit with a no. 6 or no. 4 flat bristle brush and a fairly creamy mixture of Burnt Sienna and Ultramarine Blue. Don't paint a hard edge for the outline of the rabbit. Keep the edges slightly fuzzy so you will be able to paint over it when you paint the fur in step 8.

8 Add Details to Rabbit

Let's get down to business! Block in the eye, nose and dark areas on the ears with a no. 4 flat sable and a black mixture of Burnt Sienna, Ultramarine Blue and a touch of Dioxazine Purple. Load the very end of a no. 4 flat bristle brush with a small amount of a creamy mixture of Titanium White (gesso), a touch of Cadmium Orange and a touch of Ultramarine Blue to gray it. Dry-brush the fur on the rabbit, beginning at its base. Follow the contour of the body and let some of the underpainting show through to create depth within the fur. Switch to your no. 4 flat sable to finish the head and ears.

9 Highlight Rabbit

Add a lot more Titanium White (gesso) to the highlight mixture from step 8. With this new mixture and a no. 4 flat sable brush, add accents to the areas around the eye, cheek, neck and anywhere else you want to indicate a more three-dimensional effect. Drybrush the brighter highlight on the front of the rabbit with a no. 4 round sable brush and creamy, pure Titanium White (gesso). Paint a rim around the eye, making sure it is slightly broken. Add the highlight in the pupil with a no. 4 round sable, and you've got a rabbit!

10 Drift Snow on Rabbit and Weeds

Settle the weeds and rabbit down so they don't look like they're floating. Drift the snow up against the rabbit and all of the weeds you can reach with a no. 4 flat sable brush and a very creamy mixture of Titanium White (gesso) and small amounts of Cadmium Yellow Light and Cadmium Orange. Blend the snow out into the original underpainting as you drift it so there are no hard edges.

11 Underpaint Water

Apply a dark underpainting to make the water really look wet. Paint in the water area with a hake brush and a mixture of Titanium White (gesso), Ultramarine Blue, Burnt Sienna and a little Dioxazine Purple, making sure to cover the canvas completely. Include irregular shapes along the water's edge to make it appear flatter in contrast and more interesting.

12 Add Reflections of Weeds

Scrub in the basic shapes of the weeds in the water with a no. 4 round sable brush and a creamy mixture of some of the colors you used for the original weeds. Slightly wiggle your brush as you paint them in to give the impression of a slight ripple in the water. Remember to vary the values of the weed reflections. Also paint in some highlights on the reflections of the weeds.

13 Highlight Water

Really make the water come alive in this step. Along the edge of the water, apply the snow highlight mixture from step 3 with a no. 10 flat bristle brush and vertical dry-brush strokes of various lengths and widths. Let some of these strokes blend out into the water to create some nice pockets of negative space.

14 Glaze Water

Load a no. 10 flat bristle brush evenly across the end with a wash of Titanium White (gesso) and water. Hold the brush perpendicular to the canvas and slightly drag it across the surface of the water with a slight wiggle in the stroke. Repeat this step for the effect you want.

15 Underpaint Large Foreground Weeds

Gather your courage for this step. Paint in the long, tall weeds in the foreground with a fairly inky mixture of Burnt Sienna, Ultramarine Blue and Dioxazine Purple. Use a few different brushes—a no. 4 round sable, a no. 4 flat sable and a no. 4 script liner. Pull some of these weeds all the way to the top of the canvas, leave others short and bent over and let others overlap the rabbit. Let the weeds lean at different angles and overlap each other.

16 Highlight Foreground Weeds

Paint highlights on the right sides of most of the larger weeds with one of the brushes from step 15 and a mixture of Titanium White (gesso), Cadmium Yellow Light and Cadmium Orange. You don't have to highlight every weed. Instead, add some light-colored weeds against some of the darker areas of the background and the rabbit.

17 Add Final Details and Highlights

Now is your opportunity to enhance your painting with highlights and miscellaneous details. Add brighter highlights to the rabbit. Drift snow against the foreground weeds. Add some bright highlights along the water's edge. Put final highlights on the snowdrifts and piles of snow along the shoreline with a mixture of Titanium White (gesso) and a touch of Cadmium Yellow Light.

I hope this painting taught you to paint with softness and subtle value changes. I look forward to working with you on the next one.

Moonlight Canadians
16" × 20" (41cm × 51cm)

Moonlight Canadians

This painting offers all kinds of wonderful learning opportunities. You've heard me say that before, but this is one of my all-time favorite paintings to do. I love the intense moonlight glow. The real challenge in this painting isn't painting the geese, as you might suspect. It's managing the variety of green tones and values that give the painting its true atmosphere. Green is one of the hardest colors to work with, especially in a painting full of green tones. Done correctly, though, it can be one of the most exciting color schemes you'll ever work with. This painting will challenge you more than most, but it's well worth the experience. Your script liner will get a workout from all of the dead trees, and the water and reflections also will provide some work. The main feature, the Canadian geese, are small and not too detailed. They appear more as silhouettes against the moonlit sky than defined objects.

1 Underpaint Background

This painting has an interesting and unique color scheme. Apply a liberal coat of gesso made creamy with water over the sky area with a hake brush and long, vertical strokes. While the gesso is still wet, again use vertical strokes to apply Hooker's Green Hue, Burnt Sienna, a touch of Dioxazine Purple, a little Cadmium Yellow Light and a little Cadmium Orange. Carefully blend these colors together on the canvas until you have created a nice, rich, dark green background with subtle color and value changes.

2 Underpaint Water

Turn your canvas upside down and paint the water the same way you painted the sky.

3 Draw Basic Sketch
Make a quick, rough sketch of the basic components of the landscape with no. 2 soft vine charcoal.

4 Add Moonlight Glow
Drybrush in a soft moonlight glow with a no. 6 flat bristle brush and a mixture of Titanium White (gesso), Cadmium Yellow Light and a very slight touch of Cadmium Orange. Carefully blend this highlight into the background so there are no hard edges. It doesn't take very much paint, so don't overload your brush.

5 Underpaint Background Bushes

Make a mixture of Hooker's Green Hue, touches of Burnt Sienna and Dioxazine Purple and just enough Titanium White (gesso) that the mixture is still slightly darker than the background. Scrub in a nice collection of soft, interestingly shaped bushes with this mixture and a no. 6 flat bristle brush.

6 Paint Dead Background Trees

Slightly darken the mixture you used in step 5 with a little Ultramarine Blue and Burnt Sienna and make it fairly inky. Paint in the dead trees across the background with a no. 4 script liner. Change the value for some to add depth to the background by adding a little Titanium White (gesso) to the mixture.

7 Underpaint Shoreline

Scrub in a rough, irregular shoreline with a no. 6 flat bristle brush and a mixture of Hooker's Green Hue and touches of Dioxazine Purple and Burnt Sienna. This mixture should be slightly darker than the background trees. As you paint the shoreline, suggest a few bushes and also smudge some of the mixture into the water to suggest reflections from the bushes.

8 Paint Dead Tree Reflections

Slightly drag a no. 4 round sable brush from the shoreline vertically down the canvas with a creamy version of the dead tree mixture from step 6. Use a slight wiggle in your brushstrokes to make the water appear wetter and rippled.

9 Add Details to Shoreline

Now you can start adding a little detail. Paint in the suggestion of rocks and other debris along the shoreline with a no. 4 flat sable brush and a creamy mixture of Titanium White (gesso), Cadmium Orange and a little Hooker's Green Hue to gray it. Keep these highlights fairly soft; they would be too obvious if they were bright. If you think they are too bright, just add a little more Hooker's Green Hue to the mixture and paint over them.

10 Underpaint Clumps of Grass

The contour of the foreground begins to take place in this step. Make a fairly creamy mixture of Hooker's Green Hue, a little Burnt Sienna and Dioxazine Purple, making sure to use enough Burnt Sienna and Dioxazine Purple to prevent the mixture from being too green. Use a no. 10 flat bristle brush and a vertical, dry-brush stroke to paint in the clumps of grass. Include pockets of negative space to give the composition good eye flow. Drybrush the reflections from each clump, making sure to keep them soft.

11 Paint Large Tree Trunks

Paint in the trunks of each of the larger trees with no. 4 round and no. 4 flat sable brushes and a very creamy mixture of Ultramarine Blue, Burnt Sienna and a little Hooker's Green Hue. Don't worry about the smaller limbs; just concentrate on what you can do comfortably with these two brushes. Use the negative space around the trees to create good balance and eye flow.

12 Paint Moon

Dab a little bit of a mixture of Titanium White (gesso) and a touch of Cadmium Yellow Light for the moon with a no. 4 flat bristle brush. Blend this color out from the moon with a dry-brush, scrubbing stroke. You may need to repeat this step to make the area bright enough. Do the same for the moon's reflection in the water.

13 **Add Tree Limbs**
Add enough water to the mixture you used to paint the trees in step 11 to make it inky. Thoroughly load a no. 4 script liner, rolling it to a point. Add limbs to the trees in the middleground. Don't be afraid to add as many as it takes. Again, keep an eye on negative space and overlap plenty of branches.

14 **Sketch Geese**
If you want to, sketch the geese on a separate piece of paper, then transfer them to the canvas with graphite paper and a pencil. Otherwise, sketch the geese directly onto the canvas with no. 2 soft vine charcoal.

15 Underpaint Geese

Underpaint the gray areas on the geese with a no. 4 round sable brush and a fairly creamy, medium-dark mixture of Burnt Sienna, Ultramarine Blue and a little Titanium White (gesso). Block in the very dark areas on the geese with an almost black mixture of Ultramarine Blue and Burnt Sienna. Paint the patches on the heads and backs near the tails with pure Titanium White (gesso).

16 Add Details to Geese

Only the suggestion of detail on the geese is necessary. Drybrush in suggestions of feathers on the wings and bodies with a no. 4 round sable and a mixture of Titanium White (gesso), a touch of Cadmium Yellow Light and a little of the dark gray mixture from step 15. Just highlight the geese to give them three-dimensional form. Individual feathers shouldn't show up from this far away. Paint silver linings on the wings and various parts of the bodies with a no. 4 script liner and a mixture of Titanium White (gesso) and a little Cadmium Yellow Light, but don't completely outline each goose.

17 **Add Tall Weeds**
Paint in the weeds in the middleground and foreground with a no. 4 script liner and an inky mixture of Hooker's Green Hue, Burnt Sienna and Dioxazine Purple. Again, keep an eye on negative space and overlap plenty of weeds. Make some of the foreground weeds fairly tall and use a variety of shapes.

18 **Add Moonlight to Trees**
Paint silver linings on the edges of many of the middleground tree trunks and on a few limbs. Apply the highlights fairly thickly so they'll be opaque and bright. Don't highlight any of the small limbs; that would make the painting too busy.

19 Add Final Details

Paint in the suggestion of rocks and other debris on the shoreline with a no. 4 flat sable brush and a mixture of Titanium White (gesso), a touch of Cadmium Orange and a touch of Hooker's Green Hue to gray it. Don't overdo it; add just enough rocks and debris to make the painting look finished. Exercise your artistic license with any other details you want to make your painting more interesting.

Prairie Giant
16" × 20" (41cm × 51cm)

Prairie Giant

My Oklahoma roots really come through in this paint-
ing. The Midwest is filled with western and Native
American traditions in which the buffalo is a symbol of
freedom and power. Herds once roamed freely across
Midwestern prairies until man's desire to industrialize
the West met them head on. They were killed off to near
extinction. With good wildlife and land management,
buffalo are making a strong comeback. About an hour
from my studio are thousands of acres of unspoiled
prairie grassland where the largest herd roams. On one
of my taping adventures for my PBS show, I pho-
tographed this large bull standing on a grassy knoll. I
have painted him several times, and I couldn't pass up
the chance to share this valuable learning experience
with you. This is not a difficult painting. Just make sure
background and accent objects don't compete with the
buffalo for attention. Keep the landscape simple. You'll
learn grass and fur techniques and, if nothing else, a bit
of buffalo history!

1 Draw Basic Sketch
Make a quick, rough sketch of the basic components of the landscape with no. 2 soft vine charcoal. Don't get carried away with detail; just keep it simple.

2 Underpaint Sky
Lightly wet the sky. Then apply a liberal coat of gesso with a hake brush. While the gesso is still wet, apply Cadmium Yellow Light and a touch of Cadmium Orange at the horizon and blend upward about three-fourths of the way to the top of the canvas. While the paint is still wet, apply a mixture of Ultramarine Blue and touches of Dioxazine Purple and Burnt Sienna at the top of the canvas. Blend down into the horizon color until you have a nice, soft underpainting.

3 Add Clouds
Make a mixture of Titanium White (gesso) and touches of Ultramarine Blue, Burnt Sienna and Dioxazine Purple. The mixture should be slightly darker than the sky. Scrub in nice collections of clouds with a no. 6 flat bristle brush. Use a well-balanced arrangement of negative space to create good eye flow. Make sure the edges of the clouds are soft and fade nicely into the background.

4 Highlight Clouds
Carefully highlight the top right-hand sides of most of the cloud formations with a no. 4 flat bristle or sable brush and a mixture of Titanium White (gesso) and a slight touch of Cadmium Orange. The clouds in the right-hand side of the sky are flatter and have silver linings instead of highlights to indicate three-dimensional form. Repeat this step once or twice if you want brighter highlights on the clouds.

5 Underpaint Background Hills

Make a mixture that is slightly darker than the color at the horizon with Titanium White (gesso) and touches of Dioxazine Purple, Burnt Sienna and Ultramarine Blue. Scrub in the shapes of the very distant hills with this mixture and a no. 4 flat bristle brush. Make the mixture slightly darker and scrub in the basic form of the closer row of background hills. Give these hills more distinct form to make them appear more rugged. The extra form and detail also will make them appear closer.

6 Underpaint Distant Trees

Add a little more Dioxazine Purple and a touch of Hooker's Green Hue to the mixture from step 5 to darken it. Scrub in the basic shapes of these distant trees with a no. 4 or no. 6 flat bristle brush. Keep these shapes simple because there are not many trees. Also make sure they have nice pockets of negative space to create good eye flow.

7 Underpaint Middleground Grass

Add a little Cadmium Orange and a bit more Titanium White (gesso) to the mixture from step 6 to create a nice, soft, midtone gray-green. Use a series of overlapping, vertical dry-brush strokes and a no. 10 flat bristle brush to underpaint the grass in the middle right of the painting. Begin at the top of this area and work your way down. Allow your brushstrokes to show, suggesting blades of grass. When you reach the bottom of the grassy area, leave an irregular edge to drift the dirt in and around.

8 Underpaint Foreground Bank

Paint the bank in the foreground with a no. 6 flat bristle brush and a mixture of Burnt Sienna and a little Dioxazine Purple. Start at the top of the bank and work your way down to the flat area using a large comma stroke. Add touches of Titanium White (gesso) and Cadmium Orange as you go. As your strokes flatten out, let them become choppy and horizontal to suggest dirt. Use a variety of light and dark values that contrast each other to give the bank depth and character. Play with the design. Just make sure the banks are darker at the top so the lighter grass that overlaps the bank will show up well when you paint it in step 9.

9 Underpaint Foreground Grass

Scatter different combinations of Titanium White (gesso), Cadmium Yellow Light, a little Hooker's Green Hue and touches of Dioxazine Purple and Burnt Sienna with vertical, dry-brush strokes. Start at the top and move across the grassy area on top of the bank. As you move forward, continue changing the combinations and values of the colors to create nice contrast. I made the bottom left corner much darker than the rest of the painting.

10 Highlight Background Hills and Trees

Highlight just enough of the background hills with a no. 4 flat sable brush and a mixture of Titanium White (gesso) and a little Cadmium Orange to give them a little three-dimensional form. Add a little more Titanium White (gesso) and a touch of Phthalo Yellow-Green to the mixture, and dab highlights on the distant trees with a no. 4 or no. 6 flat bristle brush. Again, highlight the trees just enough to provide a little form.

11 Highlight Middleground Grass

Load just a little of a fairly creamy mixture of Titanium White (gesso) and touches of Phthalo Yellow-Green and Cadmium Orange on the end of a no. 10 flat bristle brush. Add highlights to the grass with a vertical, dry-brush stroke, starting at the top of the grassy area and working your way down. Leave pockets of negative space to give the grass contour. It should have a gentle, rolling effect, so don't line the highlights up in a horizontal row.

12 Paint Clumps of Grass

Make a mixture of Hooker's Green Hue, a touch of Dioxazine Purple and enough Titanium White (gesso) to make the value fit this area of the painting. Drybrush in the individual soft clumps of grass with this mixture and a no. 6 flat bristle brush. Include good negative space and eye flow around the clumps, but don't line them up in a row. These clumps serve as the transition between the back- and foregrounds.

13 Add Foreground Rocks

Suggest the pebbles and small rocks with no. 4 round and flat sable brushes and a mixture of Titanium White (gesso), a touch of Cadmium Orange and a slight touch of Cadmium Yellow Light. Use small, rounded strokes. For the larger rocks, paint darker form shadows and then highlight them with the color you used to paint the pebbles. Don't worry about bright highlights yet.

14 Sketch Buffalo

Make an accurate sketch of the basic form of the buffalo. It doesn't need to be detailed, but the form must be accurate. Sharpen the end of a piece of no. 2 soft vine charcoal just a little to make it easier to sketch with.

15 **Underpaint Buffalo**
Block in the entire buffalo with a no. 4 flat bristle brush and a dark mixture of Burnt Sienna, Ultramarine Blue and just a little Titanium White (gesso). Darken the mixture's value to paint darker areas, such as the shadows beneath the buffalo and areas where the buffalo's body parts overlap. Avoid a hard edge or outline around the body, but cover the canvas well.

16 **Add Bushes and Grass**
Make several mixtures of different values with Titanium White (gesso), touches of Cadmium Yellow Light and Phthalo Yellow-Green and a little Cadmium Orange. Dab in the highlights on the grass in the left middleground with a no. 4 or no. 10 flat bristle brush to create small bushes and clumps of grass. Don't make this area too busy. You may even need to add some darker areas to create contrast.

17 Add Details to Buffalo

Load the very end of a no. 4 flat sable brush with a small amount of a fairly creamy mixture of Titanium White (gesso) and touches of Cadmium Orange and Cadmium Yellow Light. Starting at the top of the buffalo, suggest the hair with a very light, dry-brush stroke. Follow the contour of the body, and allow some of the background color to come through to create depth. Include light and dark areas to give the buffalo form; don't make the buffalo one tone.

18 Add More Details to Buffalo

Again darken some of the shadow areas on the buffalo to create a little more depth with a no. 4 round sable brush and a dark mixture of Burnt Sienna and Ultramarine Blue. Soften any hard edges with the same brush and a mixture of Titanium White (gesso) and touches of Cadmium Yellow Light and Cadmium Orange. Make sure all of the final highlights are opaque so they will stay nice and bright.

19 Add Foreground Rocks and Dead Bushes

Block in the dark sides of the rocks on the grass above the bank with a no. 4 flat bristle brush and a mixture of Burnt Sienna, a little Ultramarine Blue, a little Dioxazine Purple and a little Titanium White (gesso) to soften it. Add form highlights to the rocks with the same brush and a mixture of Titanium White (gesso), Cadmium Orange and a slight touch of the rock mixture from step 13 to gray it. You'll add brighter highlights in step 20. Thin the first mixture you used in this step to an inky consistency. Paint in the two dead bushes with this mixture and a no. 4 script liner.

20 Add Final Details

Give your painting some personality in this step. Add elements like taller weeds, a few wildflowers and brighter highlights on the rocks and pebbles. Highlight some of the clumps of grass, but don't make the painting too busy.

I sincerely hope you learned a lot from this painting. It was great fun sharing it with you. Keep up the good work and remember that practice, practice, practice is the key!

Covey Raider
16" × 20" (41cm × 51cm)

Covey Raider

Another memory of mine plays a role in this painting. I never was a great hunter, but one of my favorite things to do as a child was to walk through the high brush, climb over barbed wire fences and try to flush out a covey of these elusive, upland game birds. Over the years I probably have painted more quail than any other bird. This painting offers a wide range of subjects and techniques. The landscape is fairly impressionistic, so you'll have an opportunity to work on grass, brush and foreground details. Even the dirt wash and the rocks and pebbles are fun to paint, and they really add to the foreground. The old fence is another exciting subject. Just make sure you use proportions correctly as the posts recede into the background. The quail and the dog provide a challenge. Proportion, again, and location are the keys to painting these animals. Don't let the amount of activity in this painting scare you. The learning experience matters most.

1 Draw Basic Sketch

Once again, make a rough sketch of the basic components of the landscape with no. 2 soft vine charcoal.

2 Underpaint Sky

Lightly wet the sky area and apply a liberal coat of gesso with a hake brush. Apply Alizarin Crimson at the horizon and blend it all the way to the top of the canvas. Then apply a mixture of Ultramarine Blue and little touches of Dioxazine Purple and Burnt Sienna at the top of the canvas and blend downward almost to the horizon. Clean your brush a bit and go back over the sky with large, crisscross, feather strokes.

3 Underpaint Background Trees

Make a mixture that is slightly darker than the sky with Titanium White (gesso), a little Ultramarine Blue, a little Burnt Sienna and a little Dioxazine Purple. Scrub in some soft, distant trees with a no. 6 flat bristle brush. Slightly darken the mixture and scrub in another group of trees just in front of the background trees. Make sure both groups of trees produce good eye flow and have soft edges.

4 Underpaint Grassy Middleground

Scrub in the grassy area with a no. 10 flat bristle brush and a variety of mixtures of Titanium White (gesso); touches of Cadmium Yellow Light, Cadmium Orange and Phthalo Yellow-Green; and occasionally a little Burnt Sienna. Use mostly golden, earth tones. Scrub in darker, contrasting areas to suggest bushes or clumps of grass with a mixture of Burnt Sienna, touches of Dioxazine Purple and Hooker's Green Hue and a little Titanium White (gesso) to soften it. Use loose, impressionistic strokes in this step.

5 Underpaint Grassy Foreground

Paint this area the same way you painted the grass in step 4, but give more definite shape to the bushes. Paint in different bush shapes with a no. 10 flat bristle brush, using a variety of contrasting values. Add Hooker's Green Hue, Dioxazine Purple and Burnt Sienna to the mixture from step 4 to make a darker color that will provide contrast. The new mixture should be a richer, olive color just perfect for the foreground. Keep your strokes loose and free.

6 Underpaint Dirt

Starting at the little bank on the bottom right, use a no. 6 flat bristle brush and a comma stroke to apply a mixture of Titanium White (gesso), Cadmium Yellow Light, a touch of Dioxazine Purple and plenty of Burnt Sienna. As you move into the flat area, apply Titanium White (gesso), Cadmium Yellow Light and Burnt Sienna to the canvas, blending them together to create a nice, warm earth tone. Let your brushstrokes show for texture.

7 Highlight Background Trees

Carefully dab on a highlight mixture of Titanium White (gesso) and touches of Cadmium Orange and Phthalo Yellow-Green with a no. 6 flat bristle brush, being careful not to cover up the background color completely. Include pockets of negative space to provide good eye flow and form.

8 Highlight Background Bushes

Use no. 4 and no. 6 flat bristle brushes and bright highlight colors with a variety of loose, free strokes to create a late afternoon, sunlit effect on the grass and bushes on the middle left of the painting. Use no. 4 round and flat sable brushes for the smaller areas.

9 Highlight Middleground Grass
Paint this grass the same way you painted the grass in step 8. Use fairly loose, impressionistic strokes with whatever brush fits the job, but make the bushes and clumps of grass more distinct. Use fairly pure colors, such as Cadmium Orange, Cadmium Yellow Light and Phthalo Yellow-Green to create an array of grass and bushes with different textures, shapes and forms and contrasting values.

10 Add Details to Dirt
You probably know by now that I can't let you get through a painting without adding a few rocks and pebbles. Make little, rounded highlights to suggest pebbles with no. 4 round and flat sable brushes and a mixture of Titanium White (gesso), a touch of Cadmium Orange and a touch of Dioxazine Purple to slightly gray it. Place some rocks and pebbles along the edge of the grass to suggest erosion, but keep most of them around the outer edge of the dirt area. For the larger rocks, paint a form with a darker value first and then highlight it with the highlight color.

11 Sketch Foreground Bush

Draw a rough but accurate sketch of the fence posts and the dead bush on the left with no. 2 soft vine charcoal. Make sure you get the correct location and perspective of the fence in your sketch before you paint it in.

12 Underpaint Fence and Bush

Paint the fence posts with a no. 4 flat sable brush and a mixture of Burnt Sienna and Ultramarine Blue. Hold the brush perpendicular to the canvas for better control while painting the crooked post shapes. Add Titanium White (gesso) to the mixture to lighten the value for each fence post as the posts recede into the background. Thin the mixture you used for the first fence post—the darkest one—to an inky consistency and paint in the dead bush with a no. 4 script liner.

13 Add Details to Landscape

Once you paint the fence and wire, painting more details around them is difficult, so take the time right now to analyze your background. Paint the trunks on the distant trees, shadows from the fence posts, weeds, flowers, more or brighter highlights and any other additional accents you want to include.

14 Add Details to Fence

Highlight the fence posts with a no. 4 round sable brush and a mixture of Titanium White (gesso) and touches of Cadmium Orange and Cadmium Yellow Light. Use short, choppy, vertical dry-brush strokes to suggest weathered wood. Allow some of the background to show through to make the posts appear rugged. Carefully paint in the wire with a no. 4 script liner and a very inky mixture of Ultramarine Blue and Burnt Sienna. Practice this first if you need to.

15 Add More Details to Foreground

Add a variety of weeds in different colors and values to tie the painting together. Add weeds and suggest flowers to settle the fence posts. Add a few more pebbles and highlights on the dirt. Don't overwork the foreground or it will compete with the dog and quail.

16 Sketch Animals

Use a sharpened charcoal pencil to accurately sketch the animals. Practice on a sketch pad to get the shapes and forms right before drawing on the canvas.

17 Underpaint Animals

Carefully underpaint the dog with a no. 4 flat sable brush and a gray mixture of Ultramarine Blue, Burnt Sienna and a touch of Titanium White (gesso). Don't leave a hard outline around the dog's outer form. Darken the value of the mixture with more Ultramarine Blue and Burnt Sienna to paint the spots and shadow areas. Slightly lighten the new mixture with Titanium White (gesso) to underpaint the quail with a no. 4 round sable brush.

18 Add Details to Dog

Make the original under-painting color from step 17 much lighter and then add a touch of Cadmium Orange. Load just a little bit of a creamy version of this mixture on the end of a no. 4 flat sable and carefully drybrush highlights on the dog's back, following the contour of the body with a very light stroke. The highlight gradually should darken as you move downward. Add some brighter highlights along the dog's back, head, tail and legs with a no. 4 round sable brush. Don't paint a hard line around the dog.

19 Add Details to Quail

Drybrush a few highlights around the outer edges of the bodies and wings with a no. 4 round sable and a mixture of Titanium White (gesso) and a touch of Cadmium Orange to suggest form and define the wings. Add some simple, delicate highlights on the wing tips to suggest individual feathers. Add the dark accents on the heads and beaks and inside the wings and tails with a darker mixture of Burnt Sienna, Ultramarine Blue and a little Titanium White (gesso) to soften it. Use simple, quick strokes and don't overdo it. If you goof up, simply underpaint the area and reapply the highlights.

20 Add Final Highlights

Pull up a few weeds under the dog to settle it down. Add some bright, orange leaves on the bushes and maybe a brighter highlight on the top of the dog with pure Titanium White (gesso). Stand back, analyze the whole painting and make any final adjustments you want.

This was a fun experience and a great learning opportunity! In fact, this would be a great painting to try in different seasons and with different game birds like pheasants or grouse.

HOMEWARD BOUND (cropped)
16" x 20" (41cm x 51cm)

PAINT ALONG WITH **JERRY YARNELL**

LEARNING
Composition

Table of Contents

Country Getaway

Prairie Relic

Rocky Road

A Peaceful Place

Homeward Bound

Broken Pots

Rocky Waters

A Peaceful Place
16" × 20" (41cm × 51cm)

Introduction

Composition is one of the most misunderstood concepts in any form of artwork. It has been said that you can be the greatest painter in the world, but if you don't know how to compose properly, your painting will fall apart. I have had the thrill of winning numerous awards over the years, and I've asked many judges why a particular painting wins. The standard answer is that the painting has a strong composition and is well-designed. I will explore the different aspects of composition, including the three different types of composition, the principles of good design, the effective use of "eye stoppers," the proper use of negative space, how to locate the center of interest correctly and how to use thumbnail sketches. Composition is really about moving the viewer's eye. The challenge is to arrange all of the components of the composition so that it's a pleasure for the viewer to look at your painting. The demonstrations in this book will explain how good composition works, so that you too can make your paintings work.

Terms & Techniques

Before beginning the step-by-step instructions on the following pages, you may want to refresh your memory by reviewing these terms and techniques.

COLOR COMPLEMENTS

Complementary colors always appear opposite each other on the color wheel. Use complements to create color balance in your paintings. It takes practice to understand how to use complements, but a good rule of thumb is to use the complement—or form of the complement—of the predominant color in your painting to highlight, accent or gray that color.

For example, if your painting has a lot of green, use its complement, red—or a form of red such as orange or red-orange—for highlights. If you have a lot of blue in your painting, use blue's complement, orange—or a form of orange such as yellow-orange or red-orange. The complement of yellow is purple or a form of purple. Keep a color wheel handy until you have memorized the color complements.

To prepare your bristle brush for dabbing, spread out the ends of the bristles like a fan.

DABBING

Use this technique to create leaves, ground cover, flowers, etc. Take a bristle brush and dab it on your table or palette to spread out the ends of the bristles like a fan (see above example). Then load the brush with the appropriate color and gently dab on that color to create the desired effect.

DOUBLE LOAD OR TRIPLE LOAD

To load a brush this way, put two or more colors on different parts of your brush. Mix these colors on the canvas instead of your palette.

Double or triple load your brush for wet-on-wet techniques.

DRYBRUSH

Load your brush with very little paint and lightly skim the surface of the canvas with a very light touch to add, blend or soften a color.

EYE FLOW

Create good eye flow and guide the viewer's eye through the painting with the arrangement of objects on your canvas or the use of negative space around or within an object. The eye must move smoothly, or flow, through your painting and around objects. The viewer's eyes shouldn't bounce or jump from place to place. Once you understand the basic components of composition— design, negative space, "eye stoppers," overlap, etc.—your paintings will naturally achieve good eye flow.

FEATHERING

Use this technique to blend to create soft edges, to highlight and to glaze. Use a very light touch, barely skimming the surface of the canvas with your brush.

GESSO

Gesso is a white paint used for sealing canvas before painting on it. Because of its creamy consistency, and because it blends so easily, I often use gesso instead of white paint. When I use the word gesso in my step-by-step instructions, I am refer-

This is an example of good use of negative space. Notice the overlap of the limbs and the interesting pockets of space around each limb.

This is an example of poor use of negative space. Notice the limbs do not overlap but are evenly spaced instead. There are few pockets of interesting space.

ring to the color white. Use gesso or whatever white pigment you prefer.

GLAZE (WASH)

A glaze or a wash is a very thin layer of paint applied over a dry area to create mist, fog, haze or sun rays or to soften an area that is too bright. Dilute a small amount of color with water and apply it to the appropriate area. You can apply the glaze in layers, but each layer must be dry before applying the next.

HIGHLIGHTING OR ACCENTING

Highlighting is one of the final stages of your painting. Use pure color or brighter values to give your painting its final glow. Carefully apply highlights on the sunlit edges of the most prominent objects in your paintings.

MIXING

If you will be using a mixture often, premix a good amount of that color to have handy. I usually mix colors with my brush, but sometimes a palette knife works better. Be your own judge.

I also sometimes mix colors on my canvas. For instance, when I am underpainting grass, I may put two or three colors on the canvas and scumble them together to create a mottled background of different colors. This method also works well well for skies.

When working with acrylics, always mix your paint to a creamy consistency that will blend easily.

NEGATIVE SPACE

Negative space surrounds an object to define its form and create good eye flow (see above example).

SCRUBBING

Scrubbing is similar to scumbling (below), but the strokes should be more uniform and in horizontal or vertical patterns. Use a dry-brush or wet-on-wet technique with this procedure. I often use it to underpaint or block in an area.

SCUMBLING

Use a series of unorganized, overlapping strokes in different directions to create effects like clumps of foliage, clouds, hair and grass. The direction of the stroke is not important for this technique.

UNDERPAINTING AND BLOCKING IN

The first step in all paintings is to block in or underpaint the dark values. You'll apply lighter values of each color to define each object later.

VALUE

Value is the relative lightness or darkness of a color. To achieve depth or distance, use lighter values in the background and darker values closer to the foreground. Lighten a color by adding white. Make a value darker by adding black, brown or the color's complement.

WET-ON-DRY

I use this technique most often in acrylic painting. After the background color is dry, apply the topcoat by drybrushing, scumbling or glazing.

WET-ON-WET

Blend the colors together while the first application of paint is still wet. I use a large hake (pronounced haKAY) brush to blend large areas, such as skies and water, with the wet-on-wet technique.

You can lighten the value of a color by adding white.

Getting Started

Acrylic Paint

The most common criticism of acrylics is that they dry too fast. Acrylics do dry very quickly because of evaporation. To solve this problem I use a wet palette system (see pages 387–389). I also use very specific dry-brush blending techniques to make blending very easy. With a little practice you can overcome any of the drying problems acrylics pose.

Acrylics are ideally suited for exhibiting and shipping. You actually can frame and ship an acrylic painting thirty minutes after you finish it. You can apply varnish over an acrylic painting, but you don't have to because acrylic paint is self-sealing. Acrylics are also very versatile because you can apply thick or creamy paint to resemble oil paint or paint thinned with water for watercolor techniques. Acrylics are nontoxic, with very little odor, and few people have allergic reactions to them.

USING A LIMITED PALETTE

I work from a limited palette. Whether for professional or instructional pieces, a limited palette of the proper colors is the most effective painting tool. It teaches you to mix a wide range of shades and values of color, which every artist must be able to do, Second, and eliminates the need to purchase dozens of different colors.

With a basic understanding of the color wheel, the complementary color system and values, you can mix thousands of colors for every type of painting from a limited palette.

For example, mix Phthalo Yellow-Green, Alizarin Crimson and a touch of Titanium White (gesso) to create a beautiful basic flesh tone. Add a few other colors to the mix to create earth tones for landscape paintings. Make black by mixing Ultramarine Blue with equal amounts of Dioxazine Purple and Burnt Sienna or Burnt Umber. The list goes on and on, and you'll see that the sky isn't even the limit.

Most paint companies make three grades of paints: economy, student and professional. Professional grades are more expensive but much more effective. Just buy what you can afford and have fun. Check your local art supply store first. If you can't find a particular item, I carry a complete line of professional- and student-grade paints and brushes.

MATERIALS LIST

Palette

white gesso
Grumbacher, Liquitex or Winsor & Newton paints (color names may vary):

- Alizarin Crimson
- Burnt Sienna
- Burnt Umber
- Cadmium Orange
- Cadmium Red Light
- Cadmium Yellow Light
- Dioxazine Purple
- Hooker's Green Hue
- Phthalo (Thalo) Yellow-Green
- Titanium White
- Ultramarine Blue

Brushes

no. 4 flat sable brush
no. 4 round sable brush
no. 4 script liner brush
no. 6 flat bristle brush
no. 10 flat bristle brush
2-inch (51mm) hake brush

Miscellaneous Items

16" × 20" (41cm × 51cm) stretched canvas
charcoal pencil
easel
no. 2 soft vine charcoal
palette knife
paper towels
Sta-Wet palette
spray bottle
water can

Brushes

I use a limited number of brushes for the same reasons as the limited palette—versatility and economics.

2-INCH (51MM) HAKE BRUSH
Use this large brush for blending, glazing and painting large areas, such as skies and bodies of water with a wet-on-wet technique.

NO. 10 FLAT BRISTLE BRUSH
Underpaint large areas—mountains, rocks, ground or grass—and dab on tree leaves and other foliage with this brush. It also works great for scumbling and scrubbing techniques. The stiff bristles are very durable, so you can treat them fairly roughly.

NO. 6 FLAT BRISTLE BRUSH
Use this brush, a cousin of the no. 10 flat bristle brush, for many of the same techniques and procedures. The no. 6 flat bristle brush is more versatile than the no. 10 because you can use it for smaller areas, intermediate details and highlights. You'll use the no. 6 and no. 10 flat bristle brushes most often.

NO. 4 FLAT SABLE BRUSH
Use sable brushes for more refined blending, painting people and highlights, and adding details to birds and other animals. Treat these brushes with extra care because they are more fragile and more expensive than bristle brushes.

NO. 4 ROUND SABLE BRUSH
Use this brush, like the no. 4 flat sable, for details and highlights. The sharp point of the round sable, though, allows more control over areas where a flat brush will not work or is too wide. This is a great brush for finishing a painting.

NO. 4 SCRIPT LINER BRUSH
This brush is my favorite. Use it for very fine details and narrow line work, such as tree limbs, wire, weeds and especially your signature, that you can't accomplish with any other brush. Roll the brush in an ink-like mixture of pigment until the bristles form a fine point.

With this basic set of brushes, you can paint any subject.

BRUSH-CLEANING TIPS

As soon as you finish your painting, use quality brush soap and warm water to clean your brushes thoroughly before the paint dries. Lay your brushes flat to dry. Paint is very difficult to get out if you allow it to dry on your brushes or clothes. If this does happen, use denatured alcohol to soften the dried paint. Soak the brush in the alcohol for about thirty minutes and then wash it with soap and water.

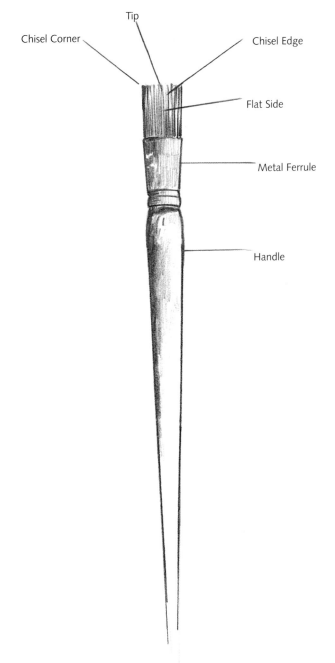

Tip

Chisel Corner

Chisel Edge

Flat Side

Metal Ferrule

Handle

Brush diagram

Palettes

Acrylics dry because of evaporation, so keeping the paints wet is critical. I use two Sta-Wet palettes made by Masterson. The first palette is a 12" × 16" (31cm × 41cm) plastic palette-saver box with an airtight lid (see page 388). Saturate the sponge that comes with the palette with water and lay it in the bottom of the box. Then soak the special palette paper and lay it over the sponge. Place your paints around the edges and you are ready to go. Use a spray bottle to mist your paints occasionally so they will stay wet all day long. When you are finished painting, attach the lid and your paint will stay wet for days.

My favorite palette is the same palette with a few alterations (see page 389). Instead of the sponge and special paper, I place a piece of double-strength glass in the bottom of the palette. I fold paper towels into quarters to make long strips, saturate them with water and lay them on the outer edges of the glass. I then place my paints on the paper towels. They stay wet for days. I occasionally mist them to keep the towels wet.

If you leave your paints in a sealed palette for several days without opening it, certain colors, such as Hooker's Green Hue and Burnt Umber, will mildew. Just replace the color or add a few drops of chlorine bleach to the water in the palette to help prevent mildew.

To clean the glass palette, allow it to sit in water for about thirty seconds or spray the glass with your spray bottle. Scrape off the old paint with a single-edge razor blade.

Setting Up Your Palette

Here are two different ways to set up your palette.

PALETTE 1

The Sta-Wet 12" × 16" (31cm × 41cm) plastic palette-saver box comes with a large sponge that you saturate with water.

Lay the sponge inside the palette box, soak the special palette paper and lay it over the sponge. Place your paints around the edges. Don't forget to mist them to keep them wet.

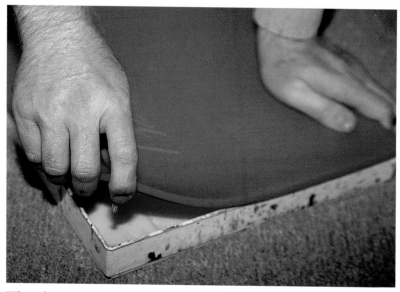

When closing the palette-saver box, make sure the airtight lid is on securely. When the palette is properly sealed, your paints will stay wet for days.

Lay the saturated paper towels around the outer edges of the glass.

Instead of using the sponge and palette paper, you can use a piece of double-strength glass in the bottom of the palette. Fold paper towels in long strips and saturate them with water.

Place your paints on the paper towel strips.

Use the center of the palette for mixing paints. Occasionally spray a mist over the paper towels to keep them wet.

To clean the palette, allow it to sit for thirty seconds in water or spray the glass with a spray bottle. Scrape off the old paint with a single-edge razor blade.

Miscellaneous Supplies

CANVAS

Canvas boards work for practicing strokes, and canvas paper pads work for studies or testing paints and brush techniques. The best surface for painting, though, is a primed, prestretched cotton canvas with a medium texture, which you can find at most art stores. As your skills advance, you may want to learn to stretch your own canvas, but 16" × 20" (41cm × 51cm) prestretched cotton canvases are all you'll need for the paintings in this book.

EASEL

I prefer a sturdy, standing easel. My favorite is the Stanrite ST500 aluminum easel. It is lightweight, sturdy and easy to fold up to take on location or to workshops.

LIGHTING

Of course, the best light is natural north light, but most of us don't have this light in our work areas. The next best lighting option is to hang 4' (1.2m) or 8' (2.4m) fluorescent lights directly over your easel. Place one cool bulb and one warm bulb in the fixture to best simulate natural light.

Studio lights

16" × 20" (41cm × 51cm) prestretched canvas

Aluminum Stanrite studio easel

SPRAY BOTTLE

I use a spray bottle with a fine mist to lightly wet my paints and brushes throughout the painting process. I recommend a spray bottle from a beauty supply store. It's important to keep one handy.

PALETTE KNIFE

I use my palette knife more for mixing than for painting. A trowel-shaped knife is more comfortable and easier to use than a flat knife.

SOFT VINE CHARCOAL

I use no. 2 soft vine charcoal for most of my sketching. It's very easy to work with, shows up well and is easy to remove with a damp paper towel.

Spray bottle

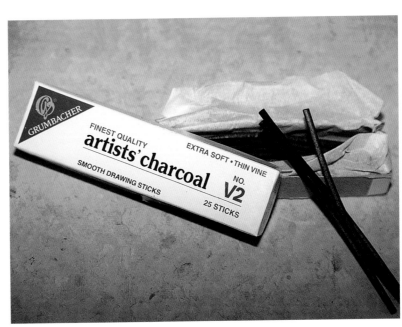

Soft vine charcoal

Palette knives

Composition and Center of Interest

A simple but accurate definition of composition is the arrangement of objects on your canvas that please the eye. That sounds simple enough, but how do you make it work?

As an artist, your main goal is to get the viewer's eye to travel through your artwork and reach the main focal point or center of interest with little or no interference from the other objects on the canvas. The three types of composition that we will discuss in the following pages are: L-shape composition, triangle-shape composition and center-type composition. Each of these types of composition has certain elements in common that make your painting work as a whole.

Elements of Composition

In the following pages we will look at some common elements that help bring a painting together and then discuss them with some examples. The following are the six common elements found in all compositions:
1. Center of interest or focal point
2. Eye stoppers
3. Negative space
4. Fillers
5. Light source and shadows
6. Overlapping

Keep in mind that each of these elements is critical to the success of your composition. They must all be present and planned in advance before you begin to paint. Remember, you may be the best painter in the world, but without a strong composition, your painting will fall apart.

Center of Interest

The first and most important aspect of composition is the focal point or center of interest, the one spot in your painting where your eye ultimately ends up.

Once you decide what your center of interest is and where you want to place it, you can begin adding all of the other elements of composition that help your eye flow through the painting. The goal in any painting is to lead the eye to your center of interest.

It takes a lot of thought and careful planning to make all the elements of composition successful. The first example shows a completed painting with the center of interest and other elements of composition working together.

Focal Points Make a Strong Composition
It's fairly obvious in this painting that the main center of interest is the redbud tree. Notice, however, that the small waterfall is also part of the focal area but is not necessarily the main interest. The waterfall does not compete with the redbud tree, but plays an important role by helping your eye stay focused on it.

Eye Stoppers

Eye stoppers are various objects placed in your painting that keep the viewer's eye from wandering off the canvas. Eye stoppers should never compete with the main eye flow or center of interest. Eye stoppers are a necessary element in all types of composition.

Elements Stop the Eye
Notice how the tall weeds in the right-hand corner stop your eye from moving off the canvas. The tall weeds are so tall that they break the plane of the horizon and help to lead your eye into the painting. Just as your eye flows around a sculpture, eye stoppers are the key factor in helping your eye flow throughout the canvas.

Effective Eye Stoppers
The weeds on the right also lead your eye back into the painting. The smaller clumps of weeds on the left serve a similar purpose. Even the dark shadow in the corner is an eye stopper. The main eye stoppers, the palm trees, stop your eye in a dramatic fashion so your attention goes right back to the center of interest—the glowing sun.

Effective Negative Space

Negative space is the empty space that surrounds an object or is within an object that gives it form. Let's look at the following examples.

Bad Negative Space
This is an example of ineffective negative space. The height of the mountain ranges and the negative space between each range are the same. All the pine trees are the same height and the same basic shape of each tree and the negative space between each tree is about the same. Overall, this example is not interesting to look at because negative space is not utilized well.

Good Negative Space
The same subjects arranged with good negative space make this example more interesting. The mountains are different shapes, and are surrounded by interesting pockets of negative space. Additionally, the pine trees are different heights and shapes and overlap each other.

Bad Negative Space

This example could be very interesting, but fails because of poor use of negative space. The tree is vertical and the limbs are evenly spaced. The clumps of grass are all the same height and shape and the bushes and rocks don't overlap. The arrangement is located on flat ground, which makes the composition static and uninteresting.

Good Negative Space

This is an example of good negative space. Using the same objects, notice how everything works together. The tree is angled. The limbs are irregular shapes and are unevenly spaced and the clumps of grass overlap and are different heights. Placing the elements on a hillside rather than on flat ground makes the whole arrangement much more interesting.

Fillers and Light Source

Fillers are the odds and ends that you use to fill up the spaces around the center of interest. However, fillers should never compete with the main subject of your painting. They may seem insignificant, but they play a crucial role in holding your composition together.

Light source and shadows are two of the most important aspects of your composition. They should be one of the first things you consider when developing your design.

Make Use of Fillers
Because this is a complicated painting, you need fillers to help you focus on the center of interest. The main fillers are the background mountain, the pine trees, the boulders and the rocks. These elements complete the painting by giving it the atmosphere of a high country landscape. Miscellaneous fillers like the clouds, grass, flowers and pebbles add the finishing touches to make this composition work. Use fillers to enhance the center of interest, but don't let them interfere with your main focal point.

Construct Strong Eye Flow
Light source is an important factor when constructing eye flow. Notice that the shadow of the large tree moves your eye off the canvas. To solve this problem, change the direction of the light source. The cast shadows will move your eye back into the main part of the painting.

Plan Your Light Source
Changing the light source in a painting can dramatically improve the eye flow in your composition. By placing the shadows in the right spot, we can make much better use of the eye stoppers and other compositional elements. Keep in mind that all shadows should fall within the main body of the composition and should never lead your eye off the canvas. Before you choose the direction of your light source, remember that light can enter your painting from the left or right, above or below, and as backlight or front light. The light source will create the cast shadows in your painting that affect your eye flow. Be sure to point your cast shadows towards your main focal point.

Shadows Can Cause Poor Composition
Many artists make this common mistake. The shadows are straight and don't follow the contour of the land. They appear to be floating. This creates a real eye flow problem, making for a poor composition.

Shadows Can Improve Composition
In the same basic composition, notice that the shadow of each fence post now follows the contour of the ground. The shadows follow the slope of the hill, then dip down the side of the gully. Shadows are deceiving. It's important to have a good understanding of how they will play into your painting's composition.

Overlapping

Overlapping helps the viewer focus on your center of interest and creates unity in your painting. Even a great painting will have very little appeal without overlapping.

Overlapping is simply the touching of two objects or overlapping of one object over another to create good negative space and effective eye flow.

Lack of Overlapping
You'll notice that none of the trunks touch or overlap each other, creating numerous pockets of dull negative space.

Better Overlapping
Overlapping the trunks and limbs dramatically changes the pockets of negative space. You can create a pleasing composition when objects overlap each other. The proper use of overlapping unifies all the elements in the painting.

Proper Use of Overlapping
When you have several objects that are similar in shape or are grouped, like this gathering of pelicans, overlapping is crucial. Separating each pelican until they are evenly spaced makes your eye bounce rather than flow from pelican to pelican. Here, your eye moves gracefully through the unified group.

Improper Overlapping
I made a rough sketch of the same group of pelicans but spaced them evenly. Notice that your eye bounces from pelican to pelican instead of moving gracefully in and around them.

Center-Type Composition

Now that you are familiar with the elements of composition, we'll discuss the three different types of composition.

The first type of composition we'll discuss is called center-type composition. This type is widely used in wildlife paintings, portraits, figure and still life paintings. As the name suggests, use this type of composition when there is one main center of interest. The drawback of using center-type composition is that it is difficult to design.

Organize the Center of Interest
The center of interest is strong in this example because it fills the canvas without the help of fillers. Miscellaneous fillers like the small pebbles, grass and shadows don't distract from the center of the composition. Because designing interesting negative space around the main center of interest is difficult, I used interesting negative space around other objects and in the shadows.

Use Overlap to Activate Negative Space
Here, as in the example above, the main challenge is composing the negative space around the pots so that your eye flows through the composition. The overlap rule is critical in activating the space in and around the pots.

Triangle-Shape Composition

Use triangle-shape compositions primarily with several competitive or repetitive subjects arranged to create effective eye flow. Unlike other compositional types, triangle compositions have more than one subject.

There are three different types of triangle-shape compositions. The first has a center of interest and several triangle-shaped objects surrounding it that together form the points of a triangle. The second uses one center of interest and several objects surrounding it to create one large triangle.

The third triangle composition involves a single center of interest with several objects that surround it that are not necessarily triangular in shape. The center of interest is situated within the window of the triangle. In this composition, eye stoppers are extremely important because they keep our eye from wandering off the canvas.

This last triangle composition works well when there are several similar objects grouped together to make the center of interest. For example, a flock of birds, a herd of animals, a group of trees, buildings or any other repetitive objects work to create a main subject.

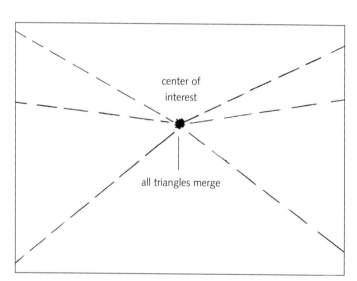

center of interest

all triangles merge

First Triangle-Shape Composition
In this very simple illustration, notice how the center of interest is surrounded by several triangle-shaped forms that merge and point towards the center of interest.

center of interest

Surround the Center of Interest with Triangles
In this painting, all of the objects that surround the center of interest form the basic shape of a triangle. The points of each triangle merge together and lead your eye towards the center of interest.

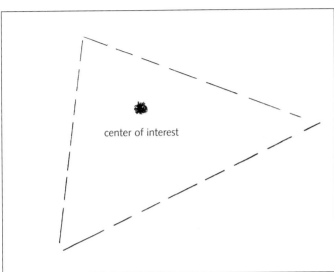

center of interest

Second Triangle-Shape Composition
The center of interest is located within the triangle. Imagine that in the area surrounding the triangle are trees, clouds, rocks, hills and mountains.

Form a Window with Objects
All of the objects that surround the center of interest form a window in the center of the triangle. These objects act as eye stoppers and fillers, but do not compete with the center of interest.

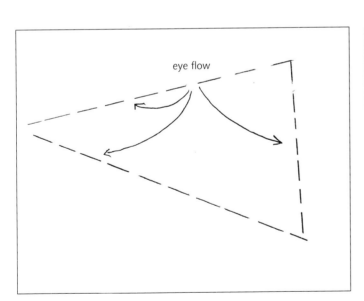
eye flow

center of interest

Third Triangle-Shape Composition
The viewer's eye flows along the shape of a triangle. Once you have established the direction of the eye flow, then you can begin adding other elements to the composition.

Eye Flow Follows Triangle
The ducks, tree stump and shoreline form the sides of the triangle. The other elements, or eye stoppers, help lead your eye around the composition and do not compete with the focal point.

L-Shape Composition

The viewer's eye follows the shape of an L in this type of composition. Generally, you can use the L-shape composition for a painting that has very few objects.

In the example below, I mainly wanted to focus on the large tree and not much else in the painting. I made the tree the largest feature in the painting and set it left of center.

In an L-shape composition locate the fillers well within the eye flow of the L. Placing the tree left of center creates pockets of good negative space.

Keep in mind that no matter how simple your painting is, you still need to be sure that all of the elements of composition apply.

center of interest

eye flow

Fillers Add Interest
The main fillers in this example are the mountain, the house and the clouds. Notice that the fillers don't compete with the main center of interest—the tree. The main purpose of fillers is to fill up space and add interest to the painting. In this case, I have used the shadows as an important element to the flow of the painting.

eye flow

Fillers Stay Within the L-Shape
The negative space around the windmill is interesting because the main elements in the painting, the windmill and the watertank, are located slightly to the right of the center of interest. The fillers—the hills, trees, rocks and fence—are within the flow of the L so as not to compete with the main subject.

center of interest

Designing a Sketch

Designing a sketch is the process of creating a balanced composition using all of the proper elements so the finished painting is pleasing to the eye. The best way to work out a good design is to do a series of thumbnail sketches. Thumbnail sketches are a great tool for working out compositional problems on a smaller scale before you begin your final painting.

Bad Design

I'm not satisfied with this sketch. I placed the large tree too far to the left of the center of interest. The mountains need to be more dominant and the space between the tree and the cabin is uninteresting. I also need to figure out how to lead your eye into the painting. It's back to the drawing board. The main problem in this sketch is poor negative space. Changing the shape of the mountain can be a possible solution.

Better Design

I am more pleased with this design, but there are still many problems with the composition. I need to change the direction of the road and adjust the pocket of negative space to the right. The large tree is still too far to the left and may work better if it were closer to the foreground.

Better Design

Now we are making progress! The overall design is much improved. To add depth, I placed the large tree in the extreme foreground. I improved eye flow by curving the road in between the tree and the cabin. Even though I'm much more satisfied I still need to make a few adjustments. In the next thumbnail sketch, I'll work out a few more details before I paint the final study.

Best Design

The main purpose of this watercolor sketch is to be absolutely sure that I'm happy with everything before I transfer the work onto a larger canvas. Adding a little color helps me see things that I may have missed. Make pencil and watercolor thumbnail sketches part of your compositional design process, and your success rate will increase dramatically. I can work out final compositional problems like negative space, proportions, light source and basic color scheme before I transfer the idea to a canvas.

More on Designing a Sketch

Bad Design

The rock formation and the lighthouse are placed in the middle of the canvas. Uninteresting pockets of negative space are on each side of the rock formation. Because of the placement, your eye does not flow through the painting. There are no eye stoppers and the waves are placed at even intervals.

Better Design

In this example, I moved the main rock formation to the left side of the canvas and gave it a more interesting shape. I added a smaller group of rocks to balance the painting and act as eye stoppers. The waves are irregular intervals to add interest and eye flow.

Good Design

I shifted the lighthouse further to the right, putting it in a more prominent position as a the center of interest. Now interesting pockets of negative space surround the lighthouse and rock formation. I moved the smaller rock formation closer to the foreground and into the right corner. A few small changes give the composition better eye flow and the rocks become dramatic eye stoppers.

Best Design

For the final adjustments, I moved the rock formation further into the background to create depth. The waves are important to the overall composition. The sailboat is added fairly close to the rock formation. All of the subjects are within the eye flow.

Final Sketch

The beauty of a color study is that you can add numerous value and color schemes that allow you to see how the final painting will take shape. By adding color, you can see more clearly the relationships between objects and the overall success of your final design. A color study will allow you to work out any compositional problems in advance.

Making a Composite

A composite is a collection of photos, sketches or ideas that you use to create one piece of art. Using certain elements from each image and then applying the rules of composition, you can create a successful composition.

By using this process, the artist has endless opportunities to create the perfect composition. Grab your camera and sketch pad and begin making some composites of your own.

Gather Reference Materials
Once you've settled on a subject, gather your reference material. Here, I've gathered several different photos, along with a sketch. Next, I'll select subjects from each photo and begin arranging them in a thumbnail sketch.

light source

Make a Rough Sketch
Sketch in the basic components of the landscape such as the location of the river, the surrounding landscape and the placement of the trees.

Locate Your Center of Interest

Find an object that you want to use for your center of interest, and sketch it into your composition. Adjust the placement of your subject and make sure it's suitable for the type of composition you've chosen. In this case, I used a triangle-shape composition.

Add Fillers

Once your center of interest is in place in your landscape, begin adding the fillers and the other elements that make up a successful composition. Remember, you may have to do several thumbnail sketches before you settle on a satisfying composition.

Final Composite

This final composite is the result of careful planning. Of course, you can make adjustments in composition, design, color, values and proportions.

eye stoppers

center of interest

fillers

Composition Tests: Painting One

Now that we've had a chance to look at the different types of composition and their basic elements, it might be fun to see if you can identify the composition types and elements used in the following paint-ings. In the space below each study, choose the type of composition already listed and the different elements of composition found in each one.

Types of Composition
Center-Type
Triangle-Shape
L-Shape

Composition Elements
Center of Interest
Eye Stoppers
Negative Space
Fillers
Light Source
Overlapping

Painting Two

Types of Composition
Center-Type
Triangle-Shape
L-Shape

Composition Elements
Center of Interest
Eye Stoppers
Negative Space
Fillers
Light Source
Overlapping

Painting Three

Types of Composition
Center-Type
Triangle-Shape
L-Shape

Composition Elements
Center of Interest
Eye Stoppers
Negative Space
Fillers
Light Source
Overlapping

Painting Four

Types of Composition
Center-Type
Triangle-Shape
L-Shape

Composition Elements
Center of Interest
Eye Stoppers
Negative Space
Fillers
Light Source
Overlapping

Painting Five

Types of Composition
Center-Type
Triangle-Shape
L-Shape

Composition Elements
Center of Interest
Eye Stoppers
Negative Space
Fillers
Light Source
Overlapping

Composition Test Answers

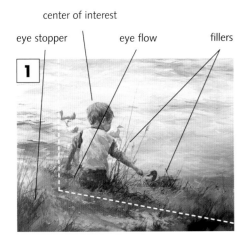

center of interest

eye stopper   eye flow   fillers

1

fillers

2

main center of interest

fillers   eye stopper

3

L-Shape Composition
The shape of the figure and the cast shadow creates an L-shape eye flow. The eye stoppers and fillers such as the weeds, ducks and sand, don't compete with the center of interest and are well within the L-shape.

Center-Type Composition
The deer is the center of interest in this composition. The grasses that surround the deer direct your eye toward the main subject. Even the tree highlights the head of the deer. The challenge in this example was simply working out the negative space in the background.

First Triangle-Shape Composition
The main subject is the center of interest and forms the triangle itself. Eye stoppers such as the bushes and shadows, keep your attention focused on the main subject.

center of interest

eye stopper   fillers

4

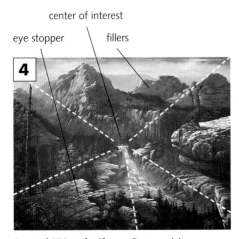

eye stopper   center of interest   fillers

5

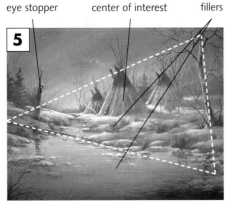

Second Triangle-Shape Composition
Here we have another triangle-shape composition. The main focal point in this painting is the waterfall. The rock formations that surround the waterfall form numerous triangles that point to the focal point. This painting needs many eye stoppers and fillers because of the complexity of its composition.

Third Triangle-Shape Composition
This is an example of another type of triangle-shape composition. The fillers and eye stoppers actually form the shape of the triangle and the center of interest is located within the triangle. The eye follows the triangle eye flow created by the dead tree, tepees and the stump.

COUNTRY GETAWAY
16" x 20" (41cm x 51cm)

Country Getaway

This painting is a simple L-shape composi-tions. You can use an L-shape for a straightforward landscape, with few sub-jects or objects. In this case, the center of interest is crucial to eye flow. For exam-ple, the large tree to the left is the main element that leads the eye through the composition. Additional elements used in the painting also must fall within the L-shape eye flow. The cabin, mountain peaks and pine trees all fall within this shape. Other fillers like the weeds, flowers and miscellaneous bushes help fill out the landscape.

1 Basic Sketch

Begin with a basic sketch of the main components of the composition, using a piece of no. 2 soft vine charcoal.

2 Underpaint Sky

Wet the sky area with a hake brush, then apply a liberal coat of gesso. While the gesso is still wet and with the same brush, begin at the horizon and paint a small amount of Cadmium Orange and a touch of Cadmium Yellow Light directly onto the canvas. At the top, paint half of the sky with Ultramarine Blue, Dioxazine Purple and a touch of Burnt Sienna. Paint downward until you meet the other color. Rinse your brush. Paint feathery brushstrokes by crosshatching the sky area. Blend the two color mixtures on the canvas until the sky is soft and hazy.

3 Add Clouds

Keep the clouds soft and simple. Mix Titanium White with a dab of Cadmium Orange until the mixture is slightly tinted. With a no. 6 flat bristle brush, rough in the clouds. Make the clouds soft, adding just enough of them for interest and atmosphere. Remember, there should be no hard edges.

4 Block in Background Mountains

The mountain is an important element in the painting but must not compete with the center of interest. Place the main peak within the L-shape eye flow. For the color of the mountain, mix Titanium White with a touch of Ultramarine Blue, Burnt Sienna and a small amount of Dioxazine Purple. Adjust the value so that the mountain is slightly darker than the sky. With a no. 6 flat bristle brush, block in the mountain, creating interesting negative space. Blend the right side of the mountain, gradually fading it out. Continue to blend away the hard edges.

5 Highlight Mountain

Mix Titanium White with just enough Cadmium Orange to make a warm, off-white tone. With a no. 4 round sable brush, layer the highlights, beginning with the right side of the mountain. Concentrate the highlights on this side first because the sunlight is coming in from the left. Make the highlights brighter at the top of the mountain and gradually fade them to the base.

6 Underpaint Background Trees

The trees create depth in this composition. Fade the trees from right to left to keep the viewer's eye from leaving the canvas. Place the trees within the L shape that you have already set up in step 4. Mix Titanium White with a touch of Hooker's Green and Dioxazine Purple. Add a touch of Burnt Sienna to warm up the mixture. With a no. 6 flat bristle brush, paint the trees with light, feathery brush-strokes. Keep the edges soft.

7 Highlight Background Trees and Sketch Cabin

For the tree highlights, mix Thalo Yellow Green with a touch of Cadmium Orange and Titanium White. To give the trees more char-acter, gently paint in highlights with a no. 6 flat bristle brush. The high-lights should not be too bright because the trees are in the back-ground. Sketch in the cabin with a piece of no. 2 soft vine charcoal.

8 Block in Pine Trees

Place the pine trees behind the cabin so that they are well within the L-shape eye flow. Mix Hooker's Green, Dioxazine Purple and a touch of Burnt Sienna. Use Titanium White to lighten the value accordingly. Paint in the trees with a no. 4 flat bristle brush. A no. 4 round sable brush will work just as well but be careful not to add too much detail with this brush. Lightly paint in the shape of the pine trees. Make interesting negative space.

9 Block in Background Meadow

For this short step, mix Hooker's Green, Titanium White and a touch of Cadmium Orange with a no. 6 flat bristle brush. Do not mix the colors on the palette. Pick them up individually and mix them together directly on the canvas. Make adjustments to the value and color as you go.

10 Underpaint Cabin

For the cabin, mix a gray tone using Titanium White, Burnt Sienna, Ultramarine Blue and a touch of Dioxazine Purple. Mix the colors to a medium-dark value. Adjust the mixture to fit the values in your own painting. Paint the dark side of the cabin with a no. 4 round sable brush. Lighten the mixture with a dab of Titanium White and paint the light side of the cabin. Make sure the cabin is in correct proportion and that all of the edges meet at right angles.

11 Underpaint Middle and Foreground Grass

For this fun step, paint quickly using lots of thick paint. Use a no. 10 flat bristle brush for the entire process. Beginning at the top of the hill, paint a thick layer of Thalo Yellow Green and a small amount of Cadmium Orange directly on the canvas. Paint a wide stripe across the horizon. Add a touch of Hooker's Green, Burnt Sienna and Dioxazine Purple to the same mixture. Mix these colors directly onto the canvas, adding them gradually. Darken the colors as you move from the background to the foreground. At this stage, you should have several rows of colors. Lay your no. 10 flat bristle brush against the canvas and pull the colors upward to the top of the hill. Paint additional rows until all the colors are blended together, giving the impression of texture.

12 Repaint Cabin

Guess what? I made a mistake. Did you catch it? I painted the cabin in step 10 with the sun coming in from the right instead of from the left. Mix a small amount of Titanium White, Burnt Sienna, Ultramarine Blue and a touch of Dioxazine Purple. With no. 4 round sable brush correct this mistake, reversing the shadow and the highlight. Since the cabin has very little detail, take this opportunity to finish painting the cabin.

13 Sketch Main Tree

Roughly sketch in the main tree trunk and branches. In this step, you can work out any proportional problems, along with any negative space issues. Refer to pages 394 and 395 for information regarding the negative space rule. Use a piece of no. 2 soft vine charcoal to complete the sketch and make corrections with a damp paper towel.

14 Underpaint Main Tree

Mix Ultramarine Blue, Burnt Sienna and a small amount of Dioxazine Purple. Block in the tree with a no. 6 flat bristle brush, mixing all of the colors directly onto the canvas. In this step you can mix the paint fairly thick. Switch to a no. 4 round or flat sable brush to paint the intermediate limbs. Leave out the smaller limbs because you will be adding them in a later step.

15 Highlight Middle Ground Grass

To add highlights to the grass, mix Thalo Yellow Green with a small amount of Cadmium Yellow and Titanium White. Paint in the highlights with a no. 10 flat bristle brush. Select areas that will add interest to your painting. Suggest small bushes and distant flowers with light, quick brushstrokes. Scatter the highlights throughout the middle ground.

16 Highlight Tree

Mix Titanium White with a hint of Cadmium Orange. Paint the bark with short vertical brushstrokes with a no. 4 flat sable brush. Enhance the texture even more by allowing some of the background to show through. Don't add too many highlights. In a few places, change the tone of the highlights by adding small amounts of Cadmium Orange.

17 Add Tree Limbs

This step may be difficult, but practice does make perfect. Practice this step first on a scrap of canvas. Mix Burnt Sienna, Ultramarine Blue and a small amount of Dioxazine Purple. Thin this mixture with water until it is the consistency of ink. Roll your no. 4 script liner through the color until the end becomes a point. Drag your brush from the trunk towards the center, overlapping the limbs with a light touch.

18 Add Tree Shadows and Bushes

Paint in the shadow of the dead tree using a no. 6 flat bristle brush and a mixture of Hooker's Green, Burnt Sienna and a small amount of Dioxazine Purple. Paint the shadow with vertical brushstrokes, following the contour of the hillside and the direction of the grass. Block in the bushes with the same mixture. The bushes should not interfere with the eye flow or the center of interest.

19 Add Details to the Foreground

This step provides a number of opportunities to be creative. Start with an inky mixture of Thalo Yellow mixed with Hooker's Green and Titanium White. Add the weeds in the foreground with a no. 4 script liner. Paint in the tree limbs and add some dead bushes and darker weeds with the same mixture. Next, load a middle-value green onto the bushes with a no. 6 flat bristle brush. Finish by embellishing the scene with a few flowers.

20 Final Details and Highlights

It is not unusual to be satisfied with the painting at this point. Nevertheless, it is a good idea to stand back and study it from a distance. Adjust the highlights by making some darker or lighter than others. Add more flowers or bring out a few more details in the cabin. For a final touch, use a no. 4 flat sable brush to add a reflective highlight to the left side of the tree. Mix Ultramarine Blue, Dioxazine Purple and Titanium White and drybrush the back side of the tree. For this last step, remember to accentuate the L-shape in the composition.

PRAIRIE RELIC
16" x 20" (41cm x 51cm)

Prairie Relic

Here, we have another L-shape composition. The windmill and water tank are strong images that form the entire L-shape eye flow. Several fillers, like the distant hills and trees, help fill out the composition. Clumps of grass, rocks and pebbles complete the middle and foreground and the dead bushes and the tall weeds work as eye stoppers. Now it is time to get to work, so let's get started.

1 Basic Sketch
Make a rough sketch of the basic elements in the painting with a piece of no. 2 soft vine charcoal.

2 Underpaint Sky
This is one of my favorite color schemes. Apply a generous amount of gesso with a hake brush. While the gesso is still wet, begin at the horizon and add Cadmium Orange. Blend upwards to the top of the canvas until it is a soft, peach color. Mix Dioxazine Purple with a touch of Ultramarine Blue. This time, begin at the top of the canvas and paint downward with large criss-cross brushstrokes. Keep the sky soft. The sky should have light, middle and dark values. Clouds are not necessary for this composition, but you may scatter a few soft clouds as long as they don't compete with your center of interest.

3 Underpaint Background Hills

Mix Titanium White and Ultramarine Blue with a touch of Burnt Sienna and Dioxazine Purple. Darken the hills with a touch more Ultramarine Blue, Burnt Sienna and Dioxazine Purple so that they are a darker value than the sky. Paint in the first hill in with a no. 6 or no. 4 flat bristle brush. Darken the mixture and block in the smaller hill. Make the edges of the hills are soft.

4 Underpaint Background Trees

This is a fairly simple step. Darken the same mixture that you mixed in step 3 with a small amount of Ultramarine Blue, Burnt Sienna and Dioxazine Purple. Add a touch of Hooker's Green to this mixture. Block in the shape of the trees with a no. 6 flat bristle brush. The trees act as eye stoppers and are slightly higher than the hills on each side of the canvas. Remember that they shouldn't compete with your center of interest or interfere with the L-shape eye flow.

5 Highlight Hills and Trees

For these simple highlights, mix Cadmium Yellow with a small amount of Titanium White until the mixture is a creamy consistency. Load a small amount onto your brush and drybrush the top of the distant hill with a no. 4 flat sable brush. Add a touch of Cadmium Orange to the mixture and paint a subtle highlight onto the second hill. Next, add Thalo Yellow Green to the mixture and dab highlights onto the trees with a no. 6 flat bristle brush.

6 Underpaint Ground

For this step, mix the colors directly onto the canvas. Apply Titanium White with touches of Burnt Sienna, Cadmium Yellow and Cadmium Orange to the horizon and at the base of the trees. Paint long horizontal brushstokes with a no. 10 flat bristle brush. Apply the paint thick enough to cover the canvas. Add more Burnt Sienna and Dioxazine Purple to the foreground. The foreground should have a fairly rich, dark value. Do not blend the brushstrokes completely because variations in strokes and texture give the ground a realistic look.

7 Add Pebbles with Toothbrush

This is probably one of the more exciting steps! Mix a dark color; any dark color you choose will be fine for this step. Thin the mixture until it is the consistency of ink. Pick up the mixture with a toothbrush and run your forefinger across the bristles, making tiny splatters for the pebbles and sand. Test the splatters first on a scrap of canvas or paper. Practice keeping the splatters small. For highlights, repeat this process with two or three lighter colors mixed with a little Titanium White. Have fun!

8 Resketch Windmill

Resketch the rough sketch that you have made of the windmill with a no. 2 soft vine charcoal. At this stage you need to be very accurate with the lines of the windmill. A ruler or a yard stick may come in handy here. If you have a hard time sketching directly on the canvas, you may want to sketch the windmill on a sketchpad and then transfer the drawing to the canvas with graphite paper.

9 **Underpaint Rocks**
Paint the many small rocks scattered throughout the middle and foreground with a no. 4 flat sable brush. Mix Burnt Sienna with a touch of Ultramarine Blue and Dioxazine Purple. Block in several rocks, beginning at the windmill and coming into the foreground. Don't let these rocks get too dark in your painting. If they do, lighten them with a little Titanium White. Keep the values consistent.

10 **Highlight Rocks**
Mix Burnt Sienna with a touch of Ultramarine Blue and Dioxazine Purple. Add Titanium White and a touch of Cadmium Orange to this mixture. Load a small amount onto your brush and drybrush each rock with a no. 4 flat sable brush. Switch to a no. 4 round sable brush for the smaller rocks. Keep the highlights subtle.

11 Underpaint Windmill

This step is very difficult, but with a little practice you can do it. Mix Burnt Sienna, Ultramarine Blue and a little Titanium White until the mixture is creamy. Block in the windmill with a no. 4 round sable brush. To keep your hand steady, use a mahl stick and a stedi-rest system. To see how to use this gadget, refer to book 3 of this series.

12 Highlight Windmill

Mix Titanium White with a touch of Cadmium Orange and a small amount of the mixture used in step 11. Mix the colors until they are a creamy consistency. Add the highlights to the right side of the windmill and any other hard edges that require a highlight with a no. 4 flat or no. 4 round sable. Brighten this highlight later.

13 **Underpaint Water Tank**
Paint the water tank in three different values.
Mix the base value to a dark gray with Burnt Sienna,
Ultramarine Blue and a little Titanium White. Paint the
shadow of the tank with a no. 4 flat bristle brush.
Suggest boards by painting single vertical brushstrokes
from the top to the bottom of the tank. Continue blocking in the water tank, adding more Titanium White as
needed for the lighter values.

14 **Highlight Water Tank**
Mix Titanium White with a touch of Cadmium
Orange. Drybrush the highlight with a no. 4 flat sable
brush, using vertical brushstrokes. Gradually fade the
color into the shadow of the water tank. Paint the highlight at the top of the tank with a no. 4 round sable
brush. Add the band around the tank.

15 Underpaint Fence and Miscellaneous Items

Mix Burnt Sienna, Ultramarine Blue and a little Titanium White for this step. Underpaint the fence and any other boards with a no. 4 round or flat sable brush. Lighten the value of the fence as it recedes into the distance. Adjust the proportions and location of other objects so that they stay well within the L-shape eye flow.

16 Highlight Fence

This is a very simple and quick step. Mix Titanium White with a touch of Cadmium Orange. Highlight the fence posts with a no. 4 round sable brush. Brighten this highlight by adding a touch more of Titanium White. Repeat the process two or three times or until the value matches the surrounding area.

17 Add Clumps Of Grass

The clumps of grass are an important fillers for this painting. Mix Hooker's Green with Dioxazine Purple and a small amount Titanium White. Apply the grayish-green mixture with a no. 6 flat bristle brush. Carefully plan the location of each clump, using the overlap rule. Drybrush in the basic shape. The placement of the grass should not compete with the L-shape eye flow or center of interest. Adjust the value according to the location of the grass in the painting.

18 Miscellaneous Highlights and Details

For this step, paint in all of the details and highlights that will give the painting its snap. Add the dead bushes in the corners as eye stoppers. Brighten the highlights on some of the rocks and on the windmill and the tank. Highlight the wire on the fence. Paint the wire and dead bushes with a no. 4 script liner brush and a dark inky mixture of Burnt Sienna and Ultramarine Blue. Mix Thalo Yellow Green and a touch of Cadmium Orange and paint the highlights on the grass. Have fun, but don't overdo it!

ROCKY ROAD
16" x 20" (41cm x 51cm)

Rocky Road

Unlike an L-shape composition, a triangle-shape compositions may have many different elements present that can effect eye flow. In this painting, the deer is center of interest and the other objects like the pine trees, are arranged to lead your eye to the deer. If you look closely, many of the elements such as, fillers and eye stoppers, suggest triangles. Now that you get the idea of what a basic triangle-shape composition is, let's get started!

1 Basic Sketch
Make a rough sketch with a piece of no. 2 soft vine charcoal of the basic landscape elements.

2 Underpaint Sky
Wet the sky area and apply a liberal coat of gesso with a hake brush. While the gesso is still wet, paint Cadmium Yellow Light onto the horizon and blend it halfway up the canvas. Rinse your brush. Next, paint Ultramarine Blue at the top of the canvas and blend it downward until you meet the area that you painted Cadmium Yellow. Rinse your brush again and feather the two colors together with a criss-cross brushstroke.

3 Underpaint Background Mountains

The distant mountains give the painting depth. Mix Titanium White with a little Dioxazine Purple, a touch of Burnt Sienna and a very small amount of Ultramarine Blue. The mixture should have a purple tone with a value that is slightly darker than the sky. Paint in the shape of the mountains with a no. 6 flat bristle brush. Keep the shapes soft and simple.

4 Underpaint Large Mountain

This step is identical to step 3, except for the color value. Darken the mixture used in step 3 by adding Dioxazine Purple, Burnt Sienna and Ultramarine Blue. I like to use my no. 6 flat bristle brush for this step. Paint in the mountain, giving it a unique shape. Cover the canvas well, keeping the edges of the mountain soft.

5 Highlight Large Mountain

Mix Titanium White with a touch of Cadmium Yellow and a small amount of Cadmium Orange. Highlight the mountain with a no. 4 flat sable brush. Use a small amount of the mixture to complete this step. Paint the highlight from right to left. Keep the highlight soft and hazy to suggest sunlight.

6 Underpaint Distant Pine Trees

If you have painted with me even for a short time, you have probably painted dozens of pine trees by now. Mix Hooker's Green, Titanium White, Dioxazine Purple and a touch of Burnt Sienna until the mixture becomes a greenish gray. Adjust the value until it is about two shades darker than the mountain. Paint a nice collection of trees on each side of the canvas with a no. 6 flat bristle brush. Paint more trees on the right than on the left.

7 Underpaint Road

For this easy step, mix Burnt Sienna and Dioxazine Purple. Mix a second mixture of Titanium White and a small amount of Cadmium Orange and Cadmium Yellow Light. Paint in the dark side of the road with a no. 6 flat bristle brush. Paint in the sunlit side of the road with the light mixture in short, choppy horizontal strokes to suggest dirt. Blend the two values together in make a third value in the center of the road. Cover the canvas well.

8 Underpaint Meadows

This is a very impressionistic step and a lot of fun to do. Use a no. 10 flat bristle brush to apply a thick mixture of Thalo Yellow Green and a little Cadmium Orange to the top of one of the hills. Darken the mixture with Hooker's Green, Dioxazine Purple and Burnt Sienna. Paint the mixture just below the one you just finished. Don't mix the colors too much, but push them downward, holding the brush flat against the canvas. Continue pushing the colors down in rows until they begin to blend. Keep the grass light, airy and textured.

9 Detail the Road

In this step you will add ruts and highlights to the road. Mix Titanium White and a touch of Cadmium Orange. Highlight the road with a no. 6 flat bristle brush. Paint the side of the road with short, choppy brushstrokes to suggest an eroded bank. Do the same on the shadow side. Blend both values with short horizontal brushstrokes. Darken the mixture with a touch of Ultramarine Blue, Burnt Sienna and Dioxazine Purple. Drybrush the ruts with a no. 6 bristle brush, keeping the shadows lighter in the background and darker in the foreground.

10 Underpaint Dead Pine Trees

For this step, begin with the pine trees in the background. Mix Burnt Sienna with a touch of Ultramarine Blue and Titanium White. Adjust the value of this color to fit the value of the surrounding area. Thin the mixture and paint several small dead pine trees with a no. 4 script liner brush. Mix Burnt Sienna, a touch of Dioxazine Purple and Ultramarine Blue and block in the large pines with a no. 6 flat bristle brush. Use short, choppy, vertical brushstrokes to give the trees a light texture. Finish the trees by adding the limbs with a no. 4 script liner brush.

11 Add Pebbles with Toothbrush

You have probably done this fun technique before. Use any colors you want as long as you use a good range of lights and darks. Thin Burnt Umber, Burnt Sienna and Ultramarine Blue for your dark colors. Thin Cadmium Yellow Light, and Cadmium Orange and Cadmium Red Light for your light colors. Add a touch of Titanium White to make the light colors a little opaque. Load the paint onto your toothbrush and splatter each color separately until the road is covered. Cover this area well.

12 Underpaint Rocks

Mix Burnt Sienna with a little Ultramarine Blue and Dioxazine Purple. Block in a variety of rocks and rock formations with a no. 6 flat bristle brush. Remember to overlap the rocks and use the negative space to your advantage. Lighten the mixture to paint the rocks in the background. The title of this painting is "Rocky Road," so don't be afraid to paint plenty of fun rocks.

13 Highlight Rocks

Mix Titanium White with a touch of Cadmium Orange. Add a small amount of Thalo Yellow Light if you want the highlight to have a yellow tint. Paint the highlight with a no. 4 flat sable brush. Don't make it too bright. Add a little water to make the mixture more transparent, so that the underpainting shows.

14 Highlight Distant Trees and Large Pine Tree

Mix Titanium White with a little Hooker's Green and a touch of Ultramarine Blue. Or for a warmer tone, mix Titanium White with Hooker's Green and a touch of Cadmium Orange. Add the highlights to the distant trees with a no. 6 flat bristle brush. Avoid making them too solid and let some of the background color show through. For the large dead pine tree, mix Titanium White with a touch of Cadmium Orange and a touch of Burnt Sienna. Paint the bark in short, choppy, vertical strokes and a no. 4 flat sable brush.

15 Add Miscellaneous Details

Your no. 4 script liner brush will get quite a workout in this step. Mix a dark value with Hooker's Green, Burnt Sienna and a small amount of Dioxazine Purple for the tall dark weeds. Thin this mixture until it is the consistency of ink. Paint in the tall dark weeds. Mix Thalo Yellow Green and Cadmium Orange or Cadmium Yellow and Cadmium Orange. Thin the mixture and paint in the lighter weeds. Thin a mixture of Burnt Sienna and Ultramarine Blue to paint in the dead bushes. These elements are very important eye stoppers so don't be afraid to make a bold statement.

16 Final Highlights and Flowers

Let your imagination and artistic license take over here, but be careful not to overdo it. Now it's time to add the flowers and brighten the highlights on the rocks and dead pine trees. Study the overall values in your painting and have some fun with them. Apply these final highlights, so that your painting has continuity. You will know if you overdo it. If so, simply tone it down.

17 Add Deer

You can use any subject you like here, but remember to place your subject within the main eye flow of the triangle. A deer is a good choice because it is a simple subject to use and works well in a triangle-shape composition. In this case, the deer is located where all of the triangles merge. The deer must be placed within the main eye flow of the painting. To underpaint the deer, mix Titanium White with Burnt Sienna and a touch of Ultramarine Blue. Block in the basic shape with a no. 4 flat or round sable brush. Paint the highlights with a mixture of Titanium White and Cadmium Orange. Add shadows with a no. 4 round sable brush.

A PEACEFUL PLACE
16" x 20" (41cm x 51cm)

A Peaceful Place

The farm buildings are the center of interest in this painting. However, this composition is a little different because there are no ground formations, mountains, or other fillers used to lead your eye to the center of interest. I had to find a way keep the focus on the main subject, so I chose to use large trees in the foreground to form a window into the painting. This window suggests a single triangle with the center of interest in the middle. The fillers I used are the water, grass, rocks, weeds and leaves.

1 Basic Sketch

Sketch the basic elements of the composition and the contours of the landscape with a piece of no. 2 soft vine charcoal.

2 Paint Sky

Wet the sky area and then apply a liberal coat of gesso with a hake brush. While the gesso is still wet, paint pure Dioxazine Purple onto the horizon and blend the color halfway up the canvas. Next, paint pure Ultramarine Blue at the top and blend downward until you meet the Dioxazine Purple area. Rinse your brush. Paint large, feathery brush-strokes across the sky, blending the two colors together.

3 Underpaint Water

Repeat the same blending technique that you used in step 2, altering it slightly. In this step you switch the colors. The Dioxazine Purple tone is at the top of the water area and the Ultramarine Blue is at the bottom. Notice that I painted the water area larger than I did in the sketch. This is because the water area will shrink when you add the grass.

4 Underpaint Background Trees

Keep the trees soft and simple so that you can add depth to your painting. Mix Titanium White with Hooker's Green and Dioxazine Purple. Adjust this mixture until the color is slightly darker and more purple than the sky. Paint the trees into the background with a no. 6 flat bristle brush. Blend well and keep the edges soft.

5 Underpaint Hillside

This hill doesn't need a lot of detail because it divides the background and the foreground. However, it does need three values. Mix Titanium White with a touch of Thalo Yellow Green, Cadmium Orange and Hooker's Green. Paint on a thick layer of this mixture to the top of the hillside with a no. 10 flat bristle brush. Darken the value by adding more Hooker's Green and Dioxazine Purple until the mixture is fairly dark at the water's edge. While these colors are still wet, with a no. 10 flat bristle brush, push the colors upwards until each layer runs together.

6 Underpaint Reflections

Mix a soft greenish gray using Titanium White, Hooker's Green and a touch of Dioxazine Purple. Thin the mixture with water until it is a creamy consistency. Paint the first layer of reflections with a small amount of this mixture and a no. 6 flat bristle brush. Blend the edges well.

7 Paint Shoreline

This is a fun step because the little details begin to appear. Mix Hooker's Green, Burnt Sienna and Dioxazine Purple until fairly dark. Paint this color along the shoreline in short, choppy brushstrokes with a no. 6 flat bristle brush. Avoid painting a hard straight line. Add details by suggesting bushes above the water's edge. Next, add a little Titanium White and Cadmium Orange to the mixture. Paint in a few rocks or rough areas for an interesting shoreline.

8 Sketch In Buildings

Sketch in the buildings with a piece of no. 2 soft vine charcoal. Keep the sketch rough, but correctly work out the proportions and perspective of the buildings.

9 Underpaint Buildings

Mix a soft gray with Titanium White, a small amount of Ultramarine Blue and a touch of Burnt Sienna. Adjust the value to match the rest of this area in your painting. Block in the shadows of the buildings with a no. 4 flat sable. Add more Titanium White and a touch of Cadmium Orange to the gray mixture. Block in all of the light sides of the buildings. Adjust the shapes that you have just blocked in.

10 Detail Buildings

Use your artistic license in this step. Mix a shadow color with Ultramarine Blue, Burnt Sienna and Dioxazine Purple. Move or adjust the location of the doors and windows. Add all of the overhanging shadows on the roofs. For the highlights, mix Titanium White with a touch of Cadmium Yellow. With a no. 4 round and flat sable and a script liner brush, brighten the highlighted areas. Drybrush a small amount on the dark side of the buildings to suggest weathered wood.

11 Add Foreground Tree Limbs

Mix a medium gray color with Titanium White, Burnt Sienna and Ultramarine Blue. Adjust the value of this mixture to match the area just above the water's edge and then thin the mixture until it is the consistency of ink. Paint the tree trunks with a no. 4 script liner brush. Avoid making these trees too dark or too large. Surround the center of interest with them.

12 Drybrush Leaves on Limbs

Mix Hooker's Green, Titanium White and Cadmium Orange until the mixture is a soft olive green. Drybrush scattered leaves with a no. 10 flat bristle brush. Leave some patches of sky showing through so that the trees aren't too overwhelming. Use interesting negative space.

13 Paint Final Reflections

For this step, mix a dark olive green color by mixing Hooker's Green, Burnt Sienna and a small amount of Cadmium Orange. Paint in the darker value with a no. 6 flat bristle brush. Paint in the bushes just above the water's edge. Keep the edges soft.

14 Paint Foreground Grass

For the grass, mix Thalo Yellow Green with a little Cadmium Orange and Cadmium Yellow Light. Paint this mixture in an irregular shape along the water's edge with a no. 10 flat bristle brush. Push the color upward along the edge to form clumps of grass. While this area is still wet, mix Hooker's Green, Burnt Sienna and Dioxazine Purple. Paint this mixture fairly thick along the bottom of the canvas. Place the flat of your brush against the canvas and push this color into the grass.

15 Paint Tree Trunks

It's rare that Burnt Umber comes in handy, but you'll need it for this step. Use pure Burnt Umber and make it slightly creamy. Block in the main tree trunks with a no. 4 flat sable. Thin the mixture until it becomes inky. Paint in all of the miscellaneous limbs connected to the trunks with a no. 4 script liner brush. Place the limbs at the outer edges of the triangle-shape composition.

16 Add Dark Leaves and Brush

Mix Hooker's Green, Dioxazine Purple and a little Burnt Sienna until the mixture is creamy. Paint in all the leaves at the base of the first tree with a no. 6 flat bristle brush. Switch to a no. 4 round sable and paint in individual leaves. Scatter them on the trees, grouping some for interest. Use interesting negative space and allow plenty of sky to show through.

17 Highlight Water

Thin a small amount of Titanium White with clean water. Glaze the entire surface of the water area with a no. 10 flat bristle brush. Let the area dry. Highlight the water with pure Titanium White along the edges and in the main body of water with a no. 4 round sable.

18 Highlight Grass and Bushes

There is not much to this step, but it is still important because you add the highlights to give these areas more form. Mix Thalo Yellow Green and Titanium White, or Thalo Yellow Green with a touch of Cadmium Orange. Paint the highlights onto the clumps of grass, bushes and the hillside with a no. 10 or no. 6 flat bristle brush. The highlights add form to these areas.

19 Final Details and Highlights

As with all other final steps, let your artistic license work for you. Add taller weeds to the foreground and brighten some of the rocks along the shoreline. Add a few brighter highlights to the buildings. Voila! You're finished.

HOMEWARD BOUND
16" x 20" (41cm x 51cm)

Homeward Bound

The triangle-shape composition is widely used by wildlife artists, especially those who paint ducks, geese and other water-fowl. What makes this composition so unique is that the main center of interest (the ducks), the main eye stopper (the large dead tree on the right side) and the fillers (the weeds and cattails on the lower left) form a triangle. Use a triangle-shape composition to capture birds in flight.

1 Basic Sketch
Make a rough sketch of the basic elements of the landscape with a piece of no. 2 soft vine charcoal.

2 Underpaint Sky
This is a really unique color scheme. Before you begin, practice this step on a scrap of canvas. Wet the sky area and apply a liberal coat of gesso with a hake brush. Cover the sky well. While the sky is still wet, apply Cadmium Orange, dragging the color across the horizon, and blend it to the top of the canvas. While the sky is still wet, apply Ultramarine Blue across the top of the canvas and blend downward. Blend both areas with a light, feathery brushstroke.

3 Underpaint Water

In this step, paint the water with the same technique you used in step 2. The water reflects the sky, so reverse the location of the Cadmium Orange and Ultramarine Blue and feather both colors together. The Cadmium Orange horizon is now at the top of the water and the Ultramarine Blue is at the bottom. To make this step easier, turn the canvas upside down.

4 Underpaint Background Trees

Let the sky area dry before you begin this step. Mix a small amount of Titanium White, Ultramarine Blue and Cadmium Orange in equal parts. Mix these colors until they are creamy. Adjust the value of the mixture until it is slightly darker than the horizon. Paint in the trees, keeping them soft and subtle, with a no. 6 flat bristle brush. Block in the background with the same mixture. Next, darken the same mixture with more Ultramarine Blue. Paint in a second layer of trees. Keep them soft.

5 Paint Distant Tree Limbs

For this step, darken the same color that you used in step 4 with Cadmium Orange and Ultramarine Blue until it is slightly darker than the background trees. Thin it to an inky consistency. Paint in a collection of delicate trees across the horizon with a no. 4 script liner brush. Paint a variety of shapes and sizes for interesting negative space and overlap. Make sure that you don't go too dark.

6 Block In Shoreline

Mix Ultramarine Blue and Cadmium Orange with a little bit of Titanium White. Make the value three shades darker than the background trees. Block in the irregular shoreline with a no. 6 flat bristle brush. Don't paint the shoreline in a straight line. Instead, overlap some of the shoreline over the background trees. Suggest reflections by dragging a little bit of color through the water.

7 Add Middle ground Clumps of Grass

For this step, lighten the same mixture of Cadmium Orange and Ultramarine Blue that you used in step 2 with a small amount of Titanium White. Make the middle ground a lighter value than the background. Add small amounts of Titanium White until the value is a middle tone. Paint in clumps of grass, creating a nice variety of sizes and shapes with a no. 6 flat bristle brush. Block in the reflections.

8 Add Intermediate Tree Trunks

Mix Cadmium Orange and Ultramarine Blue. Darken the mixture slightly with a small amount of Ultramarine Blue and thin it to an inky consistency. Paint in the intermediate trees and grass along the shoreline with a no. 4 script liner brush. I know you are probably tired of my mentioning this, but use interesting negative space. Overlap the tree limbs in a variety of shapes, sizes and heights.

9 Reflect Intermediate Tree Trunks

Mix Cadmium Orange and Ultramarine Blue and thin it until the mixture becomes creamy. Paint in the reflections of the trees, beginning where each one is located, with a no. 4 round sable brush. Paint the reflection with a wiggly brushstroke for the trees' reflections.

10 Highlight Water

Make a milky glaze with a small amount of Titanium White and clean water. Drybrush the mixture carefully across the surface of the water with a no. 10 flat bristle brush. The idea here is to soften the reflections that you have just painted. Paint a few thin highlights along the shoreline for added sparkle with pure Titanium White and a no. 4 round sable brush.

11 Underpaint Foreground Grass

Darken the same mixture of Cadmium Orange and Ultramarine Blue that you used in earlier steps with a touch more of Ultramarine Blue. Depending on the overall value of your painting, add Titanium White to lighten the mixture. Paint in the grass with a no. 10 flat bristle brush. Cover the area well with a thick layer of paint. Keep the edges soft and irregular.

12 Underpaint Large Dead Tree

Mix Ultramarine Blue, Cadmium Orange and a little Burnt Sienna until fairly dark. Block in the main tree trunk with a no. 6 flat bristle brush. Cover the area well with a thick layer of paint. Apply the paint in short, choppy vertical strokes. Thin the same mixture until it is an inky consistency. Paint the main tree limbs with a no. 4 round sable brush. Finish the smaller limbs with a no. 4 script liner brush. Once again, make interesting the negative space and overlap a few of the branches.

13 Add Light Source

To add the light source, mix Titanium White with a touch of Cadmium Orange. Block in the area of sun and then add highlights to the trees with a no. 6 flat bristle brush. Add some of this color to the water directly below the sun. Paint the reflection using short, choppy, horizontal brushstrokes no wider than 1" (2.5cm).

14 Paint Tall Weeds in Foreground

Thin a mixture of Cadmium Orange and Ultramarine Blue until it is creamy. At the base of the largest tree, paint in the tall weeds with a no. 4 script liner brush. Add the cattails with a no. 4 round sable brush. Overlap some of the longer stalks for depth. There is no real technique for these cattails.

15 Highlight Painting

Mix Cadmium Orange and Titanium White until the mixture is very creamy. Accent the left side of each tree with a no. 4 round sable brush. Keep the highlights thin and opaque. Thin the mixture again with water and paint the taller weeds located at the base of the largest tree with a no. 4 script liner brush.

16 Sketch In Ducks

Make an accurate outline of the ducks. If a piece of no. 2 soft vine charcoal is too thick for you to make an accurate sketch, use a soft charcoal pencil or a Conté crayon.

17 Underpaint Ducks

Mix Ultramarine Blue, Cadmium Orange and just enough Titanium White to create a middle value. Block in the ducks, covering the canvas well with a no. 4 round or flat sable brush. Avoid adding too many details. The ducks are an important element in the composition, but they should not compete with the other components that you have added.

18 Highlight Ducks

To highlight the ducks, mix a warm gray using Cadmium Orange, Titanium White and a small amount of Ultramarine Blue. Drybrush the mixture onto the wings and bodies with a no. 4 round sable brush for the feathers. With the same mixture, add even more highlights by painting a thin accent around the outline of the ducks with a no. 4 script liner brush. Paint just enough of an accent to make the ducks stand out.

BROKEN POTS
16" x 20" (41cm x 51cm)

Broken Pots

This painting is a center-type composition, which is used primarily for close-up paintings like still life and portraits. You guessed it! The pots are the center of interest. Unlike the traditional subjects of triangle and L-shape compositions, center-type paintings use the center of interest to keep the viewer's attention. The pots overlap each other to create interesting pockets of negative space. The eye flows around this composition instead of bouncing from object to object. Fillers like the grass and shadows help tie the composition together. Even with a simple subject, this type of composition can be quite effective and fun.

1 Underpaint Background

This background is mottled, which means that you blend the colors directly on the canvas. After applying a liberal coat of gesso, scatter pure colors all over the surface with a hake brush. Use Dioxazine Purple, Hooker's Green, Ultramarine Blue, Burnt Sienna and Cadmium Yellow. Rinse your brush. Feather the colors together with large, criss-crossing brushstrokes.

2 Basic Sketch

Sketch the shape, location and proportion of the pots with a piece of no. 2 soft vine charcoal. Because there is little room for compositional changes, it is very important that you accurately capture the subject of this painting.

3 Underpaint Background Grass

Mix Hooker's green, Burnt Sienna and a small amount of Cadmium Yellow and Titanium White. Mix the value about two or three shades darker than the background. Mix the colors to a creamy consistency. Block in the background grass behind the pots with a no. 10 flat bristle brush. Keep the edges very soft so that you can easily blend in other elements.

4 Add Tall Background Weeds

Darken the color mixture you used in step 3 with a little more Hooker's Green and Burnt Sienna. Thin it to an inky consistency. Paint in a variety of weeds with a no. 4 script liner brush, overlapping some longer weeds for added depth. Lighten the mixture with Cadmium Yellow and a touch of Titanium White. Paint in lighter weeds to break up the darker weeds in the background.

5 Underpaint Back Pot

Begin with the shadow side of the pot. Mix Burnt Umber with a small amount of Titanium White. Block in the color at the base with a no. 6 flat bristle brush. Paint along the contour to make the pot round. As you paint across the pot, lighten the value by adding small amounts of Titanium White. Leave the brushstrokes on the pot visible. After you have finished the base of the pot, paint the neck of the pot with the same color mixture and with a no. 4 script liner that you used in the previous section. Paint the inside of the pot, placing the darkest shadow on the left.

6 Highlight Back Pot

Mix Titanium White and a small amount of Cadmium Yellow to the Burnt Umber mixture you used for step 5. Drybrush the mixture onto the left side of the pot with a no. 6 flat bristle brush. Blend the color well. Repeat the step several times to brighten the highlight. After you highlight the main body, paint both the neck and the inside of the pot. Using the same mixture you used to paint the outside of the pot, highlight the rim with a no. 4 round sable brush.

7 Detail Back Pot

Use your artistic license for this easy step. Sketch a simple design onto the pots with a piece of no. 2 soft vine charcoal. Thin pure Titanium White until it is creamy. Paint the design, using short, choppy brushstrokes and a no. 4 script liner brush. Remember that these are old pots and the design may be faded out in some areas, especially on the dark side. Paint the cracks with a small amount of Burnt Umber and a no. 4 round sable brush.

8 Underpaint Middle Pot

Paint this pot using the same blending technique you used in step 5. Mix Ultramarine Blue with a touch of Burnt Sienna and a small amount of Titanium White. Paint from the dark side across to the light side, adding Titanium White to create a second and third value.

9 Highlight Middle Pot

Mix Titanium White with Cadmium Orange. Paint the rim of the pot with this mixture using a no. 4 round sable brush. Keep the highlight soft. Repeat this step several times until the highlight is bright.

10 Detail Middle Pot

Sketch a simple design onto the middle pot. Mix Cadmium Orange and Titanium White. Paint in the design with a no. 4 script liner brush. Add some cracks and broken spots so that the pots appear old. Define the thickness of the walls by adding a final accent to the rim and edges of the cracks.

11 Underpaint Front Pot

Paint pure Burnt Sienna onto the left side of the pot. Next, mix Titanium White with a small amount of Cadmium Yellow and add this mixture to the side that you painted with Burnt Sienna. Blend the two values across the contour of the pot, using short, choppy brushstrokes to suggest texture. Keep the edges soft. For the inside of the pot, reverse the lights and darks, painting Burnt Sienna on the right side instead of the left. Add Titanium White and Cadmium Yellow to the light area and blend the values together from right to left.

12 Highlight Front Pot

Mix Titanium White with a little Cadmium Yellow and a touch of Burnt Sienna. Keep the mixture thick so that the highlight doesn't mix with the underpainting. Paint a broken line on the inside of the pot with no. 4 round sable brush.

13 Detail Front Pot

Mix Burnt Sienna with a little Ultramarine Blue and a very small amount of Titanium White. Paint in any design you want with a no. 4 round sable brush. Keep the design soft and avoid making a solid outline. Highlight the top rim of the pot with pure Titanium White.

14 Add Shadows

For the shadow, mix Burnt Sienna with a little Dioxazine Purple and a touch of Titanium White. Paint the shadows with a no. 6 flat bristle brush. Add the shadow next to the pots and paint it out towards the edges of the composition. Paint the shadow in short, choppy brushstrokes, for movement and texture. Lighten the mixture with Titanium White and a touch of Cadmium Orange. Paint in the lightest part of the shadow.

15 Add Foreground Grasses

Mix Hooker's Green with a small amount of Burnt Sienna, a touch of Dioxazine Purple and a little Titanium White. Paint in the soft clumps of background grass with a no. 6 flat bristle brush. Scatter the grass throughout the composition. The grass acts as an eye stopper, helping the viewer focus on the pots.

16 Miscellaneous Highlights and Details

Thin the mixture used in step 15 until it is an inky consistency. Paint the taller weeds with a no. 4 script liner brush, making sure to overlap some of the weeds for interest and depth. Don't be afraid to make these weeds very tall. Lighten the mixture with Cadmium Yellow and Titanium White. Add some lighter weeds for variety and to add contrast to the darker weeds. Next, add some miscellaneous highlights to the grassy areas. Paint a few small flowers in the foreground in any color you would like. Paint highlights as needed onto the pots, sand and weeds.

ROCKY WATERS
16" x 20" (41cm x 51cm)

Rocky Waters

This is a difficult painting because of the many different elements involved in making it. The painting is designed so that the cabin is the center of interest. The other elements act as fillers and eye stoppers to help complete the painting. It is important that all the elements work together so that the painting can be a success.

1 Basic Sketch

Make a rough sketch of the basic elements in the painting. A simple sketch of the landscape is sufficient to establish the placement of the objects.

2 Underpaint Background

For the mottled background, apply touches of pure colors directly onto the canvas. Scatter small amounts of Hooker's Green, Dioxazine Purple, Cadmium Red Light and Thalo Yellow Green across the surface of the canvas. Blend the colors until you have made varied tones in your background. Keep the center of the background lighter than the outer edges.

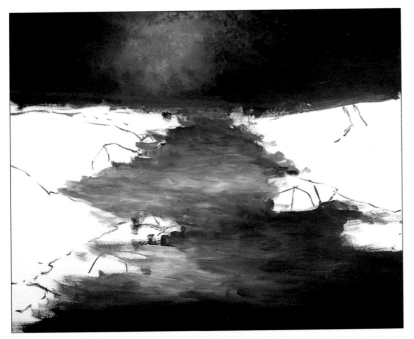

3 Underpaint Water

Begin with the the river. Mix Titanium White with touches of Hooker's Green, Ultramarine Blue, Burnt Sienna and a little Dioxazine Purple. Block in the water with a no. 6 flat bristle brush. Paint shorty, choppy brushstrokes for texture. Remember that you will need to make the value slightly lighter in the foreground.

4 Underpaint Middle and Background Grass

Mix Thalo Yellow Green with touches of Cadmium Orange, Burnt Sienna and a little Hooker's Green with a no. 10 flat bristle brush directly onto the canvas. Mix the tones until they are on the warm side. Paint the foreground by adding more Hooker's Green and Burnt Sienna to darken the value. Cover the canvas in loose brushstrokes to suggest wild grasses.

5 Underpaint Rocks

This is not a difficult step, but it is a bit intimidating. Mix Ultramarine Blue, Burnt Sienna and a touch of Dioxazine Purple on your palette. Lighten the mixture with a small amount of Titanium White. Block in the rocks with a no. 6 flat bristle brush, covering the canvas well. Darken the value of each rock with a bit more of Ultramarine Blue and Burnt Sienna as you recede into the background. Keep the rocks in the foreground lighter in value.

6 Underpaint Background Tree Trunks

For this step, add Titanium White to the mixture used in step 5 to block in the rocks. Keep in mind that the value should be slightly darker than the background. Add Ultramarine Blue if it's necessary to darken the value. Thin the mixture to an inky consistency. Paint in the background trunks with a no. 4 script liner brush. Make negative space interesting by keeping the trees outside the center of interest.

7 Highlight Rocks

For this difficult step, mix a highlight by combining Titanium White, a small amount of Cadmium Orange and a little Ultramarine Blue. Thin this mixture until it is creamy. Drybrush this color onto the top left side of each rock with a no. 6 flat bristle brush. Leave visible brushstrokes for texture. Don't make the rocks too bright in this step.

8 Highlight Water

Mix Titanium White with small amounts of Ultramarine Blue and Hooker's Green. Mix the colors until they are creamy. Paint short, choppy, horizontal brushstrokes across the water area with a no. 4 flat sable brush. Paint in loose brushstrokes for movement in the water's surface.

9 Add Light Leaves on Background Trees

Use several combinations of colors for this step. Mix Thalo Yellow Green with a touch of Cadmium Orange. Mix Cadmium Yellow with Cadmium Orange or use pure Cadmium Yellow and pure Cadmium Orange. Make the mixtures creamy and paint in the highlights with a no. 10 or no. 6 flat bristle brush. Avoid making the highlight too solid. Paint the leaves letting the underpainting show through.

10 Add Dark Leaves on Background Trees

This step is identical to the step 9. Mix Hooker's Green, a touch of Burnt Sienna and a little Dioxazine Purple. Make this mixture lighter in value than the background color. Paint in the darker leaves with a no. 10 or no. 6 flat bristle brush. Place these leaves at the outer edges of the canvas so that your eye remains in the center. Keep the leaves light and airy, allowing some of the underpainting to show through.

11 Add Large Tree Trunks

Plan the placement of the tree before you begin this step. Also, you have a couple of choices of color here. Mix Ultramarine Blue and Burnt Sienna for a rich brown, or use pure Burnt Umber. Make the mixtures creamy and block in the main shape of the larger tree trunks with a no. 4 round sable brush and a no. 4 flat sable brush. Overlap the limbs for depth. Paint the smallest branches with a no. 4 script liner brush.

12 Paint Large Leaves

Mix Hooker's Green with a little bit of Burnt Sienna and Dioxazine Purple. Mix this color until it is a very dark greenish-brown. Make the mixture creamy and with a no. 4 round sable brush paint the leaves using quick, overlapping brushstrokes. Arrange the leaves so that the tree has an even balance. Leave areas open for interesting negative space.

13 Highlight Middle and Background Grasses

You can use almost any light color or combination of colors that you want in this step. Some possible color choices are a mixture of Cadmium Yellow and Cadmium Orange, pure Cadmium Yellow or Cadmium Yellow mixed with Titanium White. Don't use bright greens and keep your colors on the warm side. Paint in the highlights throughout the middle ground and background with a no. 6 flat bristle brush. Avoid making the highlights too solid and allow some of the background to show through.

14 Underpaint Foreground Grass

This step is quick and easy. Mix Hooker's Green, Burnt Sienna, and Dioxazine Purple. Drybrush the grass by pulling the paint upward to make soft edges with a no. 10 flat bristle brush. Cover the canvas well. You may need to repeat this step a couple of times to get enough of the foreground grass in place.

15 Detail and Highlight Water

Make a small amount of pure Titanium White creamy and paint highlights around the edges of the rocks and the top of each waterfall with a no. 4 round sable brush. Paint in the highlights heavily so that they are bright and opaque.

16 Detail and Highlight Rocks

Mix Titanium White and Cadmium Orange. If you prefer this mixture to be on the yellow side, add a small amount of Cadmium Yellow. Make this mixture creamy. Highlight the top left side of each rock with a no. 4 flat sable brush. Let some of the underpainting show through. Darken the mixture with a small amount of Burnt Sienna and Ultramarine Blue. Suggest cracks and adjust some of the shapes in the rocks. Keep the rocks in the center brighter in value than those on the edges of the composition.

17 Add Tall Weeds in Foreground

No surprise here! Mix a dark mixture of Hooker's Green, Dioxazine Purple and Burnt Sienna. Thin this mixture until it's inky. Paint in the dark tall weeds with a no. 4 script liner brush. Lighten the value by adding small amounts of Titanium White. Overlap some of the weeds, painting some at different lengths. Place most of the taller weeds on the left side of the painting and around the rocks.

18 Sketch the Cabin and Final Highlights

Scatter the wild flowers here and there for a nice touch. Lighten the color of some weeds for contrast. Brighten orange leaves on the large tree to help bring it forward. Brighten the highlights on a few rocks for variety. Brighten the highlights on the water. Again, be careful not to overdo it. Sketch in the cabin with a piece of no. 2 soft vine charcoal.

19 Add Center of Interest

Although this is the most important part of the painting, it is one of the easiest to paint. Mix Ultramarine Blue, a little Burnt Sienna and Titanium White to make a light gray. Lighten the value by adding more Titanium White. The value should match the surrounding area of interest. Block in the dark side first with a no. 4 flat sable brush. Lighten the mixture with a little more Titanium White and a touch of Cadmium Orange, and block in the light side. Add the doors, windows, overhanging shadows and miscellaneous details. Paint in a few small bushes at the base of the cabin with a mixture of Cadmium Yellow and Cadmium Orange. To finish the cabin, add a white fence and a little smoke from the chimney.

Gallery

Texas Bluebonnets
15" × 30" (38cm × 77cm)

Tossed by the Waves
16" × 20" (40.6cm × 50.8cm)

Patient Fisherman
16" × 20" (40.6cm × 50.8cm)

Misty Morning Sunrise
16" × 20" (40.6cm × 50.8cm)

You Can See Forever
16" x 20" (41cm x 51cm)

Summer Dreams
16" x 20" (41cm x 51cm)

The material in this compilation appeared in the following previously published North Light Books, and appears here by permission of the authors. (The initial page numbers given refer to pages in the original work; page numbers in parentheses refer to pages in this book.)

Yarnell, Jerry	Paint Along With Jerry Yarnell: Painting Magic c. 2002	Pages 1, 4–125 (5–127, 504–505)
Yarnell, Jerry	Paint Along With Jerry Yarnell: Painting Techniques c. 2002	Pages 1–3, 6–125 (128–251, 502–503, 506–507)
Yarnell, Jerry	Paint Along With Jerry Yarnell: Painting Adventures c. 2002	Pages 1, 4–125 (252–375, 500–501, 508–511)
Yarnell, Jerry	Paint Along With Jerry Yarnell: Learning Composition c. 2003	Pages 1, 4–125 (376–499)

 Published by North Light Books, an imprint of F+W Publications, Inc., 4700 East Galbraith Road, Cincinnati, Ohio 45236. (800) 289-0963. First edition.

Other North Light Books are available from your local bookstore, art store or direct from the publisher.

09 08 07 06 05 5 4 3 2 1

Painting Landscapes With Jerry Yarnell / edited by North Light Books–1st ed.
p. cm.
ISBN 1-58180-740-6 (hc.: alk. paper)

Cover designer: Clare Finney
Production Editor: Jennifer Ziegler
Production Coordinator: Kristen Heller